Word-by-Word Translations of Songs and Arias

Part I - German and French

A Companion to
The Singer's Repertoire

by

Berton Coffin
Werner Singer
Pierre Delattre

The Scarecrow Press, Inc.

New York   1966

SCARECROW PRESS, INC.

Published in the United States of America
by Scarecrow Press, Inc.
A wholly owned subsidiary of
The Rowman & Littlefield Publishing Group, Inc.
4501 Forbes Boulevard, Suite 200
Lanham, Maryland 20706
www.scarecrowpress.com

PO Box 317
Oxford
OX2 9RU, UK

Copyright 1966, by Berton Coffin
Werner Singer
Pierre Delattre
L. C. Card No. 66-13746

ISBN 0-8108-0149-3
ISBN 978-0-8108-0149-3

Preface

Word-by-Word Interpretative Translations of Songs and Arias, Part I, German and French has been prepared by the authors for the use of English-speaking singers, teachers, coaches and accompanists that their art may be more meaningful and more communicative to their public.

During the fabled days of the Bel Canto era, singers studied their art for an extended period of time and were able to pursue their careers with the knowledge of only one language - their own - Italian. In the 20th century we are living in a vastly more complicated age. Now we have a limited amount of time to accomplish more - the attaining of a vocal technique suitable for many styles of performance, the performance of an expanded repertoire of several centuries in several languages, and the performance of musical scores of great vocal and musical complexity.

How can such challenges be met? - only by the use of more efficient aids in the teaching and study of singing. This book has been formulated to assist in the interpretation of German and French languaged texts. (It is planned that a second volume of translations in other languages will follow).

Interpretation! W. J. Henderson, famed music critic and author of The Art of Singing (Dial Press, 1938, New York), has given one of the most definitive statements of our art, "Singing is the interpretation of text by means of musical tones produced by the human throat." But how does one interpret a text if it is in a foreign language in which the singer is not conversant? Obviously he must first know the exact meaning of every word he sings. Master teachers of the past have told their students to look up each word of a song in the dictionary, placing the translated meaning over the word. What a monumental task, especially for those who have little time and few language skills! Such efforts can only be partially successful because of the changing forms of the verbs in the various tenses and because of poetic and occasional archaic language usage. Frequently linguistic scholars have great difficulty in creating meaningful translations.

One may ask, why not use the translations already in existence? The translations known to the authors have been made to be singable and are both rhythmed and rhymed. Such artistic problems eliminate the synchronization of meanings with the text.

It is believed that this volume of translations will be of immense value for all singers, from the beginner to the artist-singer. Many artists have evidenced interest in its preparation. The more advanced the singer, the more necessary this information is to him, because his is an endless search for meanings, colors, and nuances seemingly newly created in each performance.

Richard Strauss, one of the immortal Lieder and operatic composers as well as one of the leading operatic conductors of his day, wrote in 1942 in an essay about his career that the struggle between word and music had been the problem of his life right from the beginning. This statement also defines a continuing problem for every singer, accompanist, and conductor. One must know the meaning of the words as well as the meaning of the music before one can know the integral and ensemble values of the vocal line and the accompaniment. It can be said that too many recitals heard today are based upon musical interpretations by both the singer and accompanist. For the singer, the performance of any song or aria entails the setting of the stage in one's mind and the subsequent characterization of the song within that framework. Such characterization begins with poetic performance and implies the stressing of the descriptive sounds of a language as well as its accents. This coloring must involve both singer and accompanist. Sometimes the music is predominant - sometimes the poetry. Only with the sensitive interplay of word and music can one attain that Elysian level of interpretation which is above and beyond vocalization, musicianship, intelligence, taste and discrimination. This is the artistic level at which a performance becomes not only a human but a spiritual experience.

The Singer's Repertoire Series (Scarecrow Press, N. Y.) began in 1956 with multiple listings for coloratura soprano, lyric soprano, dramatic soprano, mezzo soprano, contralto, lyric tenor, dramatic tenor, baritone and bass. The second edition of The Singer's Repertoire was enlarged and includes over 1,000 lists published in four volumes, Volume I, Soprano, Volume II, Mezzo Soprano and Contralto, Volume

III, Lyric Tenor and Dramatic Tenor, and Volume IV, Baritone and Bass. Volume V, Program Notes for The Singer's Repertoire (Coffin & Singer, Scarecrow Press, N. Y.) listed over 1,000 program notes that could be used in concert and recital programs. Volume VI on pronunciation of repertoire, Phonetic Readings of Songs and Arias (Coffin, Errolle, Singer & Delattre, Pruett Press, Boulder, Colorado) gives the classical pronunciation of songs in Italian, German and French. Word-by-Word Translations becomes Volume VII.

The Singer's Repertoire Series has been most fortunate in its co-authors. In this volume of German and French translations, we again have had the services of Werner Singer and Pierre Delattre. Their backgrounds are as follows:

Werner Singer, Coach-Accompanist of New York City, is German-born and was trained at the Statliche Hochschule für Musik, Berlin. He has conducted operas at the Hamburg Volksoper and the Theatro Municipal, Rio de Janeiro, Brazil. In this country he is widely known, having been a coach and/or accompanist to Mmes. Barbieri, Berger, Leider, Loevberg, Tebaldi and Yeend, and Messrs. Bernac, de Luca, Gedda, London, Svanholm, Tagliavini and Vinay. In the academic field, Mr. Singer has established and has been successfully holding summer classes in "Repertoire for Singers" at the University of Colorado.

Pierre Delattre, Professor of French and Director of the Research Laboratory of Experimental Phonetics, University of California, Santa Barbara. Formerly Professor of French at the University of Colorado. Born in France, he was trained at the University of Paris and at the University of Michigan. He was head of the Department of Phonetics at Middlebury summer schools for 20 years and has been phonetics editor of the French Review since 1939. He has probably built the best experimental phonetics laboratory, for the analysis of accents in foreign languages and the acoustic analysis of vowels and consonants, in the United States. Contributor to Bulletin, National Association of Teachers of Singing, Volume XV, No. 1, October 1958, "Vowel Color and Voice Quality" (most important for comparison of speech and singing vowel qualities and vocal positions); Volume XVIII, No. 4, May 1962, "Effect of Pitch on the Intelligibility of Vowels." Lecturer at

NATS Workshops. French editor for Webster Dictionaries since 1941.

We extend our thanks to the following publishers who have allowed their lyrics to be used in this volume: Franco Colombo, Inc. (Ricordi), Boston Music Company, and G. Schirmer.

Berton Coffin, Professor and
Head, Division of Voice
University of Colorado
Boulder, Colorado

January 18, 1966

Procedures to follow in using these translations

When forming these word-for-word translations it has been found necessary to add words and to delete words for clarification of meaning. The rule for use is as follows:

In line two read the words in parentheses ( ) and omit the words in square brackets [ ].

Frequently the poetry included in this volume resists word-by-word translation. One of the great problems arises in the German text where a verb and its prefix may be separated by as much as two or three lines (i. e., Mach. . . zu). (Machen would mean "make," zu - "to," but zumachen would mean "close.") When verb and prefix are separated, the translation has been made under the verb (i. e., Mach (close) and a symbol [-] placed under the prefix since the qualifying influence of the prefix has been indicated in the word under the verb. Many times certain words should be left out when reading the word-by-word translation, because these words are meaningless in the English language. Therefore, bracketed words should be omitted, i. e., "Through the darkness steals [itself] bright sunshine." Frequently words need to be rearranged to give clarity of meaning. So the preceeding translation when rearranged becomes more meaningful when read, "Bright sunshine steals through the darkness." It is important that punctuation marks be observed when rereading lines for meanings. Frequently inversion in our language indicates a question - be sure and note whether there is a question mark before accepting a meaning, i. e., "Kăm' er zu mich," means "came he to me." Since there is no question mark the meaning is, "he came to me." Where the meaning of the word-by-word translation is obscure, an explanatory third line has been added.

Indexes

The texts in this volume are listed alphabetically by composer. An index of titles and first lines appears in the back of the book.

Bach   Bist du bei mir
                 Are you with me
                 (If you are with me)

Bist du bei mir, geh ich mit Freuden
Are you with me, go I with joy
(If you are with me)

zum Sterben und zu meiner Ruh!
to [the] dying and to my rest!

Ach, wie vergnügt wär so mein Ende,
Oh, how pleasant would be thus my end,

es drückten deine lieben Hände
it closed your beloved hands
(if your beloved hands close)

mir die getreuen Augen zu!
me the faithful eyes [shut]!
(my faithful eyes)

Bach   Komm, süsser Tod
                  Come, sweet death

Komm, süsser Tod, komm, sel'ge Ruh'!
Come, sweet death, come, blessed rest!

Komm, führe mich in Friede,
Come, lead me into peace,

weil ich der Welt bin müde.
since I of the world am tired.

Ach komm, ich wart' auf dich,
Oh, come, I wait for you,

komm bald und führe mich,
come soon and lead me,

drück' mir die Augen zu.
Press me the eyes shut.
(close my eyes)

Komm, sel'ge Ruh'!
Come, blessed rest!

Bachelet   Chère Nuit
                            Dear Night

Voici l'heure bientôt
Here is the hour soon,
(The time will soon come)

Derrière la colline
Behind the hill

Je vois le soleil qui décline
I see the sun that wanes
(I see the sun setting)

Et cache ses rayons jaloux.
And hides its rays jealous.
(And hiding its jealous rays)

J'entends chanter l'âme des choses
I hear sing the soul of things
(I hear the soul of things singing)

Et les narcisses et les roses
And the narcissi and the roses

M'apportent des parfums plus doux!
Bring me some perfumes more sweet!
(Bring me sweeter perfumes)

Chère nuit aux clartés sereines,
Dear night to the clarities serene
(Dear night with serene clearness)

Toi qui ramènes le tendre amant
You that bring back the tender lover.

Ah! descends et voile la terre
Ah! descend and veil the earth

De ton mystère, calme et charmant.
With your mystery, calm and charming.

Mon bonheur renaît sous ton aile,
My happiness is reborn under thy wing,

O nuit plus belle que les beaux jours:
O night more beautiful than beautiful days

Bachelet   Chère Nuit (Continued)

Ah! lève-toi! Pour faire encore
Ah! Arise! To make again

Briller l'aurore de mes amours!
Shine the dawn of my loves!
(The day of my loves dawn)

Beethoven　　　　　　　　Abscheulicher...

Abscheulicher!　wo eilst du hin?　from "Fidelio"
Abominable (one)!　where hurry you to?

Abscheulicher!　wo eilst du hin?
Abominable (one)!　where hurry you to?

was hast du vor in wildem Grimme?
what have you intended in wild fury?

Des Mitleids Ruf, der Menschheit Stimme,
[The] pity's call, [the] humanity's voice,

rührt nicht mehr deinen Tigersinn.
touches not anymore your tiger-sense.

Doch toben auch wie Meereswogen
Still roar also like sea-waves
(Still anger and rage roar)

dir in der Seele Zorn und Wuth,
you in the soul anger and rage,
(in your soul like sea-waves)

so leuchte mir ein Farbenbogen,
so shines (on) me a colorbow,
　　　　　　　　　　(bow of colors) (rainbow)

der hell auf dunklen Wolken ruht.
which brightly upon dark clouds rests.

Der blickt so still', so friedlich nieder,
It looks so quiet, so friendly down,

der spiegelt alte Zeiten wieder,
it mirrors old times again,
(it flashes back old times)

und neu besänftigt wallt mein Blut.
and newly soothed flows my blood.

Komm, Hoffnung, lass den letzten Stern
Come, hope, let the last star

der Müden nicht erbleichen,
of the tired not turn pale,
(of the despairing ones not turn pale)

13

o komm, erhell' mein Ziel, sei's noch so fern,
oh come, light up my goal, be it still so distant,

die Liebe, sie wird's erreichen.
[the] love, it will it reach.
(love will reach it)

Komm, o komm, komm, o Hoffnung!
Come, oh come, come, oh hope!

Lass den letzten Stern
Let the last star

der Müden nicht erbleichen!
of the tired not turn pale!
(of the despairing ones not turn pale)

Erhell' ihr Ziel, sei's noch so fern,
Light up their goal, be it still so distant,

die Liebe wird's erreichen.
[the] love will it reach.
(love will reach it)

Ich folg dem innern Triebe,
I follow the inner drive,

ich wanke nicht,
I stagger not,

mich stärkt die Pflicht
me strengthens the duty
(the duty of true wife's love)

der treuen Gattenliebe.
of true wife's love.
(will strengthen me)

O du, für den ich alles trug,
Oh you, for whom I everything endured,

könnt' ich zur Stelle dringen,
could I [to] the place invade,

wo Bosheit dich in Fessein schlug,
where malice you in chains put,

und süssen Trost dir bringen!
and (could) sweet consolation to you bring!

Beethoven   Adelaide
                        Adelaide

Einsam wandelt dein Freund im Frühlingsgarten,
Lonely walks your friend in the Spring-garden,

mild vom lieblichen Zauberlicht umflossen,
mildly by gentle magic-light surrounded,

das durch wankende Blütenzweige zittert,
which through swaying flower-branches trembles,
                               (shimmers)

Adelaide!
Adelaide!

In der spiegelnden Fluth, im Schnee der Alpen,
In the mirroring flood, in the snow of the Alps,

in des sinkenden Tages Goldgewölke,
in the sinking day's golden clouds,

Im Gefilde der Sterne strahlt dein Bildnis,
In the fields of stars shines your image,

Adelaide!
Adelaide!

Abendlüftchen im zarten Laube flüstern,
Evening-breezes in the tender foliage whisper,

Silberglöckchen des Mai's im Grase säuseln,
silver-bells of May in the grass rustle,

Wellen rauschen und Nachtigallen flöten:
waves roar and nightingales sing:

Adelaide!
Adelaide!

Einst, o Wunder! entblüht auf meinem Grabe
Once, oh miracle! blooms upon my grave

eine Blume der Asche meines Herzens,
a flower from the ashes of my heart,

Beethoven   Adelaide (Continued)

deutlich schimmert auf jedem Purpurblättchen:
clearly glitters upon each purple-leaf:

Adelaide!
Adelaide!

Beethoven   Der Floh
                 The flea

Es war einmal ein König,
There was once a king,

der hatt' einen grossen Floh,
who had a big flea,

den liebt' er garnicht wenig,
whom loved he not little
(whom he loved not little)

als wie seinen eig'nen Sohn.
just like his own son.

Da rief er seinen Schneider,
Then called he his tailor,

der Schneider kam heran:
the tailor came near:

Da miss dem Junker Kleider,
There measure (for) the squire clothes,

und miss ihm Hosen an!
and measure him (for) trousers [-]!

In Sammet und in Seide
In velvet and in silk

war er nun angethan,
was he now dressed,

hatte Bänder auf dem Kleide,
had ribbons on his coat,

hatt' auch ein Kreuz daran,
had also a cross thereon,
        (medal)

und war sogleich Minister,
and was (made) at once minister of State,

und hatt' einen grossen Stern,
and had a big star,
        (decoration)

17

da wurden seine Geschwister
then became his brothers and sisters

bei Hof auch grosse Herr'n.
at court also big people.

Und Herr'n und Frau'n am Hofe,
And gentlemen and ladies at the court,

die waren sehr geplagt,
they were much plagued,

die Königin und die Zofe
the Queen and the lady's maid

gestochen und genagt,
(were) stung and bitten,

und durften sie nicht knicken,
and could them not pinch,
(and were not allowed to pinch them)

und weg sie jucken nicht.
and away them scratch not.
(and not scratch them away)

Wir knicken und ersticken
We pinch and smother

doch, doch gleich, wenn einer sticht.
surely, but immediately, if one stings.
                                  (bites)

Beethoven   Die Ehre...

Die Ehre Gottes aus der Natur
The honor of God from [the] nature
    (Glory)

Die Himmel rühmen des Ewigen Ehre,
The heavens praise the Eternal's honor,

ihr Schall pflanzt seinen Namen fort.
their sound proclaims His name.

Ihn rühmt der Erdkreis,
Him praises the globe,

ihn preisen die Meere, vernimm, o Mensch,
Him praise the oceans, hear, oh man,

ihr göttlich Wort!
their divine word!

Wer trägt der Himmel unzählbare Sterne?
Who carries the heavens innumerable stars?

Wer führt die Sonn' aus ihrem Zelt?
Who leads the sun from its tent?

Sie kommt und leuchtet und lacht uns von ferne
It comes and shines and smiles us from afar
(the sun)   (at us)

und läuft den Weg gleich als ein Held.
and strides the road just as a hero.

Beethoven   Die Trommel gerühret
               The drum beat
               (Beat the drum)

Die Trommel gerühret, das Pfeifchen gespielet!
The drum beat, the pipe play!
(Beat the drum, play the pipe)

Mein Liebster gewaffnet den Haufen befiehlt,
My beloved armed the crowd commands,
(In arms my beloved commands the soldiers)

die Lanze hoch führet, die Leute regieret.
the lance high lifts, the people rules.
(he lifts high the lance and rules the people)

Wie klopft mir das Herz!   Wie wallt mir das Blut!
How beats me the heart!   How boils me the blood!
(How my heart beats!   How my blood boils)

O hätt' ich ein Wämslein und Hosen und Hut!
O, had I a little shirt and trousers and hat!

Ich folgt' ihm zum Thor 'naus mit muthigem Schritt,
I (would) follow him to the gate [out] with courageous step,

ging' durch die Provinzen, ging' ürberall mit.
would go through the provinces, would go everywhere with
   (them).

Die Feinde schon weichen, wir schiessen da drein;
The foes already retreat, we shoot into them;

welch' Glück sondergleichen, ein Mannsbild zu sein!
what joy unparalleled, a boy to be!

Beethoven   Freudvoll und leidvoll
                       Joyful and sorrowful

Freudvoll und leidvoll, gedankenvoll sein;
Joyful and sorrowful, thoughtful (to) be;
(To be joyful and sorrowful, to be thoughtful)

Langen und bangen in schwebender Pein;
(to) long (for) and (to) care (for) in hovering torment;

himmelhoch jauchzend; zum Tode betrübt;
skyhigh rejoicing; to death saddened;
(to rejoice skyhigh; to be saddened to death)

glücklich allein ist die Seele, die liebt!
happy alone is the soul, which loves!

21

Beethoven　　　　　Gott! welch' Dunkel hier! from "Fidelio"
　　　　　　　　　　God! what darkness here!

Gott! welch' Dunkel hier!
God!　what darkness here!

O grauenvolle Stille!
O horrible silence!

Öd' ist es um mich her:
Dreary is it around me:

Nichts, nichts lebet ausser mir.
Nothing, nothing lives except me.

O schwere Prüfung!
O heavy trial!

Doch gerecht ist Gottes Wille!
But just is God's will!

Ich murre nicht:
I grumble not:

das Mass der Leiden steht bei dir!
the measure of suffering stands with thee!

In des Leben's Frühlingstagen
In [the] life's Spring days

ist das Glück von mir gefloh'n.
is [the] happiness from me fled.
(has happiness gone from me)

Wahrheit wagt' ich kühn zu sagen,
Truth dared I courageously to tell,

und die Ketten sind mein Lohn.
and the chains are my reward.

Willig duld' ich alle Schmerzen,
Willingly suffer I all pains,

ende schmählich meine Bahn;
(willingly) end (I) ignominiously my path;

süsser Trost in meinem Herzen:
sweet consolation in my heart:

22

Beethoven   Gott! welch' Dunkel hier! (Continued)
meine Pflicht hab' ich gethan!
my duty have I done!

Und spür' ich nicht linde, säuselnde Luft?
And feel I not gentle, rustling air?
                         (breeze)

Und ist nicht mein Grab mir erhellet?
And is not my grave [me] brightened?

Ich seh', wie ein Engel im rosigen Duft
I see, how an angel in rosy fragrance

sich tröstend mir zur Seite stellet,
[itself] consoling me at the side places,
(consolingly places itself at my side)

ein Engel, Leonoren, der Gattin, so gleich,
an angel, Leonore, the spouse, so alike,
(which is so like Leonore, the spouse)

der führt mich zur Freiheit in's himmlische Reich.
who guides me to freedom in the heavenly kingdom.

Beethoven   Ich liebe dich
                         I love you

Ich liebe dich, so wie du mich,
I love you, so as you me,
                (just as you love me)

am Abend und am Morgen,
in the evening and in the morning,

noch war kein Tag, wo du und ich
there was no day, where you and I

nicht theilten uns're Sorgen.
not shared our sorrows.

Auch waren sie für dich und mich
Also were they for you and me
(Shared by you and me they were)

getheilt leicht zu ertragen;
shared easy to endure;
(easy to endure)

du tröstetest im Kummer mich,
you comforted in sorrow me,

ich weint' in deine Klagen,
I cried in your laments,

D'rum Gottes Segen über dir,
Therefore God's blessing upon you,

du meines Lebens Freude,
you, my life's joy.

Gott schütze dich, erhalt' dich mir,
God protect you, keep you me,
                (keep you for me)

schütz' und erhalt' uns beide!
protect and keep us both!

Beethoven   Mailied
                  May-song

Wie herrlich leuchtet mir die Natur,
How splendid shines (to) me [the] nature,
(How splendid shines nature to me)

wie glänzt die Sonne, wie lacht die Flur!
how gleams the sun, how smiles the field!

Es dringen Blüten aus jedem Zweig
It brings blossoms from each branch

und tausend Stimmen aus dem Gesträuch,
and thousand voices from the shrub,

und Freud' und Wonne aus jeder Brust:
and joy and bliss from each breast:

o Erd', o Sonne, o Glück, o Lust!
oh Earth, oh sun, oh happiness, oh delight!

O Lieb', o Liebe, so golden schön,
Oh love, oh love, so golden beautiful,
           (so beautifully golden)

wie Morgenwolken auf jenen Höh'n!
as morning-clouds upon those hills!

Du segnest herrlich das frische Feld,
You blessed splendidly the fresh field,

im Blütendampfe die volle Welt.
in the vapor of flowers - the whole world.
        (scent of flowers)

O Mädchen, Mädchen, wie lieb ich dich!
Oh maiden, maiden, how love I you!

wie blickt dein Auge, wie liebst du mich!
how looks your eye, how loves you me!
(how your eyes look, how you love me)

So liebt die Lerche Gesang und Luft,
so loves the lark song and air,

und Morgenblumen den Himmelsduft,
and morning-flowers the heaven's scent,
(and flowers in the morning the perfume of heaven)

25

Beethoven   Mailied   (Continued)

wie ich dich liebe mit warmem Blut,
how I you love with warm blood,

die du mir Jugend und Freud' und Muth
who you me youth and joy and courage
(you who give me youth and joy and courage)

zu neuen liedern und Tränen gibst.
for new songs and tears gives.
(for new songs and tears)

Sei ewig glücklich, wie du mich liebst!
Be eternally happy, as you me love!
                    (for your love to me)

Beethoven   Mignon
                 Mignon

Kennst du das Land, wo die Citronen blüh'n,
Know you the land, where the lemons bloom,

im dunkeln Laub die Goldorangen glüh'n,
(where) in the dark foliage the golden oranges glow,

ein sanfter Wind vom blauen Himmel weht,
(where) a gentle breeze from the blue sky blows,

die Myrthe still und hoch der Lorbeer steht?
(where) [the] myrtle silent and high [the] laurel grow?

Kennst du es wohl?
Know you it perhaps?

Dahin möcht' ich mit dir, o mein Geliebter, zieh'n,
To that place want I with you, oh my beloved, (to) go.

Dahin!
To that place!

Kennst du das Haus?   Auf Säulen ruht sein Dach,
Know you the house?   On pillars rests its roof,

es glänzt der Saal, es schimmert das Gemach,
[it] shines the hall, [it] shimmers the chamber,
                        (light shimmers in the chamber)

und Marmorbilder steh'n und seh'n mich an:
and marble statues stand and look (at) me:

was hat man dir, du armes Kind, gethan?
what has one to you, you poor child, done?

Kennst du es wohl?
Know you it perhaps?

Dahin möcht' ich mit dir, o mein Beschützer, zieh'n.
To that place want I with you, oh my protector, (to) go.

Dahin!
To that place!

Kennst du den Berg und seinen Wolkensteg?
Know you the mountain and its clouded path?

27

Beethoven   Mignon (Continued)

Das Maulthier sucht im Nebel seinen Weg;
The mule seeks in the mist its road;

in Höhlen wohnt der Drachen alte Brut;
in caves dwells the dragon's old brood;

es stürzt der Fels und über ihn die Fluth.
[it] falls the rock and over it the flood.

Kennst du ihn wohl?
Know you it perhaps?

Dahin geht unser Weg!
To that place goes our road!

o Vater, lass uns zieh'n!
oh Father, let us move on!

Dahin lass uns zieh'n!
To that place let us move on!

Beethoven   Mit einem gemalten Band
                With a painted ribbon

Kleine Blumen, kleine Blätter
Small flowers, small leaves

streuen mir mit leichter Hand
strew [me] with light hand
(are strown with light hand)

gute junge Frühlingsgötter
good young Spring-Gods
(by the young gods of spring)

tändelnd auf ein luftig Band.
jestingly upon an airy ribbon.
(forming an airy ribbon of flowers)

Zephyr, nimm's auf deine Flüget,
Zephyr, carry it upon your wings,

schling's um meiner Liebsten Kleid;
entwine it around my beloved's dress;

und so tritt sie vor den Spiegel
and thus steps she before the mirror

all' in ihrer Munterkeit.
all in her liveliness.
(in all her liveliness)

Sieht mit Rosen sich umgeben,
Sees with roses herself surrounded,
(with roses surrounded, she herself)

selbst wie eine Rose jung.
herself as a rose young.
(looks like a young rose)

Einen Blick, geliebtes Leben!
One glance, beloved life!
(One glance from you, beloved one)

und ich bin belohnt genug.
and I am rewarded enough.

Fühle, fühle, was dies Herz empfindet,
Feel, feel, what this heart senses,

29

reiche frei mir deine Hand,
give freely (to) me your hand,

und das Band, das uns verbindet,
and the ribbon, which us unites,

sei kein schwaches Rosenband!
be no fragile band of roses!

Beethoven   Wonne der Wehmut
                   Joy of melancholy

Trocknet nicht, Thrähen der ewigen Liebe!
Dry not, tears of eternal love!

Ach, nur dem halb getrockneten Auge
Ah, only to the half-dried eye
(Ah, to the half-dried eyes)

wie öde, wie tot die Welt ihm erscheint!
how empty, how dead the world for it appears!
(the world seems empty and dead)

Trocknet nicht, Thränen unglücklicher Liebe.
Dry not, tears (of) unhappy love.

Berlioz   L'absence
            Absence

Reviens, reviens, ma bien-aimée!
Return, return, my beloved!

Comme une fleur loin du soleil,
Like a flower far from the sun,

La fleur de ma vie est fermée
The flower of my life is closed
(The flower of my life has folded)

Loin de ton sourire vermeil,
Far from thy smile ruby,
(Far from thy ruby smile)

Entre nos coeurs quelle distance!
Between our hearts such distance!

Tant d'espace entre nos baisers!
So much space between our kisses!

O sort amer!   O dure absence!
O fate bitter! O hard absence!
(O bitter fate! O harsh separation)

O grands désirs inapaisés!
O great desires unappeased!
(O unfulfilled great passions)

D'ici là-bas que de campagnes,
From here to there so many countrysides,
(Between here and there, so many countrysides)

Que de villes et de hameaux,
So many cities and hamlets,

Que de vallons et de montagnes,
So many valleys and mountains,

A lasser le pied des chevaux!
To weary the foot of the horses!
(To weary the horses' feet)

Bizet   Habanera, from "Carmen"

L'amour est un oiseau rebelle
Love is a bird rebellious
(Love is a wild bird)

Que nul ne peut apprivoiser,
That no one is able to tame,
(That cannot be tamed)

Et c'est bien en vain qu'on l'appelle,
And it is quite in vain that one him calls,
(And it is quite in vain that one calls him)

S'il lui convient de refuser.
If it him suits to refuse.
(If it suite him to refuse)

Rien n'y fait, menace ou prière,
Nothing is to be done, threat or prayer,
(Nothing avails, threat or prayer)

L'un parle bien, l'autre se tait;
One speaks well, the other is silent;

Et c'est l'autre que je préfère
And it is the other that I prefer

Il n'a rien dit; mais il me plait.
He has nothing said; but he me pleases.
(He said nothing; but I like him)

L'amour est enfant de Bohême,
Love is child of Bohemia,
(Love is free like a gypsy)

Il n'a jamais, jamais connu de loi,
It has never, never known any law,

Si tu ne m'aimes pas, je t'aime;
If you me do not love, I you love;
(If you do not love me, I love you)

Si je t'aime, prends garde à toi!
If I you love, take care to yourself!
(If I love you, beware)

33

Mais si je t'aime, si je t'aime, prends garde à toi!
But if I love you, if I love you, beware!

L'oiseau que tu croyais surprendre
The bird that you thought to surprise
(The bird that you thought you were capturing)

Battit de l'aile et s'envola;
Fluttered his wings and took flight;

L'amour est loin, tu peux l'attendre;
Love is far, you can it expect;
(When love is distant, you expect it in vain)

Tu ne l'attends plus, il est là!
You expect it no longer, it is here!
(When you no longer expect it, it is here)

Tout autour de toi, vite, vite,
All around you, quickly, quickly,

Il vient, s'en va, puis il revient;
It comes, it goes away, then it returns;

Tu crois le tenir, il t'évite;
You think it to hold, it you avoids;
(When you think you hold it, it evades you)

Tu crois l'éviter, il te tient!
You think it to avoid, it you holds!
(When vou think you evade it, it holds you)

Bizet   Je dis...

Je dis que rien ne m'épouvante, from "Carmen"
I say that nothing frightens me, from "Carmen"

C'est des contrebandiers le refuge ordinaire.
This is of smugglers the refuge regular.
(This is the regular hide-out of smugglers)

Il est ici, je le verrai
He is here, I him will see
(He is here, I will see him)

Et le devoir que m'imposa sa mère
And the duty that on me imposed his mother
(And the task that his mother placed upon me)

Sans trembler je l'accomplirai.
Without to tremble I it will accomplish
(I will accomplish without trembling)

Je dis que rien ne m'épouvante,
I say that nothing me frightens,
(I say that nothing frightens me)

Je dis, hélas! que je réponds de moi;
I say, alas! that I answer of myself;
(I say, alas! that I can answer for myself)

Mais j'ai beau faire la vaillante,
But I have in vain to make the brave one,
(But no matter how brave I act)

Au fond du coeur je meurs d'effroi!
At the bottom of the heart I am dying of fright!
(Deep in my heart I am dying of fright)

Seule en ce lieu sauvage,
Alone in this place wild,
(Alone in this wild place)

Toute seule j'ai peur, mais j'ai tort d'avoir peur;
All alone I have fear, but I have wrong to have fear;
(All alone I am afraid, but I am wrong to be afraid)

Vous me donnerez du courage,
You me will give some courage,
(Thou wilt give me courage)

35

Bizet   Je dis que   rien... (Continued)

Vous me protégerez, Seigneur!
You me will protect, Lord!
(Thou wilt protect me, Lord)

Je vais voir de près cette femme
I am going to see closely that woman
(I am going to see that woman face-to-face)

Dont les artifices maudits
Of whom the guiles accursed
(Whose evil charms)

Ont fini par faire un infâme
Have ended by to make an infamous one
(Have succeeded in making a villain)

De celui que j'aimais jadis!
Of him that I loved of old!

Elle est dangereuse, elle est belle!
She is dangerous, she is beautiful!

Mais je ne veux pas avoir peur! Non ---
But I do not want to have fear! No ---
(But I do not want to be afraid! No)

Je parlerai haut devant elle
I will speak up before her
(I will speak boldly before her)

Ah! vous me protégerez! donnez-moi du courage!
Ah! you me will protect! give me some courage!
(Ah! Thou wilt protect me! Give me courage)

Bizet   La fleur...

La fleur que tu m'avais jetée, from "Carmen"
The flower which you to me had thrown

La fleur que tu m'avais jetée
The flower which you to me had thrown,

Dans ma prison m'était restée,
In my prison to me had remained,
(I kept in my prison)

Flétrie et sèche, cette fleur
Withered and dry, this flower

Gardait toujours sa douce odeur;
Kept always its sweet odor;
(Never lost its sweet scent)

Et pendant des heures entières,
And during (some) hours entire,
(And for hours on end)

Sur mes yeux, fermant mes paupières,
On my eyes, closing my lids,

De cette odeur je m'enivrais
With this scent I myself intoxicated

Et dans la nuit je te voyais!
And in the night I you saw!

Je me prenais à te maudire,
I myself found you damning,
(I found myself condemning you)

A te détester, à me dire:
At you detesting, to myself saying:

Pourquoi faut-il que le destin
Why must it be that the destiny
(Why is it that fate)

L'ait mise là sur mon chemin!
Her has put there on my road!
(Placed her there in my path)

37

Puis je m'accusais de blasphème,
Then I myself accused of blasphemy,

Et je ne sentais en moi-même,
And I not felt in myself,
(And within myself I only felt)

Je ne sentais qu'un seul désir,
I felt but one sole desire,

un seul désir, un seul espoir:
One lone desire, one lone hope:

Te revoir, ô Carmen, oui, te revoir!
You to see again, oh Carmen, yes, you to see again!

Car tu n'avais eu qu'à paraître,
For you had only to appear,

Qu'à jeter un regard sur moi,
Only to throw a glance on me,
(Only to cast me a glance)

Pour t'emparer de tout mon être,
In order to take possession of all my being,

O ma Carmen!   Et j'étais une chose à toi!
Oh my Carmen!   And I was a thing to you!
(Oh my Carmen!   And I belonged to you!)

Carmen, je t'aime!
Carmen, I you love!

Bizet   Ouvre ton coeur
                             Open your heart

La marguerite a fermé sa corolle,
The daisy has closed its corolla,

L'ombre a fermé les yeux du jour.
Shadow has closed the eyes of the day.

Belle, me tiendras-tu parole?
Beauty, to me will hold you word?
(Beautiful one, will you keep your promise to me)

Ouvre ton coeur à mon amour,
Open your heart to my love,

O jeune ange, à ma flamme,
Oh young angel, to my flame,

Qu'un rêve charme ton sommeil,
That a dream charm your slumber,
(Let a dream grace your sleep)

Je veux reprendre mon âme,
I want to recapture my soul,

Ouvre ton coeur, ô jeune ange, à ma flamme,
Open your heart, oh young angel, to my flame,

Comme une fleur s'ouvre au soleil!
As a flower opens to the sun!

Bizet   Seguidilla, from "Carmen"

Près des remparts de Séville,
Near the barricades of Seville,

Chez mon ami Lillas Pastia
By my friend Lillas Pastia
(At my friend Lillas Pastia's house)

J'irai danser la Séguedille
I shall go dance the Seguidilla

Et boire du Manzanilla.
And drink some Manzanilla.

J'irai chez mon ami Lillas Pastia
I shall go by my friend Lillas Pastia
(I shall go to my friend Lillas Pastia's house)

Oui, mais toute seule on s'ennuie,
Yes, but all alone one gets bored,

Et les vrais plaisirs sont à deux;
And the true pleasures are for two;
(Real pleasures are those which are shared)

Donc, pour me tenir compagnie,
So, in order to me hold company,
So, to keep me company,

J'emmènerai mon amoureux!
I shall bring my lover!

Mon amoureux il est au diable,
My lover he is with the devil,

Je l'ai mis à la porte hier!
I him have put at the door yesterday!
(Yesterday I threw him out)

Mon pauvre coeur très consolable,
My poor heart very consolable,
(My poor heart is easily consoled)

Mon coeur est libre comme l'air!
My heart is free as the air!
(My heart is as free as the wind)

40

Bizet   Seguidilla... (Continued)

J'ai des gallants à la douzaine,
I have (some) gallants by the dozen,
(I have dozens of admirers)

Mais ils ne sont pas à mon gré.
But they are not to my liking.

Voici la fin de la semaine:
Here is the end of the week:

Qui veut m'aimer? je l'aimerai!
Who wants me to love? I him shall love!
(Who wants to love me? I shall love him)

Qui veut mon âme? Elle est à prendre!
Who wants my soul? It is to take!
(Who wants my soul? It is free)

Vous arrivez au bon moment!
You arrive at the right moment!

Je n'ai guère le temps d'attendre,
I have hardly the time to wait,
(There is no time to lose)

Car avec mon nouvel amant, . . .
For with my new lover, . . .

Votre toast, je peux vous le rendre, from "Carmen"
Your toast, I can to you it return,

Votre toast, je peux vous le rendre,
Your toast, I can to you it return,

Señors, señors, car avec les soldats
Señors, señors, for with (the) soldiers

Qui, les Toréros peuvent s'entendre;
Yes, (the) Toreros can get together;

Pour plaisirs, pour plaisirs, ils ont les combats!
For pleasures, for pleasures, they have (the) combats!
(For pleasure, for pleasure, they fight)

Le cirque est plein, c'est jour de fête!
The arena is full, it is (a) day of feast!

Le cirque est plein du haut en bas;
The arena is full from top to bottom;

Les spectateurs, perdant la tête,
The spectators, losing their heads,

Les spectateurs s'interpellent à grand fracas!
The spectators challenge each other with a great uproar!

Apostrophes, cris et tapage
Apostrophes, shouts and loud noises

Poussés jusques à la fureur!
Pushed up to (the) furor!
(Raised to a furious pitch)

Car c'est la fête du courage!
For it is the holiday of courage!

C'est la fête des gens de coeur!
It is the holiday of people with heart!
(It is a day for courageous men)

Allons! en garde! ah!
Come! on guard! ah!

Toréador, en garde!
Toreador, on guard!

Et songe bien, oui, songe en combattant,
And think well, yes, think in fighting,
(And remember, yes, remember as you fight)

Qu'un oeil noir te regarde, et que l'amour t'attend,
That an eye black you looks at, and that love for you waits,
(That dark eyes are fixed upon you, and that love awaits you)

Toréador, l'amour t'attend!
Toreador, love you awaits!

Tout d'un coup, on fait silence. . .
All at a blow, one makes silence. . .
(All at once, it is quiet. . .)

Ah! que se passe-t-il?
Ah! what is happening?

Plus de cris, c'est l'instant!
No more cries, it is the instant!
(No more shouting, now is the time)

Le taureau s'élance en bondissant hors du Toril!
The bull springs forth (in) bounding out of the pen!

Il s'élance, il entre, il frappe!
He leaps, he enters, he strikes!

Un cheval roule, entraînant un Picador,
A horse rolls, dragging (along) a Picador,

"Ah! bravo! Toro!" hurle la foule!
"Ah! bravo! Toro!" cries the crowd!

Le taureau va, il vient, et frappe encore!
The bull goes, he comes, and strikes again!

En secouant ses banderilles,
While shaking his banderillas,

Plein de fureur, il court! Le cirque est plein de sang!
Full of fury, he runs! The arena is full of blood!

On se sauve, on franchit les grilles!
People run away, they climb the grates!

43

Bizet   Votre toast... (Continued)

C'est ton tour maintenant! Allons! en garde! ah!
It is your turn now! Come! on guard! ah!

Bohm   Still wie die Nacht
                        Calm as the night

Still wie die Nacht, tief wie das Meer
Calm as the night, deep as the sea

soll deine Liebe sein!
shall your love be!

Wenn du mich liebst, so wie ich dich,
If you me love, so as I you,

will ich dein eigen sein.
will I your own be.

Heiss wie der Stahl und fest wie der Stein
Hot as [the] steel and firm as [the] stone

soll deine Liebe sein!
shall your love be!

Brahms   Am Sonntag Morgen
                           On Sunday morning

Am Sonntag Morgen, zierlich angetan,
On Sunday morning, neatly dressed,

wohl weiss ich, wo du da bist hingegangen,
well know I, where you then have gone,

und manche Leute waren, die dich sah'n,
and many people [were], who you have seen,
                              (have seen you)

und kamen dann zu mir, dich zu verklagen.
[and] came then to me, you to accuse.

Als sie mir's sagten, hab ich laut gelacht,
As they to me it spoke, have I loudly laughed,

und in der Kammer dann geweint zur Nacht.
and in the room then wept at night.

Als sie mir's sagten, fing' ich an zu singen,
As they to me it spoke, began I to sing,

um einsam dann die Hände wund zu ringen.
for lonely then the hands sore to wring.
(but when alone, I wrung my hands till sore)

46

Brahms   An die Nachtigall
                  To the nightingale

Geuss' nicht so laut der liebentflammten Lieder
Pour not so loud the love-kindled songs'

tonreichen Schall
tone-rich sound

vom Blütenast des Apfelbaums hernieder,
from the blossom-branch of the apple tree [down],

o Nachtigall!
oh nightingale!

Du tönest mir mit deiner süssen Kehle
You sound me with your sweet throat
(with the sound of your sweet throat)

die Liebe wach;
the love awake;
(you awaken love)

denn schon durchbebt die Tiefen meiner Seele
for already passes through the depths of my soul

dein schmelzend "Ach."
your melting "Ach."

Dann flieht der Schlaf von neuem dieses Lager,
Then flees the slumber from anew this bed,

ich starre dann
I stare then

mit nassem Blick und totenbleich und hager
with wet glance and death-pale and haggard
(to the heaven with tearful eyes, deathly pale)

den Himmel an.
the heaven on.
(and haggard)

Fleuch, Nachtigall, in grüne Finsternisse,
Fly, nightingale, into green darknesses,

ins Haingesträuch,
into the grove's thicket,

47

und spend' im Nest der treuen Gattin Küsse,
and give in the nest of the faithful spouse kisses,
(and in the nest give kisses to the faithful spouse)

entfleuch!
fly away!

Brahms An eine Aeolsharfe
To an aeolian harp

Angelehnt an die Efeuwand dieser alten Terrasse,
Leaning against the ivy-wall of this old terrace,

du, einer luftgebornen Muse geheimnisvolles Saitenspiel,
you, an airborn muse's mysterious string-instrument,

fang' an, fange wieder an deine melodische Klage.
begin [-], begin again [-] your melodic lament.

Ihr kommet, Winde, ferne herüber,
You come, winds, far across,
                (from afar)

ach! von des Knaben, der mir so lieb war,
ah! from the boy, who (to) me so dear was,
(ah, from the boy's recently planted grave)

frisch grünende Hügel.
fresh greening mound.
(from the boy who was so dear to me)

Und Frühlingsblüten unterwegs streifend,
And spring-blossoms on the way brushing,
(The wind brushing the spring-blossoms on the way)

übersättigt mit Wohlgerüchen,
over-saturated with fragrances,
(becomes over-saturated with fragrances)

wie süss bedrängt ihr dies Herz!
how sweetly oppress you this heart!
(which sweetly oppress this heart)

Und säuselt her in die Saiten,
And whispers [thence] in the strings,

angezogen von wohllautender Wehmut,
attracted by harmonious melancholy,

wachsend im Zug meiner Sehnsucht
swelling in the track of my longing
(the sound swells, caused by my longing)

und hinsterbend wieder.
and dying again.
(sound which then dies again)

Aber auf einmal, wie der Wind heftiger herstösst,
But suddenly, as the wind more violently blows,

ein holder Schrei der Harfe
a gentle cry of the harp

wiederholt mir zu süssem Erschrecken
repeats (to) me in sweet alarm

meiner Seele plötzliche Regung.
my soul's sudden emotion.

Und hier, die volle Rose streut geschüttelt
And here, the full rose scatters, shaken (by the wind)

all' ihre Blätter vor meine Füsse!
all its petals at my feet!

Brahms   Auf dem Kirchhofe
                At the cemetery

Der Tag ging regenschwer und sturmbewegt,
The day went rain-heavy and storm-moved,
(The day was stormy and had heavy rains)

ich war an manch' vergess'nem Grab' gewesen,
I had at many a forgotten grave been,

verwittert Stein und Kreuz, die Kränze alt,
weather-beaten stone and cross, the wreathes old,

die Namen überwachsen, kaum zu lesen.
the names overgrown, hard to read.

Der Tag ging sturmbewegt und regenschwer,
The day went storm-moved and rain-heavy,

auf allen Gräbern fror das Wort: Gewesen.
upon all graves froze the word: has been.

Wie sturmestot die Särge schlummerten,
Like storm-dead the coffins slumbered,

auf allen Gräbern taute still: Genesen.
upon all graves thawed quietly: Healed.

Brahms   Botschaft
                        Message

Wehe, Lüftchen, lind und lieblich
Blow, little breeze, gently and charmingly

um die Wange der Geliebten,
around the cheeks of the beloved,

spiele zart in ihrer Locke,
play tenderly in her lock(s),

eile nicht, hinweg zu flieh'n.
hurry not, away to flee.

Tut sie dann vielleicht die Frage,
Does she ten perhaps (ask) the question,

wie es um mich Armen stehe,
how it around me poor one stands,
(how it is with me, poor one)

sprich: "Unendlich war sein Wehe,
speak: "Endless was his sorrow,

höchst bedenklich seine Lage;
highly doubtful his plight;

aber jetzo kann er hoffen,
but now can he hope,

wieder herrlich aufzuleben,
again joyfully to revive,

denn du, Holde, denkst an ihn. "
for you, lovely one, think of him. "

Brahms   Das Mädchen spricht
                      The maiden speaks

Schwalbe, sag' mir an,
Swallow, tell me,

ist's dein alter Mann
is it your old man
            (venerable husband)

mit dem du's Nest gebaut?
with whom you the nest built?

oder hast du jüngst erst dich ihm vertraut?
or have you recently only yourself to him wedded?

Sag', was zwitschert ihr,
Say, what warble you,

sag', was flüstert ihr
say, what whisper you

des Morgens so vertraut?
in the morning so intimately?

Gelt, du bist wohl auch noch nicht lange Braut.
Say, you are probably also yet not long ago bride.
(Say, you have probably not been a bride for very long)

Brahms   Dein blaues Auge
                          Your blue eye(s)

Dein blaues Auge hält so still,
Your blue eye(s) hold so tranquil,
            (are so tranquil)

ich blicke bis zum Grund.
I look till the ground.
            (into their depths)

Du fragst mich, was ich sehen will?
You ask me, what I (to) see desire?
            (what I want to see)

Ich sehe mich gesund.
I see myself recover.
(I look into them till I recover)

Es brannte mich ein glühend Paar,
[there] burned me a glowing pair, (of eyes)

noch schmerzt das Nachgefühl:
still pains the after-effect:

das deine ist wie ein See so klar
that of you is like a lake so clear
(those of yours are like a lake so clear)

und wie ein See so kühl.
and like a lake so cool.

54

Brahms   Der Schmied
                The blacksmith

Ich hör' meinen Schatz,
I hear my darling,

den Hammer er schwinget,
the hammer he swings,

das rauschet, das klinget,
that roars, that clangs,

das dringt in die Weite,
that penetrates (into) the distance,

wie Glockengeläute,
like bell's ringing,

durch Gassen und Platz.
over alleys and market-square.

Am schwarzen Kamin,
At the black hearth,

da sitzet mein Lieber,
there sits my beloved,

doch geh' ich vorüber,
[but] go I past,

die Bälge dann sausen,
the bellows [then] roar,

die Flammen aufbrausen,
the flames lick,

und lodern um ihn.
and blaze around him.

Brahms   Der Tod, das ist die kühle Nacht
                  [The] death, [that] is the cool night

Der Tod, das ist die kühle Nacht,
[the] death, [that] is the cool night,

das Leben ist der schwüle Tag.
[the] life is the sultry day.

Es dunkelt schon, mich schläfert,
It grows dark already, me sleepy,
                        (I'm sleepy)

der Tag hat mich müd' gemacht.
(the) day has me tired made.

Über mein Bett erhebt sich ein Baum,
Above my bed lifts [itself] a tree,
                        (grows)

d'rin singt die junge Nachtigall;
in it sings the young nightingale;

sie singt von lauter Liebe,
it sings of pure love,

ich hör' es sogar im Traum.
I hear it even in the dream.

Brahms   Die Mainacht
                [The] May-night

Wann der silberne Mond durch die Gesträuche blinkt,
When the silvery moon through the shrubs shines,

und sein schlummerndes Licht über den Rasen streut,
and its slumbering light over the lawn spreads,

und die Nachtigall flötet,
and the nightingale flutes,
                (sings)

wandl' ich traurig von Busch zu Busch.
walk I sadly from bush to bush.

Überhüllet vom Laub girret ein Taubenpaar
Covered by foliage coos a pair of doves

sein Entzücken mir vor;
its enchantment me for;
(its enchantment to me)

aber ich wende mich, suche dunklere Schatten,
but I turn myself, seek darker shadows,

und die einsame Träne rinnt.
and the lonely tear flows.

Wann, o lächelndes Bild,
When, oh smiling image,

welches wie Morgenrot durch die Seele mir strahlt,
which like morning-glow through the soul [me] shines,

find ich auf Erden dich?
find I on earth you?
(do I find you on earth)

Und die einsame Träne bebt mir heisser,
And the lonely tear trembles [me] hotter,
                (flows)

heisser die Wang herab.
hotter the cheek down.
(hotter down my cheek)

57

Brahms   Feldeinsamkeit
                  Field-solitude

Ich ruhe still im hohen grünen Gras
I rest quietly in the high green grass

und sende lange meinen Blick nach oben,
and send [at length] my glance [to] upward,

von Grillen rings umschwirrt ohn' Unterlass,
by crickets around swarmed without cessation,
(crickets swarm around me without cessation)

von Himmelsbläue wundersam umwoben.
by heaven's azure wondrously surrounded.

Die schönen weissen Wolken zieh'n dahin
The beautiful white clouds travel on

durch's tiefe Blau, wie schöne stille Träume;
through the deep blue, like beautiful silent dreams;

mir ist, als ob ich längst gestorben bin
(to) me is, as if I long ago died have
(I feel, as if I have died long ago)

und ziehe selig mit durch ew'ge Räume.
and travel happily [with]through eternal spaces.
(and happily travel with them through eternal spaces)

Brahms   Immer leiser wird mein Schlummer
                       Always fainter grows my slumber

Immer leiser wird mein Schlummer,
Always fainter grows my slumber,

nur wie Schleier liegt mein Kummer
and like veils lies my sorrow

zitternd über mir.
trembling upon me.

Oft im Traume hör' ich dich
Often in dream hear I you

rufen draus' vor meiner Tür,
call outside [before] my door,

niemand wacht und öffnet dir,
nobody wakes and opens (for) you,

ich erwach' und weine bitterlich.
I awake and weep bitterly.

Ja, ich werde sterben müssen.
Yes, I [have] die must.
(Yes, I must die)

Eine Andere wirst du küssen,
Another (one) will you kiss,

wenn ich bleich und kalt;
when I pale and cold;
(when I am pale and cold)

eh' die Maienlüfte weh'n,
before the May-breezes blow,

eh' die Drossel singt im Wald:
before the thrush sings in the forest:

Willst du mich noch einmal seh'n,
Will you me once more see,

komm', o komme bald!
come, oh come soon!

Brahms   In der Fremde
                In the foreign land

Aus der Heimat hinter den Blitzen rot,
From the homeland behind the lightning red,

da kommen die Wolken her.
there come the clouds from.
(from there come the clouds)

Aber Vater und Mutter sind lange tot,
But father and mother are long ago dead,

es kennt mich dort keiner mehr.
[it] knows me there nobody anymore.

Wie bald, ach, wie bald kommt die stille Zeit,
How soon, oh, how soon comes the silent time,

da ruhe ich auch
then rest I also

und über mir rauscht die schöne Waldeseinsamkeit,
and above me rustles the beautiful forest solitude,

und keiner kennt mich mehr hier.
and nobody knows me longer here.

Brahms   In Waldeseinsamkeit
          In forest solitude

Ich sass zu deinen Füssen in Waldeseinsamkeit;
I sat at your feet in forest solitude;

Windesatmen, Sehnen ging durch die Wipfel breit.
Wind's breathing, longing went through the treetops wide.

In stummen Ringen senkt' ich das Haupt in deinen Schoss,
In mute struggle sank I the head into your lap,

und meine bebenden Hände um deine Knie ich schloss.
and my trembling hands around your knees I clasped.

Die Sonne ging hinunter, der Tag verglühte all,
The sun has set, the day faded all,

ferne, sang eine Nachtigall.
from afar sang a nightingale.

Brahms Liebestreu
    True Love

"O versenk', o versenk' dein Leid, mein Kind,
"Oh sink, oh sink your sorrow my child,

in die See, in die tiefe See!"
into the sea, into the deep sea!"

"Ein Stein wohl bleibt auf des Meeres Grund,
"A stone will stay on the ocean's floor,

mein Leid kommt stets in die Höh'. "
my sorrow comes always to the high. "
                    (surface)

"Und die Lieb', die du im Herzen trägst,
"and the love, which you in the heart carry,

brich sie ab, brich sie ab, mein Kind!"
break it off, break if off, my child!"

"Ob die Blum' auch stirbt, wenn man sie bricht,
"Whether the flower also dies, when one it breaks,

treue Lieb' nicht so geschwind. "
true love not so fast. "
(true love does not break so fast)

"Und die Treu', 's war nur ein Wort,
"And [the] fidelity, [it] was only a word,

in den Wind damit hinaus!"
into the wind with it [out]!"

"O Mutter, und splittert der Fels auch im Wind,
"Oh mother, and splinters the rock even in the wind,

meine Treue, die hält ihn aus. "
my fidelity, it holds it out. "
            (outlasts the storm)

Brahms   Mädchenlied
              Maiden's song

Auf die Nacht in der Spinnstub'n
At [the] night in the spinning-room

da singen die Mädchen,
there sing the maidens,

da lachen die Dorfbub'n,
there laugh the village boys,

wie flink gehn die Rädchen!
how fast go the wheels!
        (turn)

Spinnt jedes am Brautschatz,
Spins each one at the trousseau,

dass der Liebste sich freut.
that the beloved [himself] be happy.

Nicht lange,
Not long,

so gibt es ein Hochzeitsgeläut.
then gives it a wedding-bells pealing.
        (and we will have wedding bells pealing)

Kein Mensch, der mir gut ist,
No man, who me good is,
(No one who loves me)

will nach mir fragen;
will for me ask;

wie bang mir zu Mut ist,
how fearful me in the heart is,
(how discouraged I am)

wem soll ich's klagen?
to whom shall I [it] complain?

Die Tränen rinnen mir übers Gesicht -
The tears flow [me] over the face -

Brahms   Mädchenlied   (Continued)

wofür soll ich spinnen?
what for shall I spin?
(for whom)

Ich weiss es nicht!
I know it not!
(I don't know)

Brahms　　　　　　Meine Liebe ist grün
　　　　　　　　　My love is green

Meine Liebe ist grün wie der Fliederbusch,
My love is green as the lilac bush,

und mein Lieb ist schön wie die Sonne,
and my beloved is beautiful as the sun,

die glänzt wohl herab auf den Fliederbusch
which shines right down on the lilac bush

und füllt ihn mit Duft und mit Wonne.
and fills it with scent and with joy.

Meine Seele hat Schwingen der Nachtigall
My soul has wings of the nightingale

und wiegt sich in blühendem Flieder,
and cradles itself in the blooming lilac,

und jauchzet und singet vom Duft berauscht
and rejoices and sings of fragrance drunk
(and intoxicated with fragrance rejoices and sings)

viel liebestrunkene Lieder.
many love-drunk songs.

Brahms   Minnelied
                Lovesong

Holder klingt der Vogelsang,
Lovelier sounds the bird-song,

wenn die Engelreine,
when the virgin-angel,

die mein Jünglingsherz bezwang,
who my young man's heart conquered,

wandelt durch die Haine.
walks through the woods.

Röter blühen Tal und Au,
Redder blooms valley and meadow,

grüner wird der Wasen,
greener grows the lawn,

wo die Finger meiner Frau
where the fingers of my mistress

Maienblumen lasen.
may-flowers gathered.

Ohne sie ist alles tot,
without her is everything dead,

welk sind Blüt' und Kräuter:
withered are blossoms and herbs:

und kein Frühlingsabendrot
and no spring-evening-glow

dünkt mir schön und heiter.
seems to me beautiful and serene.

Traute, minnigliche Frau
Gentle, lovely lady

wollest nimmer fliehen,
may (you) never flee,

dass mein Herz, gleich dieser Au,
that my heart, like this meadow,

mög' in Wonne blühen.
may in bliss bloom.

Brahms   Nachtigall
                          Nightingale

O Nachtigall, dein süsser Schall,
Oh nightingale, your sweet sound,

er dringet mir durch Mark und Bein.
[it] penetrates me through marrow and leg.
                          (marrow and bone)

Nein, trauter Vogel, nein!
No, beloved bird, no!

Was in mir schafft so süsse Pein,
That which in me creates such sweet torment,

das ist nicht dein,
[that] is not your (sound),

das ist von andern, himmelsschönen,
that is of other, heavenly,

nun längst für mich verklungenen Tönen
now long for me died away sounds
(sounds which for me died away long ago)

in deinem Lied ein leiser Wiederhall!
in your song a soft echo!
(but echo softly in your song)

Brahms   Nicht mehr zu dir zu gehen
                No more to you to go

Nicht mehr zu dir zu gehen,
No more to you to go,

beschloss ich und beschwor ich,
resolved I and swore I,

und gehe jeden Abend,
and go each evening
(but)

denn jede Kraft
for each power
   (all)

und jeden Halt verlor ich.
and each strength lost I.
   (all will-power)

Ich möchte nicht mehr leben,
I wish no longer to live,

möcht augenblicks verderben,
wish instantly to perish,

und möchtedoch auch leben
and wish but also to live
(but also wish to live)

für dich, mit dir
for you, with you

und nimmer sterben.
and never to die.

Ach, rede, sprich ein Wort nur,
Ah, talk, speak one word only,

ein einziges, ein klares;
[an] only one, a clear one;

gib Leben oder Tod mir,
give life or death to me,

nur dein Gefühl enthülle mir, dein wahres!
but your feeling reveal to me, your true one!
                (feeling)

Brahms   O kühler Wald
                      Oh cool forest

O kühler Wald, wo rauschest du,
Oh cool forest, where rustles you,
(Oh cool forest in which my beloved walks)

in dem mein Liebchen geht?
in which my beloved walks?
(where do you rustle)

O Widerhall, wo lauschest du,
Oh echo, where listen you,
(Oh echo which willingly understands)

der gern mein Lied versteht?
which willingly my song understands?
(my song, where do you listen)

Im Herzen tief da rauscht der Wald,
In the heart deep there rustles the forest,
(In the depth of the heart there rustles the forest)

in dem mein Liebchen geht,
in which my beloved walks,

in Schmerzen schlief der Widerhall,
in sorrows slept the echo,

der Lieder sind verweht.
the songs are blown away.

Brahms   O liebliche Wangen
                               Oh lovely cheeks

O liebliche Wangen,
Oh lovely cheeks,

ihr macht mir Verlangen,
you make me desire,

dies rote, dies weisse
this red, this white

zu schauen mit Fleisse.
to look (at) with eagerness.

Und dies nur alleine
And this solely alone

ist's nicht, was ich meine;
is it not, what I mean;

zu schauen, zu grüssen,
to look (at), to greet,

zu rühren, zu küssen!
to touch, to kiss!

ihr macht mir Verlangen,
you make me desire,

o liebliche Wangen!
oh lovely cheeks!

O Sonne der Wonne!
Oh sun of joy!

O Wonne der Sonne!
Oh joy of the sun!

O Augen, so saugen
Oh eyes, which drain

das Licht meiner Augen.
the light of my eyes.

O englische Sinnen!
Oh angelic thoughts!

O himmlisch Beginnen!
Oh heavenly beginning!

O Himmel auf Erden!
Oh heaven on earth!

Magst du mir nicht werden,
May you me not be,
(Will you not be mine)

o Wonne der Sonne,
oh joy of the sun,

o Sonne der Wonne!
oh sun of the joy!

O Schönste der Schönen!
Oh most beautiful of the beauties!

Benimm mir dies Sehnen,
Take (from) me this longing,

komm eile, komm, komme,
come hurry, come, come,

du Süsse, du Fromme!
you sweet, you gentle (one)!

Ach Schwester, ich sterbe,
Ah sister, I die,

ich sterb', ich verderbe,
I die, I perish,

komm, komme, komm eile,
come, come, come hurry,

benimm mir dies Sehnen,
take (from) me this longing,

o Schönste der Schönen.
oh most beautiful of the beauties.

Brahms   O wüsst' ich doch den Weg zurück
                          Oh knew I [but] the way back

O wüsst' ich doch den Weg zurück,
Oh knew I [but] the way back,

den lieben Weg zum Kinderland!
the beloved way to [the] children's land!

O warum sucht' ich nach dem Glück
Oh why searched I for [the] happiness

und liess der Mutter Hand?
and left [the] mother's hand?

O wie mich sehnet auszuruh'n,
Oh how me long (to) rest,
        (I)

von keinem Streben aufgeweckt,
by no strife awakened,

die müden Augen zuzutun,
the tired eyes to close,

von Liebe sanft bedeckt!
by love gently covered!

Und nichts zu forschen, nichts zu späh'n,
And nothing to seek, nothing to look (for),

und nur zu träumen leicht und lind,
and only to dream lightly and gently,

der Zeiten Wandel nicht zu seh'n,
[the] time's change not to see,

zum zweiten Mal ein Kind!
for the second time a child!
(to be a child for the second time)

O zeigt mir doch den Weg zurück,
Oh show me [but] the way back,

den lieben Weg zum Kinderland!
the beloved way to [the] children's land!

Vergebens such' ich nach dem Glück,
In vain search I for [the] happiness,

ringsum ist öder Strand!
all around is deserted shore!

Brahms Salamander
Salamander

Es sass ein Salamander
There sat a salamander

auf einem kühlen Stein,
on a cool stone,

da warf ein böses Mädchen
then threw a wicked maiden

ins Feuer ihn hinein.
into the fire him [in].
(him into the fire)

Sie meint', er soll verbrennen,
She thought, he should burn,

ihm ward erst wohl zu Mut,
him was just good to the heart,
(but it was just good for his heart)

wohl wie mir kühlem Teufel
(as) good as to me cool devil
(as good as burning love is)

die heisse Liebe tut.
the burning love does.
(for me, poor devil)

Brahms Sandmännchen
Little sandman

Die Blümelein sie schlafen
The little flowers [they] sleep

schon längst im Mondenschein,
already [long] in the moon shine,

sie nicken mit den Köpfchen
they nod with the little heads

auf ihren Stengelein.
upon their little stems.

Es rüttelt sich der Blütenbaum,
[it] sways [itself] the blossom-tree,

er säuselt wie im Traum:
it rustles as in the dream:

Schlafe, schlaf du, mein Kindelein!
Sleep, sleep you, my little child!

Die Vögelein sie sangen
The little birds [they] sang

so süss im Sonnenschein,
so sweetly in the sunshine,

sie sind zur Ruh gegangen
they are to the repose gone
(have gone to sleep)

in ihre Nestchen klein.
in their little nests tiny.
(in their tiny little nests)

Das Heimchen in dem Ährengrund,
The cricket in the field of wheat,

es tut allein sich kund:
[it] does alone [itself] give sound:

Schlafe, schlaf du, mein Kindelein!
Sleep, sleep you, my little child!

76

Sandmännchen kommt geschlichen
Little sandman comes creeping

und guckt durchs Fensterlein,
and looks through the little window,

ob irgent noch ein Liebchen
if some still a darling
(to see if still some darling)

nicht mag zu Bette sein.
not may to bed be.
(has not gone to bed)

Und wo er nur ein Kindchen fand,
And where he then a little child found,

streut er ihm in die Augen Sand.
strews he him in the eyes sand.

Schlafe, schlaf du, mein Kindelein!
Sleep, sleep you, my little child!

Sandmännchen aus dem Zimmer,
Little sandman out of the room,

es schläft mein Herzchen fein,
it sleeps my little heart fine,

es ist gar fest verschlossen
[it] is quite firmly closed

schon sein Guckäugelein.
already its little peeping eyes.
(already the little peeping eyes)

Es leuchtet morgen mir "Willkomm"
They shine tomorrow to me "Welcome"

das Äugelein so fromm!
the little eye(s) so gentle!

Schlafe, schlaf du, mein Kindelein!
Sleep, sleep you, my little child!

Brahms   Sapphische Ode
              Sapphic Ode

Rosen brach ich nachts mir am dunklen Hage;
Roses gathered I (in) the night (for) myself at the dark hedge;

süsser hauchten Duft sie als je am Tage;
sweeter exhaled fragrance they than ever in daytime;
(they exhaled sweeter fragrance than ever in daytime)

doch verstreuten reich die bewegten Äste
yet sprinkle richly the moving branches
(yet the moving branches richly sprinkled)

Tau, der mich nässte.
dew, which me moistened.
(dew, which moistened me)

Auch der Küsse Duft mich wie nie berückte,
Also the kisses scent me as never (before) charmed,
(The scent of kisses which I gathered in the night)

die ich nachts vom Strauch deiner Lippen pflückte:
which I in the night from the hedge of your lips gathered:
(from the hedge of your lips charmed me as never before)

doch auch dir, bewegt im Gemüt gleich jenen,
but also (from) you, moved in the soul like those,
(moved as you were in the soul, thawed the tears)

tauten die Tränen.
thawed the tears.
(like the dew drops from the roses)

Brahms   Schön war, das ich dir weihte
                          Beautiful was, what I you offered

Schön war, das ich dir weihte,
Beautiful was, what I you offered,

das goldene Geschmeide;
the golden jewels;

süss war der Laute Ton,
sweet was the lute's tone,

die ich dir auserlesen;
which I (for) you had chosen;

das Herze, das sie beide darbrachte,
the heart, that them both offered,

wert gewesen wär's,
worth would have been it,
(would have been worthy)

zu empfangen einen bessern Lohn.
to receive a better reward.

Brahms   Sonntag
                     Sunday

So hab' ich doch die ganze Woche
So have I [but] the whole week

mein feines Liebchen nicht geseh'n,
my beautiful darling not seen,

ich sah es an einem Sonntag
I saw her on a Sunday
(I saw her standing at the door)

wohl vor der Türe steh'n:
[indeed] at the door standing:
(on a Sunday)

das tausendschöne Jungfräulein,
the thousand-times beautiful maiden,

das tausendschöne Herzelein,
the thousand-times beautiful little heart,

wollte Gott, ich wär' heute bei ihr!
will God, I were today with her!
(God willing)

So will mir doch die ganze Woche
So will me but the whole week
(So will not end the smile in me)

das Lachen nicht vergeh'n,
the smile not end,
(during the whole week)

ich sah es an einem Sonntag
I saw her on a Sunday
(I saw her go to church)

wohl in die Kirche geh'n:
[indeed] to [the] church go:
(on a Sunday)

das tausendschöne Jungfräulein,
the thousand-times beautiful maiden,

das tausendschöne Herzelein,
the thousand-times beautiful little heart,

Brahms   Sonntag   (Continued)

wollte Gott, ich wär' heute bei ihr!
will God, I were today with her!
(God willing)

Brahms   Ständchen
                 Serenade

Der Mond steht über dem Berge,
The moon stands over the mountain,
        (hangs)

so recht für verliebte Leut;
so right for amorous people;
(just right for people in love)

im Garten rieselt ein Brunnen,
in the garden murmurs a fountain,

sonst Stille weit und breit.
otherwise quietness far and wide.

Neben der Mauer im Schatten,
At the wall in the shadow,

da steh'n der Studenten drei
there stand [of the] students three
(there are standing three students)

mit Flöt' und Geig' und Zither
with flute and fiddle and zither

und singen und spielen dabei.
and sing and play at the same time.

Die Klänge schleichen der Schönsten
The sounds creep to the most beautiful
(The sounds creep gently into the dream)

sacht in den Traum hinein,
gentle into the dream,
(of the most beautiful)

sie schaut den blonden Geliebten
she sees the blond lover

und lispelt: "vergiss nicht mein!"
and lisps: "forget not me!"
         (forget me not)

Brahms   Therese
                   Therese

Du milchjunger Knabe, wie schaust du mich an?
You milk-young boy, how look you me at?
(You very young boy, how do you look at me)

Was haben deine Augen für eine Frage getan!
What have your eyes for a question done!
(What question have your eyes asked)

Alle Ratsherrn in der Stadt und alle Weisen der Welt
All senators in the city and all sages of the world

bleiben stumm auf die Frage, die deine Augen gestellt!
remain mute to the question, which your eyes asked!

Eine Meermuschel liegt auf dem Schrank meiner Bas':
A seashell lies upon the cabinet of my female cousin:

da halte dein Ohr d'ran, dann hörst du etwas!
there hold your ear on, then hear you something!
(to it, then you hear something)

83

Brahms   Vergebliches Ständchen
                      Fruitless Serenade

Guten Abend, mein Schatz, guten Abend, mein Kind!
Good evening, my jewel, good evening, my child!

Ich komm' aus Lieb' zu dir,
I come out of love to you,

ach, mach' mir auf die Tür.
ah, open me up the door.
(ah, open the door for me)

Mein Tür ist verschlossen, ich lass' dich nicht ein;
My door is closed, I let you not in;

Mutter, die rät mir klug,
Mother, she advised me wisely,

wärst du herein mit Fug
were you in with pretext

wär's mit mir vorbei!
were it with me over!
(it would be the end of me)

So kalt ist die Nacht, so eisig der Wind,
So cold is the night, so icy the wind,

dass mir das Herz erfriert,
that me the heart freezes,
(that my heart will freeze)

mein Lieb' erlöschen wird,
my love extinguish will,
(that my love will extinguish)

öffne mir, mein Kind!
open (for) me, my child!

Löschet dein' Lieb', lass sie löschen nur!
Extinguishes your love, let it extinguish then!

Löschet sie immerzu,
Extinguishes it still,
                  (for good)

geh' heim zu Bett, zur Ruh'.
go home to bed, to repose.

gute Nacht, mein Knab'!
good night, my boy!

Brahms   Verrat
              Betrayal

Ich stand in einer lauen Nacht
I stood in a mild night

an einer grünen Linde,
at a green linden tree,

der Mond schien hell, der Wind ging sacht,
the moon shone bright, the wind went gently,
                                  (blew)

der Giessbach floss geschwinde.
the brooklet flowed swiftly.

Die Linde stand vor Liebchens Haus,
The linden tree stood before (the) beloved's house,

die Türe hört ich knarren.
the door heard I creak.

Mein Schatz liess sacht ein Mannsbild 'raus:
My darling let gently a man out (of the door):

"Lass morgen mich nicht harren;
"Let tomorrow me not wait;
(Do not let me wait tomorrow)

lass mich nicht harren, süsser Mann,
let me not wait, sweet man,

wie hab ich dich so gerne!
how am I (of) you so fond!

Ans Fenster klopfe leise an,
At the window knock softly,

mein Schatz ist in der Ferne, ja Ferne!"
my treasure is in the distance, yes distance!"
      (husband)

Lass ab vom Druck und Kuss, Feinslieb,
Let go of hug and kiss, lover,

du Schöner im Sammetkleide,
you handsome (one) in the velvet suit,

86

nun spute dich, du feiner Dieb,
now hurry [you], you fine thief,

ein Mann harrt auf der Heide, ja Heide.
a man waits on the heather, yes heather.

Der Mond scheint hell, der Rasen grün
The moon shines bright, the lawn green
                              (the green lawn)

ist gut zu unserm Begegnen,
is good for our meeting,

du trägst ein Schwert und nickst so kühn,
you carry a sword and nod so courageously,

dein Liebschaft will ich segnen, ja segnen!
your love-making will I bless, yes bless!

Und als erschien der lichte Tag,
And when arrived the shiny day,

was fand er auf der Heide?
what found it on the heather?
                (the day)

Ein Toter in den Blumen lag
A dead one in the flowers lay
(A dead one lay in the flowers)

zu einer Falschen Leide, ja Leide.
to a false one's sorrow, yes sorrow.

Brahms   Vier Ernste Gesänge
                        Four Serious Songs

                   1)   Denn es gehet dem Menschen
                     For it goes with man

Denn es gehet dem Menschen, wie dem Vieh,
For it goes with [the] man, as with the beast,

wie dies stirbt, so stirbt er auch;
as this dies, so dies he also;
   (the beast)   (man)

und haben alle einerlei Odem;
and have all the same breath;

und der Mensch hat nichts mehr, denn das Vieh:
and [the] man has nothing more, than the beast:

denn es ist alles eitel.
for it is all futile.

Es fährt alles en einen Ort;
They go all to one place;

es ist alles von Staub gemacht,
[it] is all of dust made,

und wird wieder zu Staub.
and becomes again [to] dust.

Wer weiss, ob der Geist des Menschen aufwärts fahre,
Who knows, if the spirit of man upwards goes,

und der Odem des Viehes unterwärts unter die Erde,
and the breath of (the) beast down below the soil,

unterwärts unter die Erde fahre?
down below the soil goes?

Darum sahe ich, dass nichts bessers ist,
Therefore saw I that nothing better is,

denn dass der Mensch fröhlich sei in seiner Arbeit,
than that [the] man happy be in his work,

den das ist sein Teil.
for this is his lot.

Denn wer will ihn dahin bringen,
For who will him to it bring,
(For who will bring him to the point)

dass er sehe, was nacht ihm geschehen wird?
that he sees, what after him happen will?
(that he can see, what will happen after he is gone)

Brahms   Vier Ernste Gesänge
Four Serious Songs

2) Ich wandte mich
I turned [myself]

Ich wandte mich und sahe an alle,
I turned [myself] and looked at all,

die Unrecht leiden unter der Sonne;
who injustice suffer under the sun;

und siehe, da waren Tränen,
and behold, there were tears,

Tränen derer, die Unrecht litten
tears of those, who injustice suffered

und hatten keinen Tröster;
and had no comforter;

und die ihnen Unrecht täten, waren zu mächtig,
and those (who) them injustice did, were too powerful,

dass sie keinen Tröster haben konnten.
that they no comforter have could.
(could have)

Da lobte ich die Toten, die schon gestorben waren,
Then praised I the dead ones, who already died have,
(have died)

mehr als die Lebendigen, die noch das Leben hatten.
more than the living ones, who still [the] life had.

Und der noch nicht ist, ist besser, als alle beide,
And he (who) yet not is, is better, than all both,
(is born, has it better than both)

und des Bösen nicht inne wird,
and the bad not perceives,
(for he is not yet aware of the bad)

das unter der Sonne geschieht.
which under the sun occurs.

Brahms   Vier Ernste Gesänge
           Four Serious Songs
           3) O Tod, wie bitter bist du
               Oh death, how bitter are you

O Tod, wie bitter bist du,
Oh death, how bitter are you,

wenn an dich gedenket ein Mensch,
when of you thinks a man,

der gute Tage und genug hat
who good days and enough has
(who has good days and plenty)

und ohne Sorge lebet;
and without worries lives;

und dem es wohlgeht in allen Dingen
and who is well off in all things

und noch wohl essen mag!
and still well eat likes!
(and still likes to eat well)

O Tod, wie wohl tust du dem Dürftigen,
Oh death, how well do you (for) the needy (one),
               (good are)

der da schwach und alt ist,
who [there] weak and old is,

der in allen Sorgen steckt,
who in all worries sticks,
(who has many worries)

und nichts Bessers zu hoffen,
and nothing better to hope (for),

noch zo erwarten hat!
nor to expect [has]!

O Tod, wie wohl tust du.
Oh death, how good do you.
               (are)

Brahms   Vier Ernste Gesänge
                     Four Serious Songs
                4)   Wenn ich mit Menschen- und mit
                     Engels-zungen redete
                     Though I with men's and with Angel's-
                     tongues speak

Wenn ich mit Menschen- und mit Engels-zungen redete,
Though I with men's- and with Angel's -tongues speak,
(Though I speak with the tongues of men and of angels)

und hätte der Liebe nicht,
and had [the] love not,

so wär ich ein tönend Erz, oder eine klingende Schelle.
so were I a sounding brass, or a clanging cymbal.

Und wenn ich weissagen könnte, und wüsste alle Geheimnisse
And though I prophecy could, and knew all secrets

und alle Erkenntnisse, und hätte allen Glauben,
and all knowledge, and had all faith,

also, dass ich Berge versetzte,
so, that I mountains move,
                   (could move)

und hätte der Liebe nicht,
and had [the] love not,

so wäre ich nichts.
so were I nothing.

Und wenn ich all meine Habe den Armen gäbe,
And if I all my property (to) the poor gave,

und liesse meinen Leib brennen,
and let my body burn,

und hätte der Liebe nicht,
and had [the] love not,

so wäre mir's nichts nütze.
so were [me] it (of) no profit.

Wir sehen jetzt durch einen Spiegel
We look now through a mirror
(We see the word unclear)

in einem dunkeln Worte;
into a dark word;
(as through a mirror)

dann aber von Angesicht zu Angesichte.
then but [from] face to face.

Jetzt erkenne ich's stückweise,
Now recognize I it partly,

dann aber werd' ich's erkennen,
then [but] will I it recognize,

gleich wie ich erkennet bin.
just as I recognized am.

Nun aber bleibet Glaube, Hoffnung, Liebe, diese drei;
Now but remains faith, hope, love, these three;

aber die Liebe ist die grösseste unter ihnen.
but [the] love is the greatest among them.

Brahms   Von ewiger Liebe
                   Of eternal love

Dunkel, wie dunkel im Wald und in Feld.
Dark, how dark in the forest and in the field.

Abend schon ist es, nun schweiget die Welt.
Evening already is it, now silences the world.
                    (is silent)

Nirgend noch Licht, und nirgend noch Rauch, ja,
Nowhere [yet] light, and nowhere [yet] smoke, yes,

und die Lerche sie schweiget nun auch.
and the lark it silences now also.

Kommt aus dem Dorfe der Bursche heraus,
Comes from the village the lad [out],

gibt das Geleit der Geliebten nach Haus,
gives [the] escort to the beloved till home,

führt sie am Weidengebüsche vorbei,
guides her by the pasture hedges [past],
(guides her past the hedges of the pasture)

redet so viel und so mancherlei:
talks so much and so many a thing:

"Leidest du Schmach und betrübest du dich,
"Suffer you shame and sadden you yourself,
(if you suffer shame and if you are sad)

leidest du Schmach von andern um mich,
suffer you shame by others about me,

werde die Liebe getrennt so geschwind,
be [the] love dissolved as fast,

schnell wie wir früher vereiniget sind.
fast as we earlier united were.

Scheide mit Regen und scheide mit Wind,
Separate with rain and separate with wind,

schnell wie wir früher vereiniget sind. "
fast as we earlier united were. "

Brahms   Von ewiger Liebe

Spricht das Mägdelein, Mägdelein spricht:
Speaks the maiden, maiden speaks:

"Unsere Liebe, sie trennet sich nicht!
"Our love, [it] dissolves [itself] not!

Fest ist der Stahl und das Eisen gar sehr,
Firm is the steel and the iron very much,

unsere Liebe ist fester noch mehr.
our love is firmer still [more].

Eisen und Stahl, man schmiedet sie um,
Iron and steel, one forges [them around],

unsere Liebe, wer wandelt sie um?
our love, who changes it [about]?

Eisen und Stahl, sie können vergehn,
Iron and steel, they can decay,

unsere Liebe muss ewig, ewig bestehn."
our love must eternally, eternally exist."

Brahms Wenn du nur zuweilen lächelst
If you only sometimes would smile

Wenn du nur zuweilen lächelst,
If you only sometimes would smile,

nur zuweilen Kühle fächelst
only sometimes coolness would fan

dieser ungemessnen Glut,
(on) this boundless ardor,

in Geduld will ich mich fassen
in patience will I myself composer
(compose myself)

und dich alles treiben lassen,
and (will) you everything carry on let,
(and will let you carry on everything)

was der Liebe wehe tut.
what [the] love harm does.
(which harms you)

Brahms   Wie bist du, meine Königin
                How are you, my queen

Wie bist du, meine Königin, durch sanfte Güte wonnevoll!
How are you, my queen, through gentle kindness, joyful!
(Through gentle kindness how joyful you are, my queen)

Du lächle nur, Lenzdüfte wehn durch mein Gemüte, wonnevoll!
You smile only, spring-scents blow through my soul, joyful!
(You only smile and scents of spring pass joyfully through
   my soul)

Firsch aufgeblühter Rosen Glanz, vergleich ich ihn den
   deinigen?
Fresh unfolded roses shine, compare I it to your (lustre)?

Ach, über alles was da blüht, ist deine Blüte, wonnevoll!
Ah, above all which there blooms, is your blossom, joyful!

Durch tote Wüsten wandle hin, und grüne Schatten breiten
   sich,
Through dead deserts walk [on], and green shadows spread,
(Green shadows spread when you walk through dead deserts)

ob fürchterliche Schwüle dort ohn' Ende brüte, wonnevoll!
whether terrible sultriness there without end broods, joyful!
(even though sultriness exists there without end, joyful)

Lass mich vergehn in deinem Arm!
Let me perish in your arm!

Es ist in ihm ja selbst der Tod,
It is in it even itself the death,
(In it even death itself is joyful)

ob auch die herbste Todesqual die Brust durchwüte,
whether also the bitter deathpain the chest devastates,
(whether also the bitter pain of death the chest devastates)

wonnevoll.
joyful.

Brahms   Wiegenlied
                Lullaby

Guten Abend, gut' Nacht,
Good evening, good night,

mit Rosen bedacht,
with roses covered,

mit Näg'lein besteckt,
with lilacs bedecked,

schlupf' unter die Deck'.
slip under the cover.

Morgen früh,
Tomorrow morning,

wenn Gott will,
if God will,

wirst du wieder geweckt.
will you again (be) wakened.

Guten Abend, gut' Nacht,
Good evening, good night,

von Eng'lein bewacht,
by little angels guarded,

die zeigen im Traum
who show in the dream

dir Christkindleins Baum:
(to) you Christchild's tree:

Schlaf' nun selig und süss,
Sleep now blissful and sweet,

schau' im Traum's Paradies.
see in the dream [the] Paradise.

Brahms   Wie Melodien zieht es mir
                Like melodies goes it me

Wie Melodien zieht es
Like melodies move in
                (sings love)

mir leise durch den Sinn,
[me] softly through the mind,

wie Frühlingsblumen blüht es,
like spring-flowers blooms it,

und schwebt wie Duft dahin.
and drifts like scent on.

Doch kommt das Word und fasst es
But comes the word and takes it
(But if this is put into words)

und führt es vor das Aug',
and brings it before the eye,
(and brought to your awareness)

wie Nebelgrau erblasst es
like grey mist fades it

und schwindet wie ein Hauch.
and vanishes like a breath.

Und dennoch ruht im Reime
And yet remains in the rhyme
(But even so remains in)

verborgen wohl ein Duft,
hidden [indeed] a fragrance,
(the rhyme a fragrance)

den mild aus stillem Keime
which mildly from the quiet bud
(which a tearful eye attracts)

ein feuchtes Auge ruft.
a moist eye calls.
(from the quiet bud)

Brahms   Wir wandelten, wir zwei zusammen
                      We wandered, we two together

Wir wandelten, wir zwei zusammen,
We wandered, we two together,

ich war so still und du so stille;
I was so silent and you so silent;

ich gäbe viel, um zu erfahren,
I would give much, [for] to know,

was du gedacht in jenem Fall.
what you thought in that event.

Was ich gedacht, unausgesprochen verbleibe Das!
That which I thought, unspoken remain [that]!

Nur Eines sag' ich, eines sag' ich:
But one (thing) say I, one (only) say I:

So schön war alles, was ich dachte,
So beautiful was everything, which I thought,

so himmlisch heiter war es all'.
so heavenly serene was it all.

In meinem Haupte die Gedanken,
In my head the thoughts,

sie läuteten wie gold'ne Glöckchen;
[they] rang like golden little bells;

so wunderschön, so wunderlieblich
so strangely sweet, so strangely charming

ist in der Welt kein and'rer Hall.
is in the world no other sound.

Charpentier   Depuis le jour, from "Louise"
               Since the day

Depuis le jour où je me suis donnée,
Since the day when I myself have given,
(Since the day I gave myself)

Toute fleurie semble ma destinée.
All flowered seems my destiny.
(My fate seems strewn with flowers)

Je crois rêver sous un ciel de féerie,
I think to dream beneath a sky of enchantment,
(I think I am dreaming beneath a magic sky)

L''âme encore grisée de ton premier baiser!
The soul still intoxicated by your first kiss!
(My soul still reeling from your first kiss)

Quelle belle vie!   Mon rêve n'était pas un rêve!
What (a) beautiful life!   My dream was not a dream!

Ah!   je suis heureuse!
Ah!   I am happy!

L'amour étend sur moi ses ailes!
Love spreads over me its wings!

Au jardin de mon coeur chante une joie nouvelle!
In the garden of my heart sings a joy new!
(A new joy sings in the garden of my heart)

Tout vibre, tout se réjouit de mon triomphe!
All vibrates, all rejoices at my triumph!
(Everything trembles and exults with my triumph)

Autour de moi tout est sourire, lumière et joie!
Around me all is smile, light and joy!

et je tremble délicieusement
and I tremble deliciously

au souvenir charmant du premier jour d'amour!
at the memory charming of the first day of love!
(at the delightful memory of our first day of love)

Je suis heureuse!   trop heureuse.
I am happy!   too happy.

101

Chausson   Les papillons
                    Butterflies

Les papillons couleur de neige
The butterflies color of snow
(Snow white butterflies)

Volent par essaims sur la mer;
Fly in swarms over the sea;

Beaux papillons blancs,
Beautiful butterflies white,

Quand pourrai-je prendre le bleu chemin de l'air!
When will I be able to take the blue road of the air!

Savez-vous, ô belle des belles,
Know you, oh beautiful of the beautiful (ones),

Ma bayadère aux yeux de jais,
My dancing girl with eyes of jet,
(My dancing girl with jet-black eyes)

S'ils me voulaient prêter leurs ailes,
If they to me wanted to loan their wings,
(If they would loan me their wings)

Dites, savez-vous où j'irais?
Say, know you where I would go?

Sans prendre un seul baiser aux roses,
Without taking a lone kiss from the roses,
(Without stealing a single kiss from the roses)

A travers vallons et forêts
Across vales and forests

J'irais à vos lèvres mi-closes,
I would go to your lips half-closed
(I would fly to your half-closed lips)

Fleur de mon âme, et j'y mourrais.
Flower of my heart, and I there would die.

Chausson   Le temps des lilas
                The time of lilacs

Le temps des lilas et le temps des roses
The time of lilacs and the time of roses

Ne reviendra plus à ce printemps-ci;
Will come back no longer to this spring here;
(Will not come this spring)

Le temps des lilas et le temps des roses
The time of lilacs and the time of roses

Est passé, le temps des oeillets aussi.
Is past, the time of carnations too.

Le vent a changé, les cieux sont moroses,
The wind has changed, the skies are sad,

Et nous n'irons plus courir, et cueillir
And we will go no longer to run and to pick

Les lilas en fleur et les belles roses;
The lilacs in flower and the beautiful roses;

Le printemps est triste et ne peut fleurir.
The springtime is sad and cannot flower.

Oh! joyeux et doux printemps de l'année,
Oh! joyous and sweet spring of the year,

Qui vins, l'an passé, nous ensoleiller;
Which came, the year past, us to make sunny;
(Which came, last year, to bathe us in sunshine)

Notre fleur d'amour est si bien fanée,
Our flower of love is so well faded,
(The flower of our love is so withered)

Las! que ton baiser ne peut l'éveiller!
Alas! that your kiss cannot it awaken!

Et toi, que fais-tu? pas de fleurs écloses,
And you, what do you? no flowers blossomed,
(And as for you, what are you doing, no bursting blossoms)

Point de gai soleil ni d'ombrages frais;
No gay sunshine nor shades cool;

Le temps des lilas et le temps des roses
The time of lilacs and the time of roses

Avec notre amour est mort à jamais.
With our love is dead forever.

Debussy   Récit et...

Récit et Air de Lia, from "L'Enfant Prodigue"
Narrative and Air of Lia, from "The Prodigal Son"

L'année en vain chasse l'année!
The year in vain chases the year!
(In vain year follows year)

A chaque saison ramenée,
To each season returned,

Leurs jeux et leurs ébats m'attristent malgré moi;
Their games and their revels me sadden in spite of myself;
(Their games and revels of each returning season sadden me
   in spite of myself)

Ils rouvrent ma blessure et mon chagrin s'accroît. . .
They reopen my wound and my grief grows. . .

Je viens chercher la grève solitaire. . .
I come to seek the shore solitary. . .

Douleur involontaire!   Efforts superflus!
Pain involuntary!   Efforts superfluous!

Lia pleure toujours l'enfant qu'elle n'a plus!
Lia weeps still the child which she has no longer!

Azaël!   Azaël!   Pourquoi m'as-tu quittée?
Azaël!   Azaël!   Why me have you left?
(Azaël!   Azaël!   Why did you leave me)

En mon coeur maternel ton image est restée.
In my heart maternal your image has remained.

Azaël!   Azaël!   Pourquoi m'as-tu quittée?
Azaël!   Azaël!   Why me have you left?
(Azaël!   Azaël!   Why did you leave me)

Cependant les soirs étaient doux,
However, the evenings were mild,

Dans la plaine d'ormes plantée,
In the plain of elms planted,
(In the plain planted with elms)

105

Quand, sous la charge récoltée,
When, beneath the burden harvested,
(When, loaded with the gathered harvest)

On ramenait les grands boeufs roux,
One brought back the great oxen red.
(The great red oxen were led back)

Lorsque la tâche était finie,
When the work was finished,

Enfants, vieillards et serviteurs,
Children, old men and servants,

Ouvriers des champs ou pasteurs,
Workers of the fields or shepherds,

Louaient, de Dieu la main bénie.
Praised, of God the hand blessed.
(Praised the gracious hand of God)

Ainsi les jours suivaient les jours
Thus the days followed the days

Et dans la pieuse famille,
And in the pious family,

Le jeune homme et la jeune fille
The young man and the young woman

Echangeaient leurs chastes amours.
Shared their chaste loves.

D'autres ne sentent pas le poids de la vieillesse;
Others feel not the weight of old age;

Heureux dans leurs enfants,
Happy in their children,

Ils voient couler les ans
They see flowing the years
(They watch the years flow by)

Sans regret comme sans tristesse. . .
Without regret as without sadness. . .

Aux coeurs inconsolés que les temps sont pesants! .
To hearts disconsolate how the times are weighty! . .
(How heavy weight the years on disconsolate hearts. .

Azaël! Azaël! Pourquoi m'as-tu quittée?
Azaël! Azaël! Why me have you left?
(Azaël! Azaël! Why did you leave me)

Debussy   Beau soir
                 Beautiful Evening

Lorsque au soleil couchant les rivières sont roses,
When at the sun going down the rivers are pink,
(When the rivers are red at sunset)

Et qu'un tiède frisson court sur les champs de blé,
And a tepid shudder runs over the fields of wheat,
(And a warm wind crosses the wheat fields)

Un conseil d'être heureux semble sortir des choses
An advice to be happy seems to emerge from things
(Happiness seems to fill the air)

Et monter vers le coeur troublé,
And to ascend toward the heart troubled,

Un conseil de goûter le charme d'être au monde,
An advice to taste the charm of being in the world,
(An invitation to taste the delights of being alive)

Cependant qu'on est jeune et que le soir est beau,
While one is young and the evening is beautiful,

Car nous nous en allons, Comme s'en va cette onde;
For we go away, as goes away this river;

Elle à la mer, Nous au tombeau.
It to the sea, we to the tomb.

Debussy   C'est l'Extase
               It is Ecstasy

C'est l'extase langoureuse
It is the ecstasy languid

C'est la fatigue amoureuse
It is the fatigue loving
(It is the loving weariness)

C'est tous les frissons des bois
It is all the shudders of the woods

Parmi l'étreinte des brises.
Midst the embrace of the breezes.

C'est, vers les ramures grises,
It is, by the branches gray,

Le choeur des petites voix.
The chorus of little voices.

O le frêle et frais murmure
Oh the frail and cool babbling

Cela gazouille et susurre,
It purls and whispers,

Cela ressemble au cri doux
It resembles the call soft

Que l'herbe agitée expire.
Which the grass agitated emits.
(Which restless grass emits)

Tu dirais, sous l'eau qui vire,
You would say, under the water that turns,
(As if it were, beneath the winding stream)

Le roulis sourd des cailloux.
The rolling deaf of pebbles.
(The muted rolling of pebbles)

Cette âme qui se lamente
This soul which laments

En cette plainte dormante
In this moan sleeping

C'est la nôtre, n'est-ce pas?
It is ours, is it not?

La mienne, dis, et la tienne
Mine, say, and yours

Dont s'exhale l'humble antienne
From which exhales the humble antiphon
(From which the humble song exhales)

Par ce tiède soir, tout bas.
During this tepid evening, very low.

Debussy   Chevaux de bois
           Merry-go-round

Tournez, tournez, bons chevaux de bois
Turn, turn, good horses of wood
(Circle, circle, good merry-go-round)

Tournez cent tours, tournez mille tours
Circle a hundred times, circle a thousand times

Tournez souvent et tournez toujours
Turn often and turn always
(Often go round and keep going round)

Tournez tournez au son des hautbois.
Turn turn to the sound of the oboes.
(Go round and round to the organ's refrain)

L'enfant tout rouge et la mère blanche
The child all red and the mother while

Le gars en noir et la fille en rose
The guy in black and the girl in pink

L'une à la chose et l'autre à la pose,
The one (woman) at the thing and the other at the pose,
(The first woman natural, the other posing)

Chacun se paie un sou de dimanche.
Each one himself pays a penny for Sunday.
(Each allows himself a bit of Sunday pleasure)

Tournez, tournez, chevaux de leur coeur,
Turn, turn, horses of their heart,
(Keep going round, you horses of their hearts)

Tandis qu'autour de tous vos tournois
While around all your circles

Clignote l'oeil du filou sournois
Blinks the eye of the rogue furtive
(The eyes of the stealthy crook flicker)

Tournez au son du piston vainqueur!
Turn to the sound of the piston conqueror!
(Go round to the sound of the conquering piston)

111

C'est étonnant comme ça vous soûle
It is surprising how that you intoxicates
(Strange how it intoxicates you)

D'aller ainsi dans ce cirque bête:
To go thus in this circus stupid:

Rien dans le ventre et mal dans la tête,
Nothing in the stomach and (an) ache in the head,

Du mal en masse et du bien en foule.
From the evil in a mass and the good in a crowd.
(Some evil in abundance and some good in abundance)

Tournez, dadas, sans qu'il soit besoin
Go round, (rocking) horse, without that there be need
(Rocking horse run, without the need)

D'user jamais de nuls éperons
To use ever any spurs

Pour commander à vos galops ronds.
In order to command your gallops round.
(To direct your circular course)

Tournez, tournez, sans espoir de foin
Circle, circle, without hope of hay

Et dépêchez, chevaux de leur âme
And hurry, horses of their soul

Déjà voici que sonne à la soupe
Already here it is that sounds to the soup
(Already it is suppertime)

La nuit qui tombe et chasse la troupe
The night which falls and chases the troop
(And night falls chasing the crowd)

De gais buveurs que leur soif affame.
Of gay drinkers whom their thirst starves.
(Of gay carousers hungered by their thirst)

Tournez, tournez! Le ciel en velours
Turn, turn! (For) the sky in velvet

D'astres en or se vêt lentement,
Of stars in gold itself dresses slowly,
(Is getting dressed slowly in golden stars)

L'Eglise tinte un glas tristement.
The Church rings a knell sadly.

Tournez au son joyeux des tambours, tournez.
Circle to the sound joyous of the drums, circle.

Debussy   Clair de lune
                     Moonlight

Votre âme est un paysage choisi
Your soul is a landscape chosen
(Your soul is a refined landscape)

Que vont charmant masques et bergamasques
That go charming masks and bergamasks
(Which masks and bergamasks charm)

Jouant du luth et dansant et quasi
Playing the lute and dancing and almost

tristes sous leurs déguisements fantasques,
sad beneath their disguises strange,

Tout en chantant sur le mode mineur
All in singing on the mode minor
(While singing in a minor key)

L'amour vainqueur et la vie opportune,
Love conqueror and the life opportune,
(About conquering love and the easy life)

Ils n'ont pas l'air de croire à leur bonheur,
They don't have the air of believing in their happiness,
(They don't seem to believe in their happiness)

Et leur chanson se mêle au clair de lune,
And their song itself mixes with the clear of the moon,
(And their song blends with the moonlight)

Au calme clair de lune triste et beau,
With the calm clear of the moon sad and beautiful,
(With the calm moonlight sad and lovely)

Qui fait rêver les oiseaux dans les arbres
Which makes dream the birds in the trees
(Causing the birds in the trees to dream)

Et sangloter d'extase les jets d'eau
And sob with ecstasy the jets of water
(And the fountains to sob with ecstasy)

Les grands jets d'eau sveltes parmi les marbres.
The great jets of water slender midst the marbles.
(The great slender fountains among the marble statues)

114

Debussy   De fleurs (Prose Lyriques)
                        Of flowers (Lyrical Prose)

Dans l'ennui si désolément vert de la serre de douleur,
In the boredom so drearily green of the hothouse of sadness,
(In the green depression of the hothouse)

Les fleurs enlacent mon coeur de leurs tiges méchantes.
The flowers interlace my heart with their stems mean.
(The spiteful stems of flowers ensnare my heart)

Ah! quand reviendront autour de ma tête les chères mains
Ah! when will return around my head the dear hands
(Ah! when will my head be held once more in those dear
  hands)

si tendrement désenlaceuses?
so tenderly disentangling?

Les grands Iris violets violèrent méchamment tes yeux,
The great Irises purple violated wickedly your eyes,
(Great purple Irises have wickedly betrayed your eyes)

en semblant les refléter, Eux, qui furent l'eau du songe
in seeming to them reflect, They, that were the water of the
  dream
(by seeming to reflect them, those eyes, the quiet water)

où plongèrent mes rêves
where plunged my dreams

si doucement enclos en leur couleur;
so sweetly inclosed in their color;

Et les lys, blancs jets d'eau de pistils embaumés,
And the lilies, white jets of water of pistils embaumed,
(And lilies, whose scented pistils are white fountains)

ont perdu leur grâce blanche
have lost their grace white
(have lost their pale grace)

Et ne sont plus que pauvres malades sans soleil!
And are no longer but poor sick (ones) without sun!

Soleil! ami des fleurs mauvaises,
Sun! friend of the flowers bad,
(Sun! friend of evil flowers)

115

Debussy   De fleurs   (Continued)

Tueur de rêves! Tueur d'illusions, ce pain béni
Killer of dreams! Killer of illusions, this bread blessed
(Killer of dreams! Killer of illusions, this altar bread)

des âmes misérables! Venez!
of souls miserable! Come!
(of damned souls! Come)

Les mains salvatrices brisez les vitres de mensonge,
The hands saving break the panes of lie,
(Saving hands, break the lying glass)

Brisez les vitres de maléfice, mon âme meurt de
Break the panes of malefice, my soul is dying of

trop de soleil! Mirages!
too much sun! Mirages!

Plus ne refleurira la joie de mes yeux
No longer will reflourish the joy of my eyes
(The joy of my eyes will blossom no more)

Et mes mains sont lasses de prier,
And my hands are tired of praying,

Mes yeux sont las de pleurer!
My eyes are tired of weeping!

Eternellement ce bruit fou des pétales noirs
Eternally this noise crazy of petals black
(For ever this mad noise of the black petals)

de l'ennui tombant goutte à goutte sur ma tête
of boredom falling drop by drop on my head

Dans le vert de la serre de douleur!
In the green of the hothouse of sadness!

Debussy   De grève (Prose Lyriques)
                 On the shore (Lyrical Prose)

Sur la mer les crépuscules tombent,
On the sea the twilights fall,

Soie blanche effilée.
Silk white frayed.

Les vagues comme de petites folles jasent,
The waves like little crazy (girls) chatter,

petites filles sortant de l'école,
little girls leaving school,

Parmi les frou-frous de leur robes,
Midst the swishing of their dresses,

Soie verte irisée!
Silk green iridescent!

Les nuages, graves voyageurs,
The clouds, solemn travelers,

se concertent sur le prochain orage,
get together on the next storm,

Et c'est un fond vraiment trop grave
And it's a background truly too heavy

à cette anglaise aquarelle.
for this English watercolor.

Les vagues, les petites vagues,
The waves, the little waves,

ne savent plus où se mettre,
know no longer where themselves to put,
(no longer know where to go)

car voici la méchante averse,
for here is the nasty downpour,

Frou-frous de jupes envolées,
Swishing of skirts scattered,

Soie verte affolée.
Silk green frightened.

117

Debussy   De grève   (Continued)

Mais la lune, compatissante à tous!
But the moon, compassionate to everyone!

Vient apaiser ce gris conflit
Comes to pacify this gray conflict

Et caresse lentement ses petites amies
And caresses slowly her little friends

qui s'offrent comme lèvres aimantes
who themselves offer like lips loving
(who offer themselves like loving lips)

A ce tiède et blanc baiser.
To this warm and white kiss.

Puis, plus rien, plus que les cloches attardées
Then, more nothing, more but the bells late
(Then, nothing more, nothing but the tardy bells)

des flottantes églises!
of floating churches!

Angélus des vagues, Soie blanche apaisée!
Angelus of the waves, Silk white pacified!
(Angelus of the waves, smoothed white silk)

Debussy   De rêve   (Proses Lyriques)
                  Of dreams (Lyrical Prose)

La nuit a des douceurs de femme
The night has (some) sweetnesses of woman

Et les vieux arbres, sous la lune d'or, songent!
And the old trees, beneath the moon of gold, Are dreaming

A Celle qui vient de passer, la tête emperlée
To Her who comes of passing, the head bepearled
(Of Her who just passed by, her head wreathed in pearls)

Maintenant navrée, à jamais navrée,
Now heart-broken, forever heart-broken,

Ils n'ont pas su lui faire signe.
They did not know to her to make sign.
(They knew not how to give her a signal)

Toutes! Elles ont passé: les Frêles, les Folles,
All! They have passed: the Frail (ones), the Crazy (ones),
(All of the women have gone by: the weak ones, the mad
ones)

Semant leur rire au gazon grêle, aux brises frôleuses
Sowing their laughter on the lawn thin, with breezes brushing
(Sowing their laughter on the thin lawn, with lightly blowing
breezes)

la caresse charmeuse des hanches fleurissantes.
the caress charmer of hips flourishing.
(the charming caress of flowering hips)

Hélas! de tout ceci, plus rien qu'un blanc frisson.
Alas! of all this, no longer anything but a white shiver.
(Alas! of all this, no more than a white shiver)

Les vieux arbres sous la lune d'or pleurent
The old trees beneath the moon of gold weep

leurs belles feuilles d'or!
their lovely leaves of gold!

Nul ne leur dédiera plus la fierté
No one to them will dedicate any longer the pride

Debussy   De rêve   (Continued)

des casques d'or
of the helmets of gold

Maintenant ternis, à jamais ternis.
Now tarnished, forever tarnished.

Les chevaliers sont morts sur le chemin du Grâal!
The knights died on the road (to) the Grail!

La nuit a des douceurs de femme, Des main semblent
The night has (some) sweetnesses of woman, (The) hands
    seem

frôler les âmes, mains si folles, si frêles,
to brush (over) the souls, hands so crazy, so frail,

Au temps où les épées chantaient pour Elles!
To the time when swords would sing for Them!

D'étranges soupirs s'élèvent sous les arbres.
Strange sighs rise beneath the trees.

Mon âme, c'est du rêve ancien qui t'étreint!
My soul, it is some dream ancient that you grips!

Debussy   De soir   (Proses Lyriques)
                    Evening   (Lyrical Prose)

Dimanche sur les villes, Dimanche dans les coeurs!
Sunday on the cities, Sunday in the hearts!

Dimanche chez les petites filles chantant
Sunday with the little girls singing

d'une voix informée des rondes obstinés
with a voice unformed (some) rounds obstinate
(nursery rhymes with immature voices)

où de bonnes Tours n'en ont plus que pour quelques jours!
in which some good Towers have (left) no longer than a few
   days
(to live)

Dimanche, les gares sont folles!
Sunday, the (railroad) stations are (going) mad!

Tout le monde appareille pour des banlieues d'aventure
All the world prepares for (some) outskirts of adventure
(Everyone prepares for adventures in the suburbs)

en se disant adieu avec des gestes éperdus!
in (to one another) saying goodbye with gestures bewildered!

Dimanche les trains vont vite,
(On) Sunday the trains go fast,

dévorés par d'insatiables tunnels;
devoured by insatiable tunnels;

Et les bons signaux des routes échangent d'un oeil unique
And the good signals of roads exchange with an eye unique
(And good road signs with a single eye exchange)

des impressions toutes méchaniques.
impressions all mechanical.

Dimanche, dans le bleu de mes rêves
Sunday, in the blue of my dreams

Où mes pensées tristes de feux d'artifices manqués
Where my thoughts sad of fires of artifice missed
(Where my sad thoughts of missed fire works)

121

Ne veulent plus quitter le deuil
Want no longer to take (off) the mourning (clothes)

de vieux Dimanches trépassés.
of old Sundays dead and gone.

Et la nuit à pas de velours vient endormir
And the night with feet of velvet comes to put to sleep
(And the night silently comes to put to sleep)

le beau ciel fatigué, et c'est Dimanche
the beautiful sky tired, and it is Sunday

dans les avenues d'étoiles;
in the avenues of stars;

la Vierge or sur argent
the Virgin gold over silver

laisse tomber les fleurs de sommeil!
lets fall the flowers of sleep!

Vite, les petits anges, Dépassez les hirondelles
Quick, the little angels, Overtake the swallows

afin de vous coucher forts d'absolution!
so as to go to bed strong in absolution!
(so that you may go to bed all saved)

Prenez pitié des villes, Prenez pitié des coeurs,
Have pity on the cities, Have pity on the hearts,

Vous, la Vierge or sur argent!
You, the Virgin gold on silver!

Debussy   En sourdine
                       Muted

Calmes dans le demi-jour
Calm in the half-day
(Calm in the half-light of day)

Que les branches hautes font,
That the branches high make,
(That the high branches make)

Pénétrons bien notre amour
Let us fill (well) our love

De ce silence profond.
With the silence profound.

Fondons nos âmes, nos coeurs
Let us blend our souls, our hearts

et nos sens extasiés,
and our senses enraptured,

Parmi les vagues langueurs
Midst the vague langours

Des pins et des arbousiers.
Of pines and arbutus.

Ferme tes yeux à demi,
Close your eyes to half,
(Half-close your eyes)

Croise tes bras sur ton sein,
Cross your arms over your breast,

Et de ton coeur endormi
And from your heart put to sleep
(And from your slumbering heart)

Chasse à jamais tout dessein.
Chase forever all design.

Laissons-nous persuader
Let us be persuaded.

123

Au souffle berceur et doux
To the breath rocker and soft
(By the soft and rocking wind)

Qui vient à tes pieds rider
Which comes to your feet to ripple
(Which comes to your feet, rippling)

Les ondes de gazon roux.
The waves of grass red.

Et quand solennel, le soir,
And when, solemn(ly), the night,

Des chênes noirs tombera,
From oaks black will fall,
(Will fall from black oaks)

Voix de notre désespoir,
Voice of our despair,

Le rossignol chantera.
The nightingale will sing.

Debussy   Fantoches
                     Phantoms

Scaramouche et Pulcinella
Scaramouche and Pulcinella

Qu'un mauvais dessein rassembla
Whom an evil plot brought together

Gesticulent noirs sous la lune.   la la la. . .
Gesticulate, black, beneath the moon.   la la la. . .

Cependant l'excellent docteur Bolonais
However, the excellent doctor Bolonais

Ceuille avec lenteur des simples
Picks with slowness medicinal herbs

Parmi l'herbe brune.
Among the grass brown.

Lors sa fille, piquant minois
So his daughter, (a) piquant face

Sous la charmille, en tapinois,
Beneath the bower, on the sly,

Se glisse demi-nue la la la
Glides half-naked la la la

En quête de son beau pirate espagnol,
In quest of her handsome pirate Spanish,

Dont un amoureux rossignol
For whom an amorous nightingale

Clame la détresse à tue-tête.
Proclaims the distress at the top of its voice.

Debussy   Green

Voici des fruits, des fleurs, des feuilles et des branches,
Here are fruits, flowers, leaves and branches,

Et puis voici mon coeur, qui ne bat que pour vous;
And then here is my heart, which beats only for you;

Ne le déchirez pas avec vos deux mains blanches,
Do not it tear up with your two hands white,

Et qu'à vos yeux si beaux l'humble présent soit doux.
And may to your eyes so beautiful the humble present be
    sweet.
(And may the humble present be sweet to your beautiful eyes)

J'arrive tout couvert encore de rosée
I arrive all covered still with dew

Que le vent du matin vient glacer à mon front,
That the wind of the morning comes to freeze on my brow,

Souffrez que ma fatigue à vos pieds reposée
Suffer that my fatigue at your feet rested
(Permit my weariness, resting at your feet)

Rêve des chers instants qui la délasseront.
Dream of the dear moments which will it rest.
(To dream of dear moments which will refresh it)

Sur votre jeune sein, laissez rouler ma tête,
On your young breast, let roll my head,

Toute sonore encore de vos derniers baisers.
All sonorous yet from your last kisses.
(Still ringing from your last kisses)

Laissez-la s'apaiser de la bonne tempête,
Let it calm down after the good tempest,

Et que je dorme un peu puisque vous reposez.
And that I sleep a little since you are resting.
(And let me sleep a while since you are resting)

126

Debussy   Harmonie du soir
                  Harmony of the evening

Voici venir les temps où vibrant sur sa tige
Here comes the time when, shaking on its stem

Chaque fleur s'évapore ainsi qu'un encensoir;
Each flower evaporates like a censer;

Les sons et les parfums tournent dans l'air du soir;
The sounds and the scents turn in the air of evening;

Valse mélancolique et langoureux vertige,
Waltz melancholy and languid dizziness,

Chaque fleur s'évapore ainsi qu'un encensoir;
Each flower evaporates like a censer;

Le violon frémit comme un coeur qu'on afflige,
The violin trembles like a heart that one afflicts,

Valse mélancolique et langoureux vertige,
Waltz melancholy and languid dizziness,

Le ciel est triste et beau comme un grand reposoir
The sky is sad and beautiful like a great (road-side) altar

Le violon frémit comme un coeur qu'on afflige;
The violin trembles like a heart that one afflicts;

Un coeur tendre, qui hait le néant vaste et noir!
A heart tender, that hates the void vast and black!

Le ciel est triste et beau comme un grand reposoir;
The sky is sad and beautiful like a great (road-side) altar;

Le soleil s'est noyé dans son sang qui se fige. . .
The sun has drowned in its blood which congeals. . .

Un coeur tendre, qui hait le néant vaste et noir,
A heart tender, that hates the void vast and black,

Du passé lumineux recueille tout vestige
From the past luminous collects all vestige
(Collects all remains of a luminous past)

Le soleil s'est noyé dans son sang qui se fige
The sun has drowned in its blood which congeals

127

Debussy Harmonie du soir (Continued)

Ton souvenir en moi luit comme un ostensoir.
Your memory in me glows like a monstrance.

Debussy   Il pleure dans mon coeur
                       It weeps in my heart

Il pleure dans mon coeur
It weeps in my heart

comme il pleut sur la ville.
as it rains on the city.

Quelle est cette langueur
What is this languor

Qui pénètre mon coeur?
Which penetrates my heart?

O bruit doux de la pluie
Oh noise soft of the rain

Par terre et sur les toits!
On the ground and on the roofs!

Pour un coeur qui s'ennuie
For a heart which is bored
(For a weary heart)

O le bruit de la pluie!
Oh the noise of the rain!

Il pleure sans raison
It weeps without cause

Dans ce coeur qui s'écoeure.
In this heart which is discouraged.

Quoi! nulle trahison?
What! no betrayal?

Ce deuil est sans raison.
This grief is without reason.

C'est bien la pire peine
It is truly the worst pain

De ne savoir pourquoi,
To not know why,

Sans amour et sans haine,
without love and without hatred,

Mon coeur a tant de peine.
My heart has so much grief.

Debussy   L'Echelonnement des haies
                 Rows of hedges

L'échelonnement des haies
The successive rows of hedges

Moutonne à l'infini, mer
White caps to infinity, (the) sea

Claire dans le brouillard clair
Clear in the mist clear

Qui sent bon les jeunes baies.
Which smells good of young berries.

Des arbres et des moulins
Trees and windmills

Sont légers sur le vert tendre
Are light on the green tender
(Are weightless on the tender green)

Où vient s'ébattre et s'étendre
Where comes to gambol and stretch out

L'agilité des poulains.
The agility of colts.

Dans ce vague d'un Dimanche
In this obscurity of a Sunday

Voici se jouer aussi
Here is to play also
(Here come also to frolic)

De grandes brebis, aussi
Large sheep, as

Douces que leur laine blanche.
Soft as their wool white.

Tout à l'heure déferlait
In a while broke

L'onde roulée en volutes
The wave rolled in whorls
(The twisted wave)

De cloches comme des flûtes
Of bells like (some) flutes

Dans le ciel comme du lait.
In the sky like milk.
(In the milk-white sky)

Debussy   Les cloches
               Bells

Les feuilles s'ouvraient sur le bord des branches,
The leaves opened on the edge of the branches,

Délicatement,
Delicately,

Les cloches tintaient, légères et franches,
The bells tolled, light and frank,

Dans le ciel clément.
In the sky merciful.

Rythmique et fervent comme une antienne,
Rythmic and fervent like an antiphon,

Ce lointain appel
This far-away call

Me remémorait la blancheur chrétienne,
Me reminded the whiteness Christian,
(Recalled to me the Christian whiteness)

Des fleurs de l'autel.
Of the flowers of the altar.

Ces cloches parlaient d'heureuses années,
These bells spoke of happy years,

Et dans le grand bois
And in the large forest

Semblaient reverdir les feuilles fanées
They seemed to turn green again the leaves withered

Des jours d'autrefois.
Of days of old.

Debussy   L'ombre des arbres
                 Shade of trees

L'ombre des arbres dans la rivière embrumée
The shadow of trees in the river misty

Meurt comme de la fumée,
Dies like smoke,

Tandis qu'en l'air, parmi les ramures réelles
While in the air, among the branches real

Se plaignent les tourterelles.
Lament the turtledoves.

Combien ô voyageur, ce paysage blême
How much oh traveler, this landscape wan

Te mira blême toi-même
You reflected, wan yourself

Et que tristes pleuraient dans les hautes feuillées,
And how sad(ly) wept in the high boughs,

Tes espérances noyées.
Your hopes drowned.
(Your own drowned hopes)

Debussy   Mandoline
                   Mandolin

Les donneurs de sérénades
The givers of serenades

Et les belles écouteuses
And the beautiful (lady) listeners

Echangent des propos fades
Exchange (some) words insipid

Sous les ramures chanteuses
Under the branches singing

C'est Tircis et c'est Aminte,
It is Tircis and it is Aminte,

Et c'est Damis qui pour mainte
And it is Damis who for many a

Cruelle fait maint vers tendre.
Cruel (girl) makes many a verse tender.

Leurs courtes vestes de soie,
Their short jackets of silk,

Leurs longues robes à queues,
Their long dresses with trains,

Leur élégance, leur joie
Their elegance, their joy

Et leurs molles ombres bleues,
And their soft shadows blue,

Tourbillonnent dans l'extase
Whirl in the ecstasy

D'une lune rose et grise,
Of a moon pink and gray,

Et la mandoline jase,
And the mandolin chatters,

Parmi les frissons de brise.   La la.
Midst the shudders of (the) breeze.   La la.

Debussy   Nuit d'étoiles
               Night of stars

Nuit d'étoiles sous tes voiles,
Night of stars beneath your veils,

Sous ta brise et tes parfums,
Beneath your breeze and your perfumes,

Triste lyre qui soupire,
Sad lyre that sighs,

Je rêve aux amours défunts.
I dream of loves defunct.

La sereine mélancolie
The serene melancholy

Vient éclore au fond de mon coeur,
Comes to blossom at the bottom of my heart,

Et j'entends l'âme de ma mie
And I hear the soul of my darling

Tressaillir dans le bois rêveur.
Tremble in the wood dreaming.

Je revois à notre fontaine
I see again at our fountain

Tes regards bleus comme les cieux,
Your glance blue as the heavens,

Cette rose, c'est ton haleine,
This rose, it is your breath,

Et ces étoiles sont tes yeux.
And these stars are your eyes.

Debussy   Romance

L'âme évaporée et souffrante,
The soul fleeting and suffering,

L'âme douce, l'âme odorante,
The soul gentle, the soul sweet-smelling,

Des lis divins que j'ai cueillis
Of the lilies divine that I have gathered

Dans le jardin de ta pensée,
In the garden of your thought,

Où donc les vents l'ont-ils chassée,
Where then the winds it have they chased,
(Oh where have the winds driven it)

Cette âme adorable des lis?
This soul adorable of the lilies?

N'est-il plus un parfum qui reste
Is there no longer a perfume that remains

De la suavité céleste,
Of the sweetness celestial,

Des jours où tu m'enveloppais
Of the days when you me enveloped

D'une vapeur surnaturelle,
In a vapor supernatural,

Faite d'espoir, d'amour fidèle,
Made of hope, of love faithful,

De béatitude et de paix?
Of beatitude and of peace?

Debussy   Spleen

Les roses étaient toutes rouges,
The roses were all red,

Et les lierres étaient tout noirs.
And the ivy was all black.

Chère, pour peu que tu te bouges,
Dear, for (a) little that you yourself move,
(Dear, with your slightest movement)

Renaissent tous mes désespoirs.
Are reborn all my despairs.

Le ciel était trop bleu, trop tendre,
The sky was too blue, too tender,

La mer trop verte et l'air trop doux.
The sea too green and the air too balmy.

Je crains toujours, ce qu'est d'attendre!
I fear always, what it is to wait!

Quelque fuite atroce de vous.
Some escape atrocious by you.

Du houx à la feuille vernie
Of the holly with the leaf varnished

Et du luisant buis je suis las
And of the shining box-wood I am tired

Et de la campagne infinie,
And of the countryside never-ending,

Et de tout, fors de vous. Hélas!
And of everything, except (of) you. Alas!

Delibes   Bell Song, from "Lakmé"

Ah, Où va la jeune Indoue, Fille des Parias,
Ah, Where goes the young Hindu, Daughter of the Parias,

Quand la lune se joue dans les grands mimosas?
When the moon plays in the great mimosas?

Elle court sur la mousse et ne se souvient pas
She runs on the moss and does not remember

Que partout on repousse l'enfant des Parias.
That everywhere they shun the child of the Parias.

Le long des lauriers roses, Rêvant de douces choses,
Along the oleanders pink, Dreaming of sweet things,

Ah! Elle passe sans bruit Et riant à la nuit!
Ah! She passes without noise And laughing with the night!

Là-bas dans la forêt plus sombre, Quel est ce voyageur
    perdu?
Over there in the forest more dark, Who is that traveler
    lost?

Autour de lui des yeux brillent dans l'ombre,
Around him (some) eyes glitter in the darkness,

Il marche encore au hasard, éperdu
He walks still at random, bewildered

Les fauves rugissent de joie,
The beasts roar with joy,

Ils vont se jeter sur leur proie,
They are going to throw themselves on their prey,

La jeune fille accourt et brave leurs fureurs:
The young girl runs and challenges their angers:

Elle a dans sa main la baguette,
She has in her hand the wand,

Où tinte la clochette, des charmeurs! Ah!
Where jingles the little bell, of the charmers! Ah!

L'étranger la regarde, Elle reste éblouie.
The stranger her looks at, She stands dazzled.

Il est plus beau que les Rajahs!
He is more handsome than the Rajahs!

Il rougira, S'il sait qu'il doit la vie
He will blush, If he knows that he owes his life

A la fille des Parias.
To the daughter of the Parias.

Mais lui, l'endormant dans un rêve,
But he, her putting to sleep in a dream,

Jusque dans le ciel il l'enlève,
Up to (in) the sky he her takes,

En lui disant: ta place est là!
While to her saying: your place is there!

C'était Vishnou fils de Brahma!
It was Vishnou son of Brahma!

Depuis ce jour au fond des bois,
Since that day in the depths of the forest,

Le voyageur entend parfois
The traveler hears sometimes

Le bruit léger de la baguette,
The noise light of the wand,
(The light jingling of the wand)

Où tinte la clochette, des charmeurs!
Where rings the little bell, of the charmers!

Delibes

Bonjour, Suzon!
Hello, Suzon!

Bonjour, Suzon, ma fleur des bois!
Hello, Suzon, my flower of the woods!

Es-tu toujours la plus jolie?
Are you still the most pretty?

Je reviens tel que tu me vois,
I return such as you me see,

D'un grand voyage en Italie.
From a long voyage in Italy.

Du paradis j'ai fait le tour.
Of paradise I made the rounds.

J'ai fait des vers, j'ai fait l'amour,
I made some verses, I made love,

Mais que t'importe?
But what to you does it matter?

Je passe devant ta maison, Ouvre ta porte!
I am passing before your house, Open your door!

Je t'ai vue au temps des lilas,
I you saw at the time of lilacs,

Ton coeur joyeux venait d'éclore.
Your heart joyous had just blossomed.

Et tu disais, je ne veux pas qu'on m'aime encore.
And you said, I don't want that one me loves yet.
(And you were saying, I don't wish to be loved yet)

Qu'as-tu fait depuis mon départ?
What have you done since my departure?

Qui part trop tôt revient trop tard.
(He) who leaves too early returns too late.

Mais que m'importe?
But what to me does it matter?

141

Delibes   Les filles de Cadix
                The girls of Cadiz

Nous venions de voir le taureau,
We had just seen the bull,

Trois garçons, trois fillettes,
Three boys, three (young) girls,

Sur la pelouse il faisait beau,
On the lawn it made pretty,
(On the grass it was nice)

Et nous dansions un boléro Au son des castagnettes:
And we danced a bolero To the sound of the castanets:

Dites-moi, voisin, Si j'ai bonne mine,
Tell me, neighbor, whether I have good appearance,
(Tell me, neighbor, whether I have a nice face)

Et si ma basquine Va bien ce matin.
And if my skirt Goes well this morning.
(And if my skirt looks alright this morning)

Vous me trouvez la taille fine? ah!
You me find the waist slender? ah!
(You think I have a slender waist? ah!)

Les filles de Cadix aiment assez cela, ah! la ra la.
The girls of Cadiz like well enough that, ah! la ra la.

Et nous dansions un boléro Un soir, c'était dimanche.
And we danced a bolero One evening, it was Sunday.

Vers nous s'en vient un hidalgo,
To us comes up a hidalgo,

Cousu d'or, la plume au chapeau,
Sewn with gold, a feather in (his) hat,

Et le poing sur la hanche: Si tu veux de moi,
And the fist on the hip: If you want of me,
(And his fist on his hip: "If ever you want me)

Brune au doux sourire, Tu n'as qu'à le dire.
Brunette with the soft smile, You have but it to say.
(Brunette with the soft smile, You have only to say so)

142

Delibes   Les filles de Cadix   (Continued)

Cet or est à toi.   Passez votre chemin beau sire,
This gold is to you.   Pass your road handsome sire,
(This gold is yours.   Go on your way, handsome sire)

Les filles de Cadix n'entendent pas cela,
The girls of Cadiz don't understand that,

la ra la, ah.
la ra la, ah.

Duparc   Chanson triste
      Sad song

Dans ton coeur dort un clair de lune,
In your heart sleeps a clear of moon,
(Moonlight slumbers in your heart)

un doux clair de lune d'été,
a sweet clear of moon of summer,
(Soft summer moonlight)

Et pour fuir la vie importune,
And to flee the life importunate,
(And to flee this tiresome life)

Je me noierai dans ta clarté.
I shall drown in your brightness.

J'oublierai les douleurs passées
I shall forget the sorrows past

Mon amour; quand tu berceras
My love; when you will rock
(My love; as you lull to sleep)

Mon triste coeur et mes pensées
My sad heart and my thoughts

Dans le calme aimant de tes bras!
In the calm magnet of your arms!
(In the calm attraction of your arms)

Tu prendras ma tête malade
You will take my head sick

Oh! quelquefois sur tes genoux,
Oh! sometimes on your knees,

Et lui diras une ballade,
And to it say a ballad,
(And sing to it a ballad)

Une ballade, qui semblera parler de nous,
A ballad, which will seem to speak of us,

Et dans tes yeux pleins de tristesses,
And in your eyes full of sadnesses,

144

Dans tes yeux alors je boirai
In your eyes then I shall drink

Tant de baisers et de tendresses,
So much of kisses and of tendernesses,
(So many kisses and so much tenderness)

Que peut-être je guérirai.
That perhaps I shall recover.

Duparc   Extase
                          Ecstasy

Sur un lys pâle mon coeur dort
On a lily pale my heart sleeps

D'un sommeil doux comme la mort,
Of a sleep sweet as the death,
(In a slumber sweet as death)

Mort exquise, mort parfumée
Death exquisite, death perfumed

Du souffle de la bien-aimée.
With the breath of the beloved.

Sur ton sein pâle mon coeur dort
On your breast pale my heart sleeps

D'un sommeil doux comme la mort.
In a slumber sweet as death.

Duparc   Le manoir de Rosemonde
                          The manor of Rosemonde

De sa dent soudaine et vorace,
Of its tooth sudden and voracious,
(With its sudden and voracious bite)

Comme un chien l'amour m'a mordu.
Like a dog love me has bitten.

En suivant mọn sang répandu,
In following my blood spilled,
(By tracking my spilled blood)

Va, tu pourras suivre ma trace.
Go, you will be able to follow my trail.

Prends un cheval de bonne race,
Take a horse of good race,
(Take a good horse)

Pars, et suis mon chemin ardu,
Leave, and follow my path arduous,

Fondrière ou sentier perdu,
Bog or trail lost,

Si la course ne te harasse!
If the trip doesn't you tire!

En passant par où j'ai passé,
In passing by where I have passed,

Tu verras que seul et blessé,
You will see that alone and wounded,

J'ai parcouru ce triste monde,
I traversed this sad world,

Et qu'ainsi je m'en fus mourir Bien loin,
And that thus I went away to die Far off,

sans découvrir Le bleu manoir de Rosemonde.
without discovering The blue manor of Rosemonde.

Duparc   L'invitation au voyage
                      Invitation to a voyage

Mon enfant, ma soeur, Songe à la douceur
My child, my sister, Think of the sweetness

D'aller là-bas vivre ensemble. Aimer à loisir,
Of going over there to live together. To love at leisure,
(Of going down there and living together. To love without
   refrain)

Aimer et mourir Au pays qui te ressemble!
To love and to die In the country which you resembles!
(To love and to die in the country which resembles you)

Les soleils mouillés De ces ciels brouillés
The suns dampened By those skies fogged

Pour mon esprit ont les charmes Si mystérieux
For my spirit have the charms So mysterious
(To me have the mystical charm)

De tes traîtres yeux, Brillant à travers leurs larmes.
Of your traitor eyes, Shining through their tears.

Là, tout n'est qu'ordre et beauté, Luxe, calme et volupté!
There, all is but order and beauty, Luxury, calm and
   voluptuousness

Vois sur ces canaux Dormir ces vaisseaux
See on those canals Sleeping those vessels
(See those boats Slumbering in those canals)

Dont l'humeur est vagabonde;
Whose temperament is vagabond;
(Restless boats)

C'est pour assouvir Ton moindre désir
It is to fulfill Your least desire

Qu'ils viennent du bout du monde.
That they come from the ends of the earth.

Les soleils couchants Revêtent les champs,
The suns setting clothe the fields,
(The setting suns cover the fields)

148

Les canaux, la ville entière, D'hyacinthe et d'or;
The canals, the city entire, Of hyacinthe and of gold;
(The canals, the whole city, with hyacinthe and gold)

Le monde s'endort Dans une chaude lumière!
The world goes to sleep In a warm light!

Là, tout n'est qu'ordre et beauté,
There, all is but order and beauty,

Luxe, calme et volupté!
Luxury, calm and voluptuousness!

Duparc   Lamento
              Lament

Connaissez-vous la blanche tombe
Know you the white tomb

Où flotte avec un son plaintif L'ombre d'un if?
Where floats with a sound plaintive The shadow of a yew tree?

Sur l'if une pâle colombe,
On the yew a pale dove,

Triste et seule au soleil couchant,
Sad and alone at sunset [-]

Chante son chant.
Sings its song.

On dirait que l'ame éveillée Pleure sous terre
One would say that the soul awakened Weeps beneath (the)
    earth

à l'unisson De la chanson
in unison With the song

Et du malheur d'être oubliée
And at the misfortune of being forgotten

Se plaint dans un roucoulement,
Moans in a cooing (voice),

Bien doucement.
Very softly.

Ah! jamais plus près de la tombe Je n'irai,
Ah! never more close to the tomb I will go,

quand descend le soir Au manteau noir,
when descends the night In mantle black,
(as when night in its black cloak descends)

Ecouter la pâle colombe Chanter,
Listening to the pale dove Sing,
(And I hear the pale dove sing)

Sur la branche de l'if, Son chant plaintif!
On the branch of the yew, Its plaintive song!

150

Duparc   Phidylé
                  Phidylé

L'herbe est molle au sommeil
The grass is soft to the sleep
(The grass is soft to sleep on)

sous les frais peupliers,
beneath the cool poplars,

Aux pentes des sources moussues,
On the slopes of the springs mossy,

Qui dans les prés en fleurs
Which in the fields in flowers
(Which in the blossoming fields)

germant par mille issues,
sprouting from a thousand openings,

Se perdent sous les noirs halliers.
Are lost beneath the black thickets.

Repose, ô Phidylé.
Rest, oh Phidylé.

Midi sur les feuillages Rayonne,
Noon on the foliage Shines,

et t'invite au sommeil.
and you invites to sleep.

Par le trèfle et le thym, seules,
By the clover and the thyme, alone,

en plein soleil,
in full sunshine,

Chantent les abeilles volages;
Sing the bees fickle;
(The fickle bees sing)

Un chaud parfum circule au détour des sentiers,
A warm perfume circulates at the turn of the paths,

La rouge fleur des blés s'incline,
The red flower of wheats inclines,
(The red wheatflower blends)

151

Et les oiseaux, rasant de l'aile la colline,
And the birds, shaving with the wing the hill,
(And the birds, shaving the hillside with their wings)

Cherchent l'ombre des églantiers.
Seek the shade of the wild rose.

Repose, ô Phidylé, Repose, ô Phidylé.
Rest, oh Phidylé, Rest, oh Phidylé.

Mais, quand l'Astre incliné sur sa courbe éclatante,
But, when the Star inclined over its curve flashing,
(But, when the Sun, bent low on its bright sweep)

Verra ses ardeurs s'apaiser,
Will see its desires quieted,
(Sees its heat die down)

Que ton plus beau sourire
Let your most lovely smile

et ton meilleur baiser Me récompensent,
and your best kiss Me reward,

me récompensent de l'attente!
me reward for the wait!

Duparc   Soupir
                Sigh

Ne jamais la voir ni l'entendre,
Not ever her to see nor her to hear,
(Never to see nor hear her)

Ne jamais bout haut la nommer,
Not ever all high her to name,
(Never to name her aloud)

Mais, fidèle, toujours l'attendre, Toujours l'aimer.
But, faithful, always her to await, Always her to love,
(But to wait for her always, faithfully, Always to love her)

Ouvrir les bras, et, las d'attendre,
To open the arms, and, tired of waiting,

Sur le néant les refermer,
On the void them to enclose,
(To close them on the void)

Mais encor, toujours les lui tendre, Toujours l'aimer.
But still, always them to her to stretch out, Always her to
   love.
(But still, ever to stretch them out to her, Ever to love her)

Ah! ne pouvoir que les lui tendre,
Ah! to be able but them to her to hold out,
(Ah! only to be able to hold them out to her)

Et dans les pleurs se consumer,
And in the tears oneself consume,
(And consume oneself in tears)

Mais ces pleurs toujours les répandre,
But these tears always them to shed,
(But forever to shed these tears)

Toujours l'aimer.
Always her to love.
(Ever to love her)

Fauré   Après un rêve
       After a dream

Dans un sommeil que charmait ton image
In a sleep that charmed your image
(In a sleep that your image charmed)

Je rêvais le bonheur, ardent mirage;
I dreamed the happiness, ardent mirage;
(I dreamed of happiness, warm illusion)

Tes yeux étaient plus doux, ta voix pure et sonore.
Your eyes were more soft, your voice pure and sonorous.

Tu rayonnais comme un ciel éclairé par l'aurore;
You shone like a sky lit up by the dawn;

Tu m'appelais, et je quittais la terre
You me called, and I left the earth

Pour m'enfuir avec toi vers la lumière;
To escape with you to the light;

Les cieux pour nous ent'ouvraient leurs nues,
The heavens for us parted their clouds,

Splendeurs inconnues, lueurs divines entrevues. . .
Splendors unknown, flashes divine caught sight of. . .
(Unknown splendors, divine illuminations glimpsed at. . .)

Hélas! Hélas, triste réveil des songes!
Alas! Alas, sad awakening from dreams!

Je t'appelle, ô nuit, rends-moi tes mensonges;
I you call, oh night, give back to me your lies;

Reviens, reviens radieuse,
Return, return radiant (one),

Reviens, ô nuit mystérieuse!
Return, oh night mysterious!

Fauré   Au bord de l'eau
               Beside the water

S'asseoir tous deux au bord du flot qui passe,
To sit down all two beside the water which passes,
(Both of us sitting beside the passing current)

Le voir passer;
It to see pass;
(To see it go by)

Tous deux, s'il glisse un nuage en l'espace,
All two if it glides a cloud in the space,
(Both of us, if a cloud in the sky glides by)

Le voir glisser;
It to see glide;
(To see it glide by)

A l'horizon s'il fume un toit de chaume,
On the horizon if there smokes a roof of cottage,
(If a cottage chimney smokes on the horizon)

Le voir fumer;
It to see smoke;
(To see it smoke)

Aux alentours, si quelque fleur embaume,
In the vicinity, if some flower perfumes,
(If some flower close by gives off a scent)

S'en embaumer;
With it to perfume;
(To be perfumed by it)

Entendre au pied du saule où l'eau murmure,
To hear at the foot of the willow where the water murmurs,

L'eau murmurer,
The water murmuring,

Ne pas sentir tant que ce rêve dure
Not to feel as long as this dream lasts

Le temps durer,
The time last,
(The hours last)

155

Mais n'apportant de passion profonde
But not bringing of passion deep
(But to feel no other deep passion)

Qu'à s'adorer,
Than to each other adore,
(Than to adore one another)

Sans nul souci des querelles du monde,
Without any worry about the quarrels of the world,

Les ignorer,
Them to ignore,
(Not to know about them)

Et seuls tous deux devant tout ce qui lasse,
And alone all two before all that which tires,
(And the both of alone before all that which tires)

Sans se lasser;
Without getting tired;

Sentir l'amour devant tout ce qui passe,
To feel love before all that which passes,
(To feel that love, in face of all that disappears)

Ne point passer!
Not (at all) to pass!
(Is ever constant)

Fauré   Aurore
             Aurora

Des jardins de la nuit s'envolent les étoiles,
From the gardens of the night fly the stars,

Abeilles d'or qu'attire un invisible miel;
Bees of gold that attracts an invisible honey;
(Like golden bees drawn by an invisible honey)

Et l'aube, au loin, tendant la candeur de ses toiles,
And the dawn, far away, spreading the purity of its webs,
(And dawn, far away, like a spider stretching out her fresh-spun
   webs)

trame de fils d'argent le manteau bleu du ciel.
weaves with threads of silver the cloak blue of the sky.
(weaves with silver threads the blue cloak of the sky)

Du jardin de mon coeur qu'un rêve lent enivre,
From the garden of my heart that a dream slow inebriates,
(From the garden of my heart, intoxicated by a languid dream)

S'envolent mes désirs sur les pas du matin,
Fly away my desires on the footsteps of the morning,
(Fly my desires with the coming of the morn)

Comme un essaim léger qu'à l'horizon de cuivre,
Like a swarm light that to the horizon of copper,
(Like a weightless swarm which, to the golden horizon)

appelle un chant plaintif, éternel et lointain.
calls a chant plaintive, eternal and far away.
(a plaintive chant calls, distant and timeless)

Ils volent à tes pieds, astres chassés des nues,
They fly to your feet, stars chased from the clouds,
(To your feet they fly, stars chased from the cloudy realms)

Exilés du ciel d'or où fleurit ta beauté,
Exiled from the sky of gold where flowers your beauty

Et, cherchant jusqu'à toi des routes inconnues,
And, seeking up to you some ways unknown,
(And, taking unknown paths to reach you)

Mêlent au jour naissant leur mourante clarté.
Mix with the day being born their dying clearness.
(They blend their fading brightness with the rising day)

Fauré   Automne
                    Autumn

Automne au ciel brumeux, aux horizons navrants,
Autumn with sky misty, with horizons heart-breaking,

Aux rapides couchants, aux aurores pâlies,
With rapid sunsets, with dawns pale,

Je regarde couler comme l'eau du torrent,
I watch flowing like the water of the brook,

Tes jours faits de mélancolie.
Your days made of melancholy.

Sur l'aile des regrets, mes esprits emportés,
On the wings of regret, my spirits taken away,

Comme s'il se pouvait que notre âge renaisse,
As if it could be that our age be reborn,

Parcourent en rêvant les coteaux enchantés,
Traverse in dreaming the slopes enchanted,
(Run dreaming over the enchanted hills)

Où, jadis, sourit ma jeunesse!
Where, formerly, smiled my youth!
(Where long ago I spent my happy youth)

Je sens au clair soleil du souvenir vainqueur,
I feel in the clear sun of the memory conqueror,
(I feel in the bright sun of the conquering memory)

Refleurir en bouquet les roses déliées,
Reflourish in bouquet the roses undone,
(Blooming in a fresh bouquet the fallen roses)

Et monter à mes yeux des larmes, qu'en mon coeur
And rise to my eyes (some) tears, which in my heart

Mes vingt ans avaient oubliées!
My twenty years had (all) forgotten!

Fauré   En prière
                     In prayer

Si la voix d'un enfant peut monter jusqu'à Vous,
If the voice of a child can rise up to You,

O mon Père,
Oh my Father,

Ecoutez de Jésus, devant Vous à genoux,
Listen to of Jesus, before You on his knees
(Listen to Jesus, kneeling before You)

La prière!
The prayer!
(In prayer)

Si Vous m'avez choisi pour enseigner vos lois
If You me have chosen to teach your laws

sur la terre,
on the earth,

Je saurai Vous servir, auguste Roi des rois,
I shall know You to serve, august King of kings,
(I shall know how to serve You, magnificent King of kings)

O Lumière!
Oh Light!

Sur mes lèvres, Seigneur,
On my lips, Lord,

mettez la vérité Salutaire,
place the truth Salutary,
(place the saving truth)

Pour que celui qui doute,
So that he who doubts,

avec humilité, Vous révère!
with humility, You honors!
(may humbly pray to You)

Ne m'abandonnez pas,
Me abandon not,
(Do not abandon me)

donnez-moi la douceur nécessaire,
give me the grace necessary,

Pour apaiser les maux, soulager la douleur,
To reduce suffering, to relieve the pain,

la misère!
(and) misery!

Révélez-Vous à moi, Seigneur en qui je crois,
Reveal Yourself to me, Lord in whom I believe,

et j'espère
and hope

Pour Vous je veux souffrir, et mourir sur la croix,
For You I want to suffer, and die on the cross,

Au Calvaire!
At Calvary!

Fauré   Fleur jetée
                 Flower thrown

Emporte ma folie au gré du vent,
Carry my folly to the will of the wind,
(Throw my folly to the wind)

Fleur en chantant cueillie
Flower in singing gathered
(Flower picked while laughing)

Et jetée en rêvant,
And thrown in dreaming,
(And thrown away while dreaming)

Emporte ma folie, au gré du vent,
Carry my folly, to the will of the wind,
(Throw my folly to the wind)

Comme la fleur fauchée périt l'amour.
Like the flower cut perishes love.
(Love dies like the cut flower)

La main qui t'a touchée
The hand that you has touched
(The hand that touched you)

Fuit ma main sans retour,
Flees my hand without return,
(Flees my hand forever)

Que le vent qui te sèche, ô pauvre fleur,
Let the wind that you dries, oh poor flower,

Tout à l'heure si fraîche,
All at the hour so fresh,
(So fresh a moment ago)

Et demain sans couleur,
And tomorrow without color,

Que le vent qui te sèche, ô pauvre fleur,
Let the wind that you dries, oh poor flower,

Que le vent qui te sèche,
Let the wind that you dries,

Sèche mon coeur.
Dry my heart.

Fauré   Ici-bas
               Down here

Ici-bas tous les lilas meurent,
Down here all the lilacs die,

Tous les chants des oiseaux sont courts,
All the songs of the birds are short,

Je rêve aux étés qui demeurent toujours!
I dream of summers that last forever!

Ici-bas les lèvres effleurent
Down here the lips (lightly) touch

Sans rien laisser de leur velours,
Without anything leaving of their velvet,
(Without leaving any of their softness)

Je rêve aux baisers qui demeurent toujours!
I dream of kisses that last forever!

Ici-bas, tous les hommes pleurent
Down here, all (the) men weep

Leurs amitiés ou leurs amours,
(About) their friendships or their loves,

Je rêve aux couples qui demeurent,
I dream of couples that last,

Qui demeurent toujours!
That last forever!

Fauré   Les berceaux
                  The cradles

Le long du Quai, les grands vaisseaux,
Along the Quai, the large ships,

Que la houle incline en silence,
That the swell bends in silence,
(Silently rocked by the surge)

Ne prennent pas garde aux berceaux,
Take no notice of the cradles,

Que la main des femmes balance.
That the hands of women rock.

Mais viendra le jour des adieux,
But will come the day of goodbyes,
(But the day of farewells will come)

Car il faut que les femmes pleurent,
For it must be that women weep,

Et que les hommes curieux
And that the men curious
(And curious men)

Tentent les horizons qui leurrent!
Explore the horizons that entice!

Et ce jour-là les grands vaisseaux,
And that day there the large ships,
(And on that day the large ships)

Fuyant le port qui diminue,
Fleeing the port which diminishes,

Sentent leur masse retenue
Feel their mass retained
(Will feel their weight held back)

Par l'âme des lointains berceaux,
By the soul of the distant cradles.

163

Fauré   Les roses d'Ispahan
       The roses of Ispahan

Les roses d'Ispahan dans leur gaine de mousse,
The roses of Ispahan in their covering of moss,
(The roses of Ispahan in their mossy sheath)

Les jasmins de Mossoul, les fleurs de l'oranger,
The jasmines of Mossul, the flowers of the orange trees,
(The jasmines of Mossul, the orange blossoms)

Ont un parfum moins frais, ont une odeur moins douce,
Have a perfume less fresh, have a scent less sweet,

O blanche Leïlah! que ton souffle léger.
Oh white Leilah! than your breath light.
(Oh pale Leilah! than your light breath)

Ta lèvre est de corail, et ton rire léger
Your lip is of coral and your laughter light
(Your lip is coral red, and your light laughter)

Sonne mieux que l'eau vive et d'une voix plus douce.
Sounds better than water live and of a voice more sweet.
(Sounds better that running water and has a sweeter voice)

Mieux que le vent joyeux qui berce l'oranger,
Better than the wind joyous that rocks the orange tree,

Mieux que l'oiseau qui chante au bord d'un nid de mousse.
Better than the bird that sings on the edge of a nest of moss.

O Leïlah! depuis que de leur vol léger
Oh Leilah! since that of their flight light
(Oh Leilah! ever since, on their light wings)

Tous les baisers ont fui de ta lèvre si douce
All the kisses have fled from your lip so sweet

Il n'est plus de parfum dans le pâle oranger,
There is no more of perfume in the pale orange tree,
(The pale orange tree has lost its scent)

Ni de céleste arome aux roses dans leur mousse.
Nor any celestial aroma to the roses in their moss.
(And the roses in their moss, their heavenly fragrance)

Oh! que ton jeune amour, ce papillon léger
Oh! that your young love, this butterfly light
(Oh! may your young love, this weightless butterfly)

Revienne vers mon coeur d'une aile prompte et douce,
Return toward my heart with a wing prompt and sweet,
(Return to my heart on soft and rapid wings)

Et qu'il parfume encor la fleur de l'oranger,
And may it perfume again the flower of the orange tree,
(And may it perfume again the orange blossom)

Les roses d'Ispahan dans leur gaine de mousse.
The roses of Ispahan in their covering of moss.
(The roses of Ispahan in their mossy sheath)

Fauré   Lydia
                Lydia

Lydia sur tes roses joues
Lydia on your pink cheeks

Et sur ton col frais et si blanc,
And on your neck cool and so white,

Roule étincelant L'or fluide que tu dénoues;
Rolls sparkling The gold fluid that you untie;
(Falls glittering The fluid gold that you loosen)

Le jour qui luit est le meilleur,
The day that shines is the best,

Oublions l'éternelle tombe;
Let us forget the eternal tomb;

Laisse tes baisers, tes baisers de colombe
Let your kisses, your kisses of dove
(Let your kisses, your dove-like kisses)

Chanter sur ta lèvre en fleur.
Sing on your lip in flower.
(Sing on your blossoming lips)

Un lys caché répand sans cesse
A lily hidden spreads without ceasing
(A hidden lily emits unceasingly)

Une odeur divine en ton sein;
An odor divine in your breast;
(A heavenly fragrance in your breast)

Les délices comme un essaim Sortent de toi,
The delights like a swarm Come out from you,
(Pleasures in swarms exhale from you)

jeune déesse
young goddess

Je t'aime et meurs, ô mes amours,
I you love and die, oh my loves,

Mon âme en baisers m'est ravie!
My soul in kisses (from) me is stolen!
(My soul is carried off in kisses)

Fauré   Lydia   (Continued)

O Lydia rends-moi la vie, Que je puisse mourir toujours!
Oh Lydia return to me the life, That I may die forever!
(Oh Lydia give back my life, That I may forever die)

Fauré   Mai
                 May

Puisque Mai tout en fleurs dans les prés nous réclame,
Since May all in flowers to the meadows us calls

Viens, ne te lasse pas de mêler à ton âme
Come, do you tire not to mix with your soul
(Come, grow not weary of blending with your soul)

La campagne, les bois, les ombrages charmants,
The country, the woods, the shades charming,
(The countryside, the woods, the pleasant shades)

Les larges clairs de lune au bord des flots dormants;
The wide clears of moon beside the currents sleeping;
(The wide moonlight beside the sleeping surge)

Le sentier qui finit où le chemin commence,
The path that finishes where the road begins,

Et l'air, et le printemps et l'horizon immense,
And the air, and the springtime and the horizon immense,

L'horizon que ce monde attache humble et joyeux,
The horizon which this world attaches humble and joyous,
(The horizon attached by this gay and humble world)

Comme une lèvre au bas de la robe des cieux.
Like a lip at the bottom of the dress of the heavens.
(Like a lip, to the hem of heaven's cloak)

Viens, et que le regard des pudiques étoiles,
Come, and let the gaze of the modest stars,

Qui tombe sur la terre à travers tant de voiles
That falls upon the earth across so many veils

Que l'arbre pénétré de parfums et de chants,
Let the tree penetrated by perfumes and by songs,

Que le souffle embrasé de midi dans les champs,
Let the breeze blazing at noon in the fields,

Et l'ombre et le soleil, et l'onde, et la verdure,
And the shade and the sun, and the wave, and the greenery,

Fauré   Mai   (Continued)

Et le rayonnement de toute la nature,
And the radiance of all (the) nature,

Fassent épanouir, comme une double fleur,
Cause to bloom, like a double flower,

La beauté sur ton front et l'amour dans ton coeur!
Beauty on your brow and love in your heart!

Fauré   Nell
                     Nell

Ta rose de poupre à ton clair soleil,
Your rose of purple with your bright sun,
(Your purple rose in your bright sun)

O Juin, étincelle enivrée,
Oh June, sparkles intoxicated,

Penche aussi vers moi ta coupe dorée:
Leans also toward me your cup gilded:
(Extends toward me too, your golden cup)

Mon coeur à ta rose est pareil.
My heart to your rose is similar.
(My heart is like your rose)

Sous le mol abri de la feuille ombreuse
Beneath the soft shelter of the leaf shady
(From beneath the soft shelter of the shady bough)

Monte un soupir de volupté;
Rises a sigh of voluptuousness;
(Rises a voluptuous sigh)

Plus d'un ramier chante au bois écarté,
More than one dove sings in the wood removed,
(More than one dove sings in the distant forest)

O mon coeur, sa plainte amoureuse.
Oh my heart, its lament amorous.

Que ta perle est douce au ciel enflammé,
How your pearl is soft in the sky inflamed,
(How soft is your pearl in the blazing sky)

Etoile de la nuit pensive!
Star of the night pensive!

Mais combien plus douce est la clarté vive
But how much more soft is the brightness vivid
(But how much softer is the sharp brightness)

Qui rayonne en mon coeur, en mon coeur charmé!
That radiates in my heart, in my heart enchanted!

La chantante mer, le long du rivage,
The singing sea, along the shore,

Taira son murmure éternel,
Will quiet its murmur eternal,
(Will cease its endless murmuring)

Avant qu'en mon coeur, chère amour, ô Nell,
Before that in my heart, dear love, oh Nell,
(Sooner than your image, oh Nell, dear love)

Ne fleurisse plus ton image!
Blooms no longer your image!
(Will cease to bloom in my heart)

Fauré   Prison

Le ciel est par dessus le toit, Si bleu, si calme. . .
The sky is above the roof, So blue, so calm. . .

Un arbre, par dessus le toit, Berce sa palme. . .
A tree, above the roof, Rocks its branches. . .

La cloche dans le ciel qu'on voit, Doucement tinte,
The bell in the sky that one sees, Softly tolls,

Un oiseau sur l'arbre qu'on voit, Chante sa plainte. . .
A bird on the tree that one sees, Sings his lament. . .

Mon Dieu, mon Dieu! La vie est là Simple et tranquille!
My Lord, my Lord! (The) life is there Simple and tranquil!

Cette paisible rumeur là Vient de la ville. . .
That peaceful murmur there Comes from the town. . .

Qu'as-tu fait, ô toi que voilà, pleurant sans cesse
What have you done, oh you who are there, weeping without
  ceasing

Dis, qu'as-tu fait, toi que voilà, de ta jeunesse?
Say, what have you done, you who are there, with your
  youth?

172

Fifteenth Century Song   L'amour de moi
                      My love

L'amour de moi s'y est enclose
The love of me there is enclosed
(My love has enclosed herself)

Dedans un joli jardinet,
In a pretty little garden,

Où croît la rose et le muguet
Where grows the rose and the lily of the valley

Et aussi fait la passerose.
And also does the hollyhock.
(And also grows the hollyhock)

Ce jardin est bel et plaisant,
This garden is beautiful and charming,

Il est garni de toutes fleurs.
It is garnished by all flowers.
(Decorated by all sorts of flowers)

Hélas! il n'est si douce chose
Alas! there is not such sweet thing
(Alas! there is nothing sweeter)

Que de ce doux rossignolet
Than this soft little nightingale

Qui chante au soir, au matinet:
That sings at eventide, at break of day:

Quand il est las, il se repose.
When he is tired, he rests.

Je l'ai regardée une pose:
I her have watched an instant:

Elle était blanche comme lait
She was white as milk

Et douce comme un agnelet,
And soft as a little lamb,

Vermeille et fraîche comme rose.
Bright red and fresh as (the) rose.

173

Fourdrain   Carnaval
             Carnival

Carnaval! Joyeux Carnaval!
Carnival! Happy Carnival!

On s'élance, La foule assiège
One bounds, The crowd pushes round
(People push and crowd around)

Des hérauts à pied, à cheval,
(Some) criers on foot, on horseback,

Précédant un riche cortège! Une fanfare.
Preceding a magnificent procession! A fanfare.

Des clameurs s'élèvent stridentes, sonores!
(Some) outcries rise up strident, sonorous!

Du haut des chars il pleut des fleurs
From the top of the carts there rains some flowers
(Flowers rain down from the tops of carts)

Et des papiers multicolores. Saluez!
And some papers many-colored. Salute!

Voici la Reine tenant sa marotte;
Here is the Queen holding her fancy;

Elle a sa traîne de gala,
She has her train of gala,
(She wears her festive train)

Et des cheveux couleur carotte;
And her hair color carrot;
(And red hair)

Elle taquine son bouffon
She teases her jester

Dont les lèvres restent muettes
Whose lips remain still

Elle lui montre comment
She to him shows how

174

Fourdrain   Carnaval (Continued)

"font" Font font les petites marionettes.
"work" Work work the little marionettes.
(the little puppets work)

Il lui répond: Merci, m'amour;
He to her replies, "Thank you, my love;

De ces leçons-là je me passe
Of those lessons there I have no need
(I'll do without those lessons)

J'écoute l'âme du faubourg
I am listening to the soul of the suburb

Jusqu'à toi monter dans l'espace
Up to you rise in the space.
(Soaring up to you in space)

Je vois là-haut, je vois soudain
I see there high, I see suddenly
(Suddenly I see up there)

Le soleil s'exalter lui-même
The sun exhilarate himself
(The sun grow brighter)

Reine, il baise ta main
Queen, he kisses your hand

Et fait flamber ton diadème.
And makes burn your diadem. "
(And causes your diadem to blaze)

Fourdrain   Le papillon
             The butterfly

Gai papillon, papillon d'or
Gay butterfly, butterfly of gold

Qui t'envoles rapide et frêle,
Who flies away rapid and frail,

Au bout des doigts je garde encor
On the end of fingers I keep still
(On my fingertips there yet remains)

Un peu de cendre de ton aile!
A bit of ash from your wing!

Tu venais voir la blonde enfant
You came to see the blond child

Qui babille dans ma chambrette,
Who prattles in my little room,

Tu venais, Monsieur le passant
You came, Mister passer-by

Dire bonjour à ma grisette
To say hello to my young maid

Ah! vraiment elle est bien ta soeur,
Ah! truly she is quite your sister,
(Ah! She is really quite like you)

Comme toi légère et volage,
Like you light and fickle,

Elle sait endormir le coeur Et le bercer
She knows to put to sleep the heart And it rock
(She knows how to lull the heart to sleep and rock it)

en un mirage.
in a mirage.
(in a dream)

Mais papillon, dès le printemps,
But butterfly, as soon as the spring (comes),

176

Fourdrain   Le papillon (Continued)

Elle s'enfuira la méchante,
She will flee the mean,
(She'll fly away, the mean thing)

Laissant de tous ses grands serments
Leaving of all her great promises

Un peu de poussière qui chante.
A bit of dust that sings.

Franck La procession
The procession

Dieu s'avance à travers les champs
God approaches across the fields

Par les landes, les prés, les verts taillis de hêtres.
Through the pine forests, the meadows, the green brush-
wood of beeches.

Il vient, suivi du peuple, et porté par les prêtres:
He comes, followed by the people, and carried by the
priests:

Aux cantiques de l'homme, oiseaux, mêlez vos chants!
With the hymns of man, birds, blend your songs!

On s'arrête.   La foule autour d'un chêne antique
One stops.   The crowd about an oak antique
(They stop.   Around an ancient oak the crowd)

S'incline, en adorant, sous l'ostensoir mystique:
Inclines, while adoring, beneath the monstrance mystical:
(Bows down, in adoration, beneath the mystical monstrance)

Soleil!   darde sur lui tes longs rayons couchants!
Sun! lance on it your long rays setting!
(Sun!   shine down on it your long declining rays)

Aux cantiques de l'homme, oiseaux, mêlez vos chants!
With the hymns of man, birds, blend your songs!

Vous, fleurs, avec l'encens exhalez votre arôme!
You, flowers, with the incense exhale your aroma!

O fête!   tout reluit, tout prie et tout embaume!
Oh feast! everything glitters, everything prays and everything perfumes!

Dieu s'avance à travers les champs.
God approaches across the fields.

Franck   Le mariage des roses
                The marriage of the roses

Mignonne, sais-tu comment S'épousent les roses?
Darling, know you how Wed the roses?
(Darling, do you know how roses wed)

Ah! cet hymen est charmant, cet hymen est charmant!
Ah! this marriage is charming, this marriage is charming!

Quelles tendres choses Elles disent en ouvrant
What tender things They say in opening

Leurs paupières closes!
Their lids closed!
(Their closed petals)

Mignonne, sais-tu comment S'épousent les roses?
Darling, know you how Wed the roses?
(Darling, do you know how roses wed)

Elles disent: aimons-nous! Si courte est la vie!
They say: let us love (one another) So short is life!
(They say: let us love! Life is so short)

Ayons les baisers plus doux, l'âme plus ravie!
Let us have kisses more sweet, the soul more enraptured!

Pendant que l'homme à genoux Doute, espère ou prie!
While that the man at knees Doubts, hopes or prays!
(While man, kneeling, Doubts or hopes or prays)

O mes soeurs, embrassons-nous! Si courte est la vie!
Oh my sisters, let us kiss (one another)! So short is life!

Crois-moi, mignonne, crois-moi, Aimons-nous comme elles.
Believe me, darling, believe me, Let us love as they.

Vois, le printemps vient à toi, Le printemps vient à toi.
See, the spring comes to you, The spring comes to you.

Et des hirondelles, Aimer est l'unique loi
And of the swallows, To love is the only law
(And for the swallows, Loving is the only law)

A leurs nids fidèles.
In their nests faithful.

Franck   Le marriage des roses   (Continued)

O ma reine, suis ton roi, Aimons-nous comme elles.
Oh my queen, follow your king, Let us love as they.

Excepté d'avoir aimé, Qu'est-il donc sur terre?
Except for having loved, What is there, now, on earth?

Votre horizon est fermé, Ombre, nuit, mystère!
Your horizon is closed, Darkness, night, and mystery!
(Your future is cloaked in shade and night and mystery)

Un seul phare est allumé, L'amour nous l'éclaire,
One lone beacon is lit, Love us it lights,
(Only one beacon is lit, Love lights it for us)

Excepté d'avoir aimé Qu'est-il donc sur terre?
Except for having loved, what is there, now, on earth?

Franck   Lied
                 Song

Pour moi sa main cueillait des roses A ce buisson,
For me her hand would pick (some) roses At this bush,

Comme encore à peine écloses, Chère moisson.
Like her still scarcely blossomed, (A) dear harvest.

La gerbe, hélas! en est fanée Comme elle aussi;
The bunch (of roses), alas! is withered Like her also;

La moissonneuse moissonnée Repose ici.
The harvester (girl) harvested Rests here.
(The harvest maid cut down in bloom of life lies here)

Mais sur la tombe qui vous couvre, O mes amours!
But on the tombstone that you covers, Oh my loves!

Une églantine, qui s'entre'ouvre, Sourit toujours,
An eglantine, which half-way opens, Smiles still,

Et sous le buisson qui surplombe, Quand je reviens,
And beneath the bush which overhangs, When I return,

Une voix me dit sous la tombe: "Je me souviens."
A voice to me says (from) beneath the grave: "I remember."

Gluck   Divinités du Styx, from "Alceste"
                    Dieties of the Styx

Divinités du Styx, ministres de la mort,
Dieties of the Styx, ministers of death,

je n'invoquerai point, votre pitié cruelle,
I shall not invoke, your pity cruel,

J'enlève un tendre époux à son funeste sort,
I carry away a tender husband from his deathly fate,

mais je vous abandonne une épouse fidèle.
but I to you abandon a wife faithful.

Divinitès du Styx, ministres de la mort,
Dieties of the Styx, ministers of death,

mourir pour ce qu'on aime est un trop doux effort,
to die for what one loves is a too sweet effort,

une vertu si naturelle, mon coeur est animé
a virtue so natural, my heart is animated
(such a natural virtue, my heart is stirred)

du plus noble transport!
by the most noble joy!

Je sens une force nouvelle,
I feel a force new,
(I feel new strength)

Je vais où mon amour m'appelle,
I am going where my love me calls,

mon coeur est animé du plus noble transport.
my heart is stirred by the noblest joy.

Gounod   Ah! Je veux vivre, from "Roméo et Juliette"
               Ah! I want to live

Ah! Je veux vivre Dans le rêve qui m'enivre
Ah! I want to live In the dream that me intoxicates

Longtemps encor! Douce flamme, Je te garde
(A) long time yet! Sweet flame, I you keep
(For a long time yet! Sweet flame, I will keep you)

dans mon âme Comme un trésor!
in my heart As a treasure!

Cette invresse De jeunesse Ne dure, hélas! qu'un jour.
This drunkeness Of youth Lasts, alas! but a day.

Puis vient l'heure Où l'on pleure,
Then comes the hour When one weeps,

Le coeur cède à l'amour,
The heart gives in to love,

Et le bonheur fuit sans retour.
And happiness flees without return.
(And happiness forever flees)

Loin de l'hiver morose
Far from the winter morose
(Far from the gloomy winter)

laisse-moi, laisse-moi sommeiller,
let me, let me slumber,

Et respirer la rose,
And breathe the rose,
(And breathe the scent of the rose)

respirer la rose avant de l'effeuiller.
breathe the rose before it plucking.
(breathe in its scent before I pluck its petals)

Reste dans mon âme
Stay in my heart

Comme un doux trésor Longtemps encor!
Like a sweet treasure (for a) Long time yet!

Ah! lève-toi, soleil!, from "Roméo et Juliette"
Ah! rise, sun!

L'amour! oui, son ardeur a troublé tout mon être!
Love! yes, its heat has troubled all my being!
(Love! yes, I am possessed by it completely)

Mais quelle soudaine clarté resplendit
But what sudden brightness shines

à cette fenêtre?
in that window?

C'est là que dans la nuit rayonne sa beauté!
It is there that in the night radiates her beauty!

Ah! lève-toi, soleil! fais pâlir les étoiles
Ah! raise yourself, sun! make to pale the stars
(Ah! rise, sun! cause the stars to fade)

Qui, dans l'azur sans voiles,
Who, in the azure without veils,
(Who, in the unveiled blue)

Brillent au firmament.
Glisten in the firmament.
(Shine down from heaven)

Ah! lève-toi, parais! Astre pur et charmant!
Ah! rise, appear! Star pure and charming!

Elle rêve! elle dénoue
She dreams! she loosens

Une boucle de cheveux Qui vient caresser sa joue
A curl of hair That comes to caress her cheek

Amour! porte-lui mes voeux! Elle parle!
Love! carry to her my greetings! She speaks!

Qu'elle est belle!
How she is beautiful!
(How beautiful she is)

Ah! je n'ai rien entendu!
Ah! I have nothing heard!

Gounod   Ah! lève-toi... (Continued)

Mais ses yeux parlent pour elle,
But her eyes speak for her,

Et mon coeur a répondu! Viens, parais!
And my heart has replied! Come, appear!

Gounod   Avant de quitter ces lieux, from "Faust"
                Before leaving these places

Avant de quitter ces lieux,
Before leaving these places,

Sol natal de mes aïeux
Soil native of my ancestors
(Native land of my fathers)

A toi, Seigneur et roi des cieux,
To you, Lord and king of the heavens,

Ma soeur je confie!
My sister I entrust!

Daigne de tout danger
Deign from all danger

Toujours, toujours la protéger,
Always, always her to protect,

Cette soeur si chérie;
This sister so cherished;

Daigne la protéger de tout danger.
Deign her to protect from all danger.
(Kindly protect her from all danger)

Délivré d'une triste pensée,
Delivered from a sad thought,

J'irai chercher la gloire au sein des ennemis,
I shall go seek glory among the enemy,

Le premier, le plus brave au fort de la mêlée
The first, the most brave in the strong of the mêlé
(To be the first and bravest in the confusion of the battle)

J'irai combattre pour mon pays.
I shall go to fight for my country.

Et si vers lui Dieu me rappelle,
And if to him God me calls,
(And if God calls me to him)

Je veillerai sur toi, fidèle, O Marguerite!
I will watch over you, faithful(ly), Oh Marguerita!

Gounod   Avant de quitter... (Continued)

. . . O Roi des cieux, jette les yeux,
. . . Oh king of the heavens, throw the eyes,
(. . . Oh Lord, look down upon us)

protège Marguerite, Roi des cieux!
protect Marguerita, King of the heavens!

Gounod   Faites-lui mes aveux, from "Faust"
                Confess to her my love

Faites-lui mes aveux, Portez mes voeux!
Make to her my avowals, Carry my greetings!
(Confess to her my love, Take my vows)

Fleurs écloses près d'elle, Dites-lui qu'elle est belle,
Flowers blossomed close to her, Tell her that she is
   beautiful,

Que mon coeur nuit et jour Languit d'amour!
That my heart night and day Languishes with love!

Révélez à son âme Le secret de ma flamme,
Reveal to her heart The secret of my flame,

Qu'il s'exhale avec vous Parfums plus doux!
That it exhales with you Perfumes more sweet!

Fanée! hélas! ce sorcier, que Dieu damne,
Withered! alas! this sorcerer, that God condemns,

M'a porté malheur!
Me has carried misfortune!
(Has brought bad luck to me)

Je ne puis, sans qu'elle se fane,
I cannot, without that it wither,
(I cannot touch a flower)

Toucher une fleur! Si je trempais mes doigts
Touch a flower! If I dipped my fingers
(Without making it wither! But suppose I dipped my fingers)

dans l'eau bénite!
in the water blessed!
(in the holy water)

C'est là que chaque soir vient prier Marguerite!
It is there that each evening comes to pray Marguerita!
(Each evening Marguerita comes here to pray)

Voyons maintenant! voyons vite! Elles se fanent?
Let's see now! let's see quickly! They themselves wither?
(Quick, let's see now! Do they wither)

188

non! Satan, je ris de toi!
no! Satan, I laugh at you!

C'est en vous que j'ai foi; Parlez pour moi!
It is in you that I have faith; Speak for me!

Qu'elle puisse connaître L'émoi qu'elle a fait naître,
That she can know the emotion that she has caused to be
  born,
(Let her know the passion that she has stirred in me)

Et dont mon coeur troublé N'a point parlé!
And of which my heart troubled has not spoken!

Si l'amour l'effarouche, Que la fleur sur sa bouche
If love her frightens, Let the flower on her mouth
(If she draws back from love, Let the flower at her lips)

Sache au moins déposer Un doux baiser!
Know at least to leave A soft kiss!
(At least know how to leave a tender kiss)

Gounod   Il était un Roi de Thulé, from "Faust"
          There was a King of Thule

Je voudrais bien savoir quel était ce jeune homme;
I should like much to know who was this young man;

Si c'est un grand seigneur, et comment il se nomme?
Whether he is a great lord, and how he is called?

Il était un Roi de Thulé, Qui, jusqu'à la tombe fidèle,
There was a King of Thule, Who, until the tomb faithful,
(There was a King of Thule, who, faithful till death)

Eut, en souvenir de sa belle,
Had, in memory of his beautiful,
(Kept in memory of his love)

Une coupe en or ciselé.
A goblet in gold engraved.

Il avait bonne grâce, à ce qu'il m'a semblé.
He had good grace, according to what it me seemed.
(It seemed to me that he was very gracious)

Nul trésor n'avait tant de charme,
No treasure had so much charm,

Dans les grands jours il s'en servait,
In the great days he of it made use,
(He would use it on important days)

Et chaque fois qu'il y buvait,
And each time that he there drank,
(And each time he drank from it)

Ses yeux se remplissaient de larmes!
His eyes would fill with tears!

Quand il sentit venir la mort,
When he felt coming the death,
(When he felt death approaching)

Etendu sur sa froide couche,
Stretched (out) on his cold bed,

Pour la porter jusqu'à sa bouche,
To it carry up to his mouth,
(In order to lift it to his lips)

190

Sa main fit un suprême effort!
His hand made a supreme effort!

Je ne savais que dire, Et j'ai rougi d'abord.
I knew not what to say, and I reddened at first.

Et puis, en l'honneur de sa dame,
And then, in honor of his lady,

Il but une dernière fois.
He drank one last time.

La coupe trembla dans ses doigts,
The goblet trembled in his fingers,

Et doucement il rendit l'âme!
And softly he returned the soul!
(And peacefully he gave up his soul)

Gounod   Je ris de...

Je ris de me voir si belle, from "Faust"
I laugh on seeing myself so lovely

Je ris de me voir Si belle en ce miroir, Ah!
I laugh to me see So beautiful in this mirror, Ah!
(I laugh on seeing myself so lovely in this mirror, Ah)

Est-ce toi, Marguerite, Est-ce toi?
Is it you, Marguerita, Is it you?

Réponds-moi, réponds vite!
Answer me, answer quickly!

Non! ce n'est plus toi! non,
No! it is no longer you! no,

Ce n'est plus ton visage; C'est la fille d'un roi,
It is no longer your face; It is the daughter of a king,

Qu'on salue au passage!
That one salutes at the passing!
(To whom all bow in passing)

Ah s'il était ici! S'il me voyait ainsi!
Ah if he were here! If he me saw thus!
(Ah if only he were here! If only he could see me like this)

Comme une demoiselle Il me trouverait belle,
Like a young lady He me would find beautiful
(He would find me as beautiful as a young lady)

Achevons la métamorphose.
Let us finish the metamorphosis.
(Let us complete the transformation)

Il me tarde encor d'essayer Le bracelet et le collier!
I am anxious still to try (on) The bracelet and the necklace!

Dieu! c'est comme une main, qui sur mon bras se pose!
Lord! it is like a hand, that on my arm is placed!

Gounod   Le veau d'or est toujours debout, from "Faust"
             The golden calf is still standing

Le veau d'or est toujours debout!
The calf of gold is still standing!

On encense Sa puissance,
One incenses His power,
(His power is honored)

D'un bout du monde à l'autre bout!
From one end of the earth to the other end!

Pour fêter l'infâme idole,
To feast the infamous idol,

Rois et peuples confondus,
Kings and peoples confounded,
(Kings and peoples mixed together)

Au bruit sombre des écus,
To the noise somber of the golden coins,

Dansent une ronde folle,
Dance a round crazy,
(Dance a mad round)

Autour de son piédestal!
About his pedestal!

Et Satan conduit le bal, conduit le bal!
And Satan conducts the ball, conducts the ball!

Le veau d'or est vainqueur des dieux!
The calf of gold is conqueror of gods!

Dans sa gloire Dérisoire,
In his glory Derisive,

Le monstre abject insulte aux cieux!
The monster despicable insults the heavens!
(The despicable monster reviles heaven)

Il contemple, ô rage étrange!
He contemplates, oh rage strange!
(At his feet he contemplates)

A ses pieds le genre humain,
At his feet the race human,
(The wild ragings of the human race)

Se ruant, le fer en main,
Hurling themselves, (the) sword in hand,

Dans le sang et dans la fange,
In the blood and in the mire,

Où brille l'ardent métal!
Where shines the ardent metal!

Et Satan conduit le bal, conduit le bal!
And Satan conducts the ball, conducts the ball!

Gounod Salut! demeure chaste et pure, from "Faust"
Greetings! dwelling chaste and pure

Quel trouble inconnu me pénètre?
What trouble unknown me penetrates?
(What unknown worry bothers me)

Je sens l'amour s'emparer de mon être!
I feel love laying hold of my being!

O Marguerite, à tes pieds me voici!
Oh Marguerita, at your feet here I am!

Salut! demeure chaste et pure,
Greetings! dwelling chaste and pure,

où se devine La présence d'une âme innocente et divine!
where is suspected The presence of a soul innocent and
divine!
(where the presence of an innocent and heavenly soul is felt)

Que de richesse en cette pauvreté!
What richness in this poverty!

En ce réduit, que de félicité!
In this hovel, what happiness!

O nature, c'est là que tu la fis si belle!
Oh nature, it is here that you her made so beautiful!

C'est là que cette enfant a dormi sous ton aîle,
It is here that this child has slept beneath your wing,

A grandi sous tes yeux.
And grown beneath your gaze.

Là que de ton haleine enveloppant son âme,
Here where with your breath enveloping her soul,

Tu fis avec amour épanouir la femme
You made with love blossom out the woman

En cet ange des cieux! C'est là! oui! c'est la!
Into this angel of the heavens! It is here! yes! it is
here!

195

Gounod   Sérénade
              Serenade

Quand tu chantes bercée Le soir entre mes bras,
When you sing rocked The evening between my arms,
(At evening when you sing rocked in my arms)

Entends-tu ma pensée, Qui te répond tout bas?
Hear you my thought, Which you replies all low?
(Do you hear my thoughts that very quietly reply)

Ton doux chant me rapelle Les plus beaux de mes jours.
Your sweet song me recalls The most beautiful of my days.
(Your sweet song calls back my happiest days)

Ah! Chantez, chantez, ma belle, Chantez, chantez toujours,
Ah! Sing, sing, my beautiful (one), Sing, sing forever,

Chantez, chantez, ma belle, Chantez toujours!
Sing, sing, my love, Sing forever!

Quand tu ris, sur ta bouche L'amour s'épanouit;
When you smile, on your lips Love blossoms forth;

Et soudain le farouche Soupçon s'évanouit.
And sudden(ly) mad Suspicion vanishes.

Ah! le rire fidèle Prouve un coeur sans détours.
Ah! the smile faithful Proves a heart without deviations.
(Ah! the faithful smike is indication of a loyal heart)

Ah! Riez, riez, ma belle, Riez, riez toujours,
Ah! Smile, smile, my love, Smile, smile forever,

Quand tu dors, calme et pure Dans l'ombre sous mes yeux,
As you sleep, calm and pure In the shade beneath my gaze,

Ton haleine murmure Des mots harmonieux.
Your breath murmurs Some words harmonious.
(Your lips whisper harmonious words)

Ton beau corps se révèle sans voile et sans atours.
Your beautiful body is revealed without veil and without attire.

Ah! Dormez, dormez, ma belle, Dormez, dormez toujours,
Ah! Sleep, sleep, my love, Sleep sleep forever,

Gounod   Sérénade   (Continued)

Dormez, dormez, ma belle, Dormez toujours!
Sleep, sleep, my love, Sleep (on) forever!

Gounod   Si le bonheur à sourire t'invite, from "Faust"
              If happiness causes you to smile

Si le bonheur à sourire t'invite,
If (the) happiness to smile you invites,
(If happiness causes you to smile)

Joyeux alors je sens un doux émoi;
Happy then I feel a sweet emotion;

Si la douleur t'accable, Marguerite,
If sadness you overpowers, Marguerita,

O Marguerite, je pleure alors,
Oh Marguerita, I weep then,

je pleure comme toi!
I weep like you!

Comme deux fleurs sur une même tige,
Like two flowers on a same stem,

Notre destin suivant le même cours,
Our destiny following the same course,

De tes chagrins en frère je m'afflige,
With your griefs like a brother I am afflicted,

O Marguerite, Comme une soeur je t'aimerai toujours!
Oh Marguerita, Like a sister I you will love always!
(Oh Marguerita, I shall love you always as my sister)

Gounod   Vous qui faites l'endormie, from "Faust"
                You who pretend to be sleeping

Vous qui faites l'endormie, N'entendez-vous pas,
You who act the sleeping (one), Hear you not,
(You who pretend to be sleeping, Do you not hear)

O Catherine, ma mie, N'entendez-vous pas
Oh Catherine, my dear, Do you not hear

Ma voix et mes pas?
My voice and my footsteps?

Ainsi ton galant t'appelle,
Thus your admirer you calls,

Et ton coeur l'en croit. Ah!
And your heart him trusts. Ah!

N'ouvre ta porte, ma belle,
Don't open your door, my beauty,

Que la bague au doigt!
But the ring on the finger!
(Except with the ring on your finger)

Catherine que j'adore, Pourquoi refuser
Catherine whom I adore, Why refuse

A l'amant qui vous implore,
To the lover who you implores,

Pourquoi refuser Un si doux baiser?
Why refuse A so sweet kiss?
(Why refuse so sweet a kiss)

Ainsi ton galant supplie, Et ton coeur l'en croit.
Thus your admirer supplicates, And your heart him trusts.

Ah! Ne donne un baiser, ma mie,
Ah! Don't give a kiss, my dear,

Que la bague au doigt! Ah!
But the ring on the finger! Ah!
(Except with the ring on your finger! Ah)

Grieg   Dereinst, Gedanke mein
                Some day, thought (of) mine

Dereinst, Gedanke mein,
Some day, thought (of) mine,

wirst ruhig sein.
(you) will silent be.

Lässt Liebesglut
Lets love's fervor
(If love's fire does not)

dich still nicht werden,
you quiet not become,
(let you become quiet)

in kühler Erden
in cool earth

da schläfst du gut,
there sleep you well,

dort ohne Lieb und Pein
there without love and torment

wirst ruhig sein.
(you) will quiet be.

Was du im Leben
What you in life

nicht hast gefunden,
not have found,

wenn es entschwunden,
when it disappeared,

wird's dir gegeben,
will it to you (be) given,
(it will be given to you)

dann ohne Wunden
then without wounds

und ohne Pein
and without torment

wirst ruhig sein.
(you) will silent be.

Grieg   Ein Traum
               A dream

Mir träumte einst ein schöner Traum:
Me (I) dreamt once a beautiful dream:

mich liebte eine blonde Maid,
me loved a blond maiden,
(a blond maiden loved me)

es war am grünen Waldesraum,
it was in the green forest-glade,

es war zur warmen Frühlingszeit:
it was in the warm Spring-time:

die Knospe sprang, der Waldbach schwoll,
the bud burst, the forest-brook swelled,

fern aus dem Dorfe scholl Geläut -
far from the village sounds (the) peal of bells -

wir waren ganzer Wonne voll,
we were (of) perfect joy full,
(Our hearts full of perfect joy)

versunken ganz in Seligkeit.
sunken wholly in blissfulness.

Und schöner noch, als einst im Traum
And fairer still, as once in the dream

begab es sich in Wirklichkeit:
occurred it [itself] in reality:

es war am grünen Waldesraum,
it was in the green forest-glade,

es war zur warmen Frühlingszeit;
it was in the warm Spring-time;

der Waldbach schwoll, die Knospe sprang,
the forest-brook swelled, the bud burst,

Geläut erscholl vom Dorfe her:
(the) bells' pealing sounded from the village [hither]:

Ich hielt dich fest, ich hielt dich lang -
I held you tight, I held you long -

und lasse dich nun nimmermehr!
and leave you now nevermore!

O frühlingsgrüner Waldesraum,
Oh spring-green forest-glade,

du lebst in mir durch alle Zeit!
you live in me through all time!

Dort ward die Wirklichkeit zum Traum,
There turned [the] reality into dream,

dort ward der Traum zur Wirklichkeit!
there turned [the] dream into reality!

Grieg   Im Kahne
             In the boat

Möven, Möven in weissen Flocken!
Seagulls, seagulls in white flocks!

Sonnenschein!
Sunshine!

Enten stolzieren in gelben Socken
Ducks strut in yellow socks

schmuck und fein.
neat and fine.

Fahr, fahr zum Fischerstrand,
Go, go to the fisher's beach,

ruhig ist es am Scheerenrand;
calm is it by the cliffs' rim;

rings die See liegt so stille,
around the sea lies so quiet,

wo-wo-wille.
wo-wo-wille.

Löse, löse, mein Schatz die dichte
Undo, undo, my darling, the thick

Lockenpracht,
locks' splendour,

dann lass uns tanzen die warme, lichte
then let us dance the warm, clear

Juninacht.
June-night (through).

Wart, wart, zu Sankte Hans
Wait, wait, at Saint John's

gibt es Hochzeit mit lust'gem Tanz,
gives it (a) wedding with gay dance,
(will be a wedding)

Geigen in Hülle und Fülle,
fiddles enough and to spare,

204

wo-wo-wille.
wo-wo-wille.

Wiege, wiege mich, blanke Welle,
Rock, rock me, shiny wave,

immerfort!
always!

Lieblich naht, wie die schlanke Gazelle,
Lovely approaches, like the slender gazelle,

mein Schätzlein dort.
my little darling [there].

Wieg, wieg in Traum mich ein,
Rock, rock in dream me [-],

du bist mein, und ich bin dein.
you are mine, and I am yours.

Geigen, schweiget nun stille!
Fiddles, silence now [-]!

Wo-wo-wille.
Wo-wo-wille.

Grieg   Margaretlein
              Little Margaret

Margaretlein sass spät am Abend,
Little Margaret sat late in the evening,

der Kuckuck rief in dem grünen Tann,
the cuckoo called in the green fir woods,

sie sang vor sich hin eine Weise,
she sang for herself [-] a melody,

dabei sie ihr Brautlinnen spann.
thereby she her bride-linen spun.

Margaretlein, sie sass an dem Fenster
Little Margaret, she sat by the window

und blickt auf den Ring von Gold,
and looks at the ring of gold,

senkte die Augen dann nieder
lowered the eyes then downwards

und lächelte minnighold.
and smiled lovingly.

Margaretlein legte so müd
Little Margaret laid so tired

auf des Armes schneeweisses Linnen die Wang.
upon the arm's snow-white linen the cheek.

Der Flieder duftet, sie träumet
The lilac smells sweet, she dreams

vom Herzallerliebsten gar lang!
of the beloved quite (a) long (time)!

Margaretlein löste ihr goldnes Haar,
Little Margaret undid her golden hair,

die Ruh umfing sie nun balde.
[the] rest captured her now [soon].
    (sleep)

Grieg   Margaretlein   (Continued)

Margaretlein faltete Hand in Hand,
Little Margaret folded hand in hand,

der Kuckuck rief in dem Walde.
the cuckoo called in the forest.

Grieg   Solvejgs Lied
              Solvejg's song

Der Winter mag scheiden,
[The] Winter may depart,

der Frühling vergehn,
[the] Spring disappear,

der Sommer mag verwelken,
[the] Summer may wither,

das Jahr verwehn;
the year vanish;

du kehrest mir zurücke,
you come to me back,

gewiss, du wirst mein,
surely, you will be mine,

ich hab es versprochen,
I have [it] promised,

ich harre treulich dein.
I wait faithfully (for) you.

Gott helfe dir,
God may help you,

wenn du die Sonne noch siehst.
If you the sun still see.
        (still see the sun)

Gott segne dich,
God may bless you,

wenn du zu Füssen ihm kniest.
if you at the feet (of) Him kneel
        (kneel at His feet)

Ich will deiner harren,
I will for you wait,

bis du mir nah,
till you me near,
        (come to me)

und harrest du dort oben,
and (should) wait you there above,

so treffen wir uns da!
then meet we [us] there!

Hahn   D'une prison
                        From a prison

Le ciel est par dessus le toit, Si bleu, si calme. . .
The sky is above the roof, So blue, so calm. . .

Un arbre, par dessus le toit, Berce sa palme. . .
A tree, above the roof, Rocks its branches. . .

La cloche dans le ciel qu'on voit, Doucement tinte,
The bell in the sky that one sees, Softly tolls,

Un oiseau sur l'arbre qu'on voit, Chante sa plainte. . .
A bird on the tree that one sees, Sings his lament. . .

Mon Dieu, mon Dieu! La vie est là Simple et tranquille!
My Lord, my Lord! (The) life is there Simple and tranquil!

Cette paisible rumeur là Vient de la ville. . .
That peaceful murmur there Comes from the town. . .

Qu'as-tu fait, ô toi que voilà, pleurant sans cesse
What have you done, oh you who are there, weeping without
    ceasing

Dis, qu'as-tu fait, toi que voilà, de ta jeunesse?
Say, what have you done, you who are there, with your
    youth?

Hahn   L'heure exquise
       The hour exquisite

La lune blanche Luit dans les bois;
The moon white shines in the woods;

De chaque branche Part une voix Sous la ramée
From each branch Springs a voice Beneath the arbor

O bienaimée.
Oh well-loved.
(Oh dearly beloved)

L'étang reflète, Profond miroir
The pool reflects, Deep mirror
(Like a deep mirror the pond reflects)

La silhouette Du saule noir
The silhouette Of the willow black

Où le vent pleure. Rêvons! c'est l'heure!. . .
Where the wind weeps. Let us dream! it is the hour!. . .

Un vaste et tendre Apaisement, Semble descendre
A vast and tender Calm, Seems to descend

Du firmament Que l'astre irise. . .
From the firmament That the moon makes iridescent. . .
(From the firmament made iridescent by the moon. . .)

C'est l'heure exquise.
It is the hour exquisite.

Hahn   Si mes vers avaient des ailes!
                  If my verses had wings!

Mes vers fuiraient, doux et frêles,
My verses would flee, soft and frail,

Vers votre jardin si beau
To your garden so beautiful

Si mes vers avaient des ailes Comme l'oiseau!
If my verses had (some) wings Like the bird!

Ils voleraient, étincelles,
They would fly, sparkles,

Vers votre foyer qui rit
Toward your hearth which laughs

Si mes vers avaient des ailes Comme l'esprit.
If my verses had wings Like the mind.

Près de vous, purs et fidèles,
Close to you, pure and faithful,

Ils accourraient, nuit et jour,
They would run, night and day,

Si mes vers avaient des ailes
If my verses had wings

Comme l'amour!
Like love!

Halévy   Si la rigueur, from "La Juive"
              If harshness, from "The Jewess"

Si la rigueur ou la vengeance
If harshness or vengeance

Leur font haïr ta sainte loi,
To them makes hate your holy law,
(Makes them hate your holy law)

Que le pardon, que la clémence, mon dieu,
That the pardon, that the clemency, my Lord,
(Let forgiveness and mercy, my Lord)

Les ramène en ce jour vers toi,
Them lead back in this day toward you,
(Lead them back today to you)

Rappelons-nous son précepte sacré,
Let us remember his precept sacred,

Ouvrons nos bras à l'enfant égaré,
Let us open our arms to the child astray,
(Let us welcome with open arms the lost child)

Nous rappelant son précepte sacré,
Us recalling his precept sacred,
(And remember his sacred precept)

oh, mon Dieu, les ramène vers toi,
oh, my Lord, them take back to you

en ce jour vers toi.
in this day to you.

Handel   Dank sei Dir, Herr
                  Thanks be to Thee, Lord

Dank sei Dir, Herr,
Thanks be to Thee, Lord,

Du hast Dein Volk mit Dir geführt,
Thou hast Thy people [with Thee] guided,

Israel, hin durch das Meer.
Israel, [on] through the sea.

Wie eine Herde zog es hindurch,
Like a flock moved it through,
                  (Thy people through the sea)

Herr, Deine Hand schützte es,
Lord, Thy hand protected it,

in Deiner Güte gabst Du ihm Heil.
in Thy grace gav'st Thou [it] salvation.

Dank sei Dir, Herr.
Thanks be to Thee, Lord.

Hüe   A des oiseaux
               To birds

Bonjour, bonjour les fauvettes,
Hello, hello (the) warblers,

Bonjour les joyeux pinsons,
Hello (the) happy finches,

Eveillez les pâquerettes
Awaken the daisies

Et les fleurs des verts buissons!
And the flowers of the green bushes!

Toujours votre âme est en fête,
Always your soul is in feast,
(Your hearts are always light and gay)

Gais oiseux qu'on aime à voir,
Happy birds that one likes to see,

Pour l'amant et le poète,
For the lover and the poet,

Vous chantez matin et soir!
You sing morning and evening!

Mais dans la plaine, il me semble
But in the plain, it me seems
(But in the field, it seems to me)

Qu'on a tendu des réseaux;
That one has stretched some nets;
(That nets have been set up)

Voltigez toujours ensemble:
Fly about always together:

En garde, petits oiseaux!
On guard, little birds!
(Watch out, little birds)

Penchez-vous sans toucher terre,
Swoop down without touching ground,

Voyez-vous au coin du bois,
See you in the corner of the woods,
(Do you see in the corner of the woods)

Vous guettant avec mystère,
You watching with mystery,
(Those children spying you mysteriously)

Ces enfants à l'oeil sournois?
Those children with the eye suspicious?
(With their suspicious glance)

Ah, bien vite à tire d'aile,
Ah, very fast at drawing of wing,
(Ah, very fast, with full speed)

Fuyez, fuyez leurs appâts;
Flee, flee their attractions;

Venez avec l'hirondelle,
Come with the swallow,

Qui dans son vol, suit mes pas.
Which, in its flight, follows my footsteps.

Dans mon jardin nulle crainte;
In my garden no fear;
(No need to worry in my garden)

Vous pourrez, d'un bec léger,
You can, with a beak light,
(With your light beaks you can)

Piller, piller sans contrainte,
Pillage, pillage without restraint,

Tous les fruits mûrs du verger.
All the fruits ripe of the orchard.

Bonsoir, bonsoir les fauvettes,
Goodnight, goodnight (the) warblers,

Bonsoir les joyeux pinsons,
Goodnight (the) happy finches,

216

Hüe   A des oiseaux   (Continued)

Endormez les pâquerettes
Put to sleep the daisies

Et les fleurs des verts buissons!
And the flowers of the green bushes!

Hüe   J'ai pleuré en rêve
               I wept in dreaming

J'ai pleuré en rêve: J'ai rêvé que tu étais morte;
I wept in dreaming: I dreamed that you were dead;

Je m'éveillai et les larmes coulèrent de mes joues.
I awakened and the tears flowed down my cheeks.

J'ai pleuré en rêve: J'ai rêvé que tu me quittais;
I wept in dreaming: I dreamed that you me left;

Je m'éveillai et je pleurai amèrement longtemps après.
I awakened and I wept bitterly long time after.
(I awakened and wept bitterly for a long time afterwards)

J'ai pleuré en rêve: J'ai rêvé que tu m'aimais encore;
I wept in dreaming: I dreamed that you me loved still;

et le torrent de mes larmes coule toujours, toujours.
and the torrent of my tears flows forever, forever.

218

Koechlin   Si tu le veux
                  If you desire it

Si tu le veux, ô mon amour,
If you it wish, oh my love,

Ce soir dès que la fin du jour Sera venue,
This evening as soon as the end of the day Will have come,

Quand les étoiles surgiront,
When the stars will rise,

Et mettront des clous d'or au fond
And will put (some) nails of gold in the background

Bleu de la nue,
Blue of the skies,

Nous partirons seuls tous les deux
We shall leave alone all the two
(Alone, the two of us will go)

Dans la nuit brune en amoureux,
Into the night brown as lovers,

Sans qu'on nous voie; Et tendrement je te dirai
Without that one us sees; And tenderly I to you will say
(Without being seen by anyone; And tenderly I'll sing to you)

Un chant d'amour où je mettrai Toute ma joie.
A song of love where I'll put All my joy.

Mais quand tu rentreras chez toi,
But when you return to your house,

Si l'on te demande pourquoi,
If (any) one to you asks why,

Mignonne fée, Tes cheveux sont plus fous qu'avant,
Darling nymph, Your hair is more tousled than before,

Tu répondras que seul le vent T'a décoiffée,
You will reply that only the wind Has disarranged (your hair),

Si tu le veux, ô mon amour.
If you it wish, oh my love.

219

Lalo   Aubade, from "Le Roi d'Ys"
            Aubade, from "The King of Ys"

Puisqu'on ne peut fléchir ces jalouses gardiennes,
Since one not can move these jealous guardians,
(Since these jealous guards cannot be moved)

Ah! laissez-moi conter mes peines Et mon émoi!
Ah! let me count my sorrows and my emotion!

Vainement, ma bien-aimée, On croit me désespérer;
Vainly, my well-loved, One believes me to despair;
(In vain, my beloved, do they think they can make me
    despair)

Près de ta porte fermée, Je veux encor demeurer!
Near to your door locked, I want yet to remain!

Les soleils pourront s'éteindre, Les nuits remplacer les
    jours,
The sun may be extinguished, The nights replace the days,

Sans t'accuser et sans me plaindre,
Without you accusing and without complaining
(Before I shall leave that spot)

Là je resterai toujours, toujours!
There I shall stay always, always!
(Always refusing to accuse you or complain)

Je le sais, ton âme est douce,
I it know, your heart is kind,

Et l'heure bientôt viendra,
And the hour soon will come,

Où la main qui me repousse,
When the hand that me repels,

Vers la mienne se tendra!
Toward mine itself will stretch out!
(Will be held out to me)

Ne sois pas trop tardive A te laisser attendrir!
Be not too tardy To yourself let be merciful!
(Do not be too slow in letting yourself be merciful)

Lalo   Aubade...(Continued)

Si Rozenn bientôt n'arrive,
If Rozenn soon arrives not,
(If Rozenn does not arrive soon)

Je vais hélas! mourir hélas!   mourir.
I am going alas! to die alas!   to die.

Liszt
Es muss ein Wunderbares sein
It must a wonderful (thing) be
(It must be a wonderful thing)

Es muss ein Wunderbares sein
It must a wonderful (thing) be

ums Lieben zweier Seelen,
about the love of two souls,
(hearts)

sich schliessen ganz einander ein,
themselves unite [wholly] one (with) another,

sich nie ein Wort verhehlen,
themselves never one word conceal,

und Freud und Leid und Glück und Noth
and joy and sorrow and happiness and misery

so mit einander tragen;
thus with one another bear;

vom ersten Kuss bis in den Tod
from (the) first kiss to [the] death

sich nur von Liebe sagen.
themselves only of love speak.
(to one another speak only of love)

Liszt   Oh! quand je dors
             Oh! when I sleep

Oh! quand je dors,
Oh! when I sleep,

viens auprès de ma couche Comme à Pétrarque
come to my bed as to Petrarch

apparaissait Laura.
appeared Laura.

Et qu'en passant ton haleine me touche
And let in passing your breath me touch

Soudain ma bouche S'entrouvrira!
Suddenly my mouth will open up!
(Suddenly my lips will part)

Sur mon front morne où peut-être s'achève
On my brow dreary where perhaps is finishing
(On my dreary brow, troubled perhaps too long)

Un songe noir qui trop longtemps dura,
A dream black which too long lasted,
(By a dark dream)

Que ton regard comme un astre s'élève
Let your gaze like a star be lifted
(Let your gaze fall like light from a star)

soudain mon rêve Rayonnera,
suddenly my dream Will radiate,

Rayonnera! ah,
Will radiate! ah,

Puis sur ma lèvre où voltige une flamme,
Then on my lips where floats a flame,

Eclair d'amour que Dieu même épura,
Flash of love that God himself purified,

Pose un baiser, et d'ange deviens femme.
Place a kiss, and from (an) angel become (a) woman.

Liszt   Oh! quand je dors (Continued)

Soudain mon âme S'éveillera,
Suddenly my soul Will awaken,

S'éveillera.   Oh! viens!
Will awaken.   Oh! come!

comme à Pétrarque apparaissait Laura!
as to Petrarch appeared Laura!

Liszt   Wer nie sein Brot mit Tränen ass
             Who never his bread with tears ate

Wer nie sein Brot mit Tränen ass,
Who never his bread with tears ate,

wer nie die kummervollen Nächte
who never [the] sorrowful nights

auf seinem Bette weinend sass,
on his bed weeping sat,

der kennt euch nicht, ihr himmlischen Mächte.
that one knows you not, you heavenly powers.

Ihr führt ins Leben uns hinein,
You lead into life us [in],

ihr lasst den Armen schuldig werden,
you let the poor one guilty become,

dann überlasst ihr ihn der Pein,
then hand over [you] him to [the] torment,

denn jede Schuld rächt sich auf Erden.
for every guilt avenges itself on earth.

Lully   Bois épais
                 Deep woods

Bois épais, redouble ton ombre;
Woods thick, redouble your shade;
(Deep woods, increase your shade)

Tu ne saurais être assez sombre,
You would not know to be enough dark,
(You could not be dark enough)

Tu ne peux trop cacher
You could not too much conceal
(You could not conceal too well)

Mon malheureux amour.
My unhappy love.

Je sens un désespoir
I feel a despair

Dont l'horreur est extrême,
Whose horror is extreme,

Je ne dois plus voir ce que j'aime,
I should no longer see that which I love,
(I am to see no longer what I love)

Je ne veux plus souffrir le jour.
I no longer want to suffer the day.
(I want no longer to bear the light of day)

Mahler   Blicke mir nicht in die Lieder
          Look [me] not into the songs

Blicke mir nicht in die Lieder!
Look [me] not into the songs!
(Look not into my songs before I finish them)

Meine Augen schlag' ich nieder,
My eyes lower I [-],

wie ertappt auf böser Tat.
as caught at (a) bad deed.

Selber darf ich nicht getrauen,
Myself may I not trust,
(I may not trust myself)

ihrem Wachsen zuzuschauen.
at their growth to look.

Blicke mir nicht in die Lieder!
Look [me] not into the songs!

Deine Neugier ist Verrat!
Your curiosity is betrayal!

Bienen, wenn sie Zellen bauen,
Bees, when they cells build,

lassen auch nicht zu sich schauen,
let also not at them glance,
(do not allow themselves to be observed)

schauen selbst auch nicht zu.
(they) look [themselves] also not [-].

Wenn die reichen Honigwaben
When the rich honey-combs
(When they have brought)

sie zu Tag gefördert haben,
they to (the light of) day brought have,
(the rich honey-combs to the light of day)

dann vor allen nasche du.
then before all (others) nibble you.

Mahler Der Tamboursg'sell
The drummer boy

Ich armer Tamboursg'sell!
I poor drummer boy!

Man führt mich aus dem G'wölb!
They take me [out] from the vault!
(cell)

Wär' ich ein Tambour blieben,
Had I a drummer remained,

dürft' ich nicht gefangen liegen!
would I not imprisoned lie!
(would I not be kept imprisoned)

O Galgen, du hohes Haus,
Oh gallows, you high house,

du siehst so furchtbar aus!
you look so terrible [-]!

Ich schau' dich nicht mehr an,
I look (at) you no more [-],

weil i weiss, dass i g'hör d'ran!
since I know, that I belong thereon!

Wenn Soldaten vorbei marschier'n,
When soldiers march by,

bei mir nit einquartier'n,
with me (they) not take quarters,

wenn sie fragen, wer i g'wesen bin:
when they ask, who I have been:

Tambour von der Leibkompanie!
Drummer of the first company!

Gute Nacht, ihr Marmelstein',
Good night, you marble stones,

ihr Berg' und Hügelein!
you mountains and little hills!

Mahler   Der Tamboursg'sell   (Continued)

Gute Nacht, ihr Offizier,
Good night, you officers,

Korporal und Musketier!
corporals and musketeers!

Ich schrei' mit heller Stimm':
I cry with clear voice:

Von Euch ich Urlaub nimm!
From you I leave take!
(From you I take leave)

Gute Nacht!
Good night!

Mahler   Ich atmet' einen linden Duft
                I breathed a gentle fragrance

Ich atmet' einen linden Duft.
I breathed a gentle fragrance.

Im Zimmer stand ein Zweig der Linde,
In the room stood a branch of the linden tree,

ein Angebinde von lieber Hand.
a present from dear hand.

Wie lieblich war der Lindenduft.
How lovely was the linden's fragrance.

Wie lieblich ist der Lindenduft,
How lovely is the linden's fragrance,

das Lindenreis brachst du gelinde!
the sprig of linden broke you gently!
(you gently broke the sprig of linden)

Ich atme leis im Duft der Linde
I breathe softly in the scent`of linden

der Liebe linden Duft.
[the] love's gentle fragrance.

Mahler   Ich bin der Welt abhanden gekommen
                     I have to the world lost become
                     (I have become lost to the world)

Ich bin der Welt abhanden gekommen,
I have to the world lost become,

mit der ich sonst viele Zeit verdorben;
with which I formerly much time wasted;

sie hat so lange nichts von mir vernommen,
it has so long nothing from me heard,

sie mag wohl glauben, ich sei gestorben!
it may [well] believe I had died!

Es ist mir auch gar nichts daran gelegen,
It is to me also absolutely nothing on it important,
(It is also of no importance to me)

ob sie mich für gestorben hält.
if it me [for] dead considers.

Ich kann auch gar nichts sagen dagegen,
I can also absolutely nothing say against it,

denn wirklich bin ich gestorben der Welt.
for really am I dead to the world.

Ich bin gestorben dem Weltgetümmel
I have died to the world's turmoil

und ruh' in einem stillen Gebiet.
and rest in a quiet place.

Ich leb' allein in meinem Himmel,
I live alone in my heaven,

in meinem Lieben, in meinem Lied.
in my love, in my song.

Mahler   Liebst du um Schönheit
                   Love you [for] beauty
                   (If you love beauty)

Liebst du um Schönheit, o nicht mich liebe!
Love you [for] beauty, oh not me love!

Liebe die Sonne, sie trägt ein goldnes Haar!
Love the sun, it wears [a] golden hair!

Liebst du um Jugend, o nicht mich liebe!
Love you [for] youth, oh not me love!

Liebe den Frühling, der jung ist jedes Jahr!
Love the spring, which young is each year!

Liebst du um Schätze, o nicht mich liebe!
Love you [for] treasures, oh not me love!

Liebe die Meerfrau, sie hat viel Perlen klar!
Love the mermaid, she has many pearls clear!

Liebst du um Liebe, o ja, mich liebe!
Love you [for] love, oh yes, me love!
(If it is love which you want, then love me)

Liebe mich immer, dich lieb' ich immer, immerdar!
Love me always, you love I always, forever!

Mahler   Lieder eines fahrenden Gesellen
          Songs of a wayfarer

          1) Wenn mein Schatz Hochzeit macht
             When my darling wedding makes
                                       (has)

Wenn mein Schatz Hochzeit macht,
When my darling wedding makes,
                      (has)

fröhliche Hochzeit macht,
gay wedding makes,
          (has)

hab' ich meinen traurigen Tag!
have I my sad day!

Geh' ich in mein Kämmerlein,
Go I into my little room,

dunkles Kämmerlein,
dark little room,

weine, wein' um meinen Schatz,
weep, weep for my love,

um meinen lieben Schatz!
for my dear love!

Blümlein blau!
Little flower blue!
(Blue little flower)

Verdorre nicht!
Wither not!

Vöglein süss!
Little bird sweet!
(Sweet little bird)

Du singst auf grüner Haide:
You sing on green heath:

"Ach! wie ist die Welt so schön!
"An! how is the world so beautiful!

233

Ziküth!"
Ziküth!"

Singet nicht! Blühet nicht!
Sing not! Bloom not!

Lenz ist ja vorbei!
Spring is surely gone!

Alles Singen ist nun aus!
All singing is now out!
          (has now ended)

Des Abends, wenn ich schlafen geh',
In the evening, when I (to) sleep go,

denk' ich an mein Leide!
think I of my grief!

An mein Leide!
Of my sorrow!

Mahler   Lieder eines fahrenden Gesellen
                Songs of a wayfarer

                2) Gieng heut Morgen über's Feld
                Went this morning over the field

Gieng heut Morgen über's Feld,
(I) went this morning over the field,
                . (through)

Thau noch auf den Gräsern hieng,
dew still on the grasses hung,

sprach zu mir der lust'ge Fink:
spoke to me the gay finch:

"Ei, du! Gelt?
"Hey, you! What do you think?

Guten Morgen! Ei, gelt?
Good morning! Hey, what do you think?

Du! Wird's nicht eine schöne Welt?
You! Will it not (be) a beautiful world?

Schöne Welt?
(A) beautiful world?

Zink! Zink! Schön und flink!
Zink! Zink! Beautiful and quick!

Wie mir doch die Welt gefällt!"
How me [indeed] the world pleases!"

Auch die Glockenblum' am Feld
Also the bluebell by the field

hat mir lustig, guter Ding',
has (to) me gayly, (of) good cheer,

mit den Glöckchen, klinge, kling, klinge, kling,
with the little bells, ding- dong, ding- dong,

ihren Morgengruss geschellt:
their morning greeting rung:

"Wird's nicht eine schöne Welt?
"Will it not (be) a beautiful world?

235

Schöne Welt?
(A) beautiful world?

Kling!   Kling!   Kling!   Kling!   Schönes Ding!
Ding - dong!   Ding - dong!   Beautiful thing!

Wie mir doch die Welt gefällt!   Heiah!"
How me indeed the world pleases!   Heiah!"

Und da fieng im Sonnenschein
And there began in the sunshine

gleich die Welt zu funkeln an;
at once the world to sparkle [-];

Alles, alles Ton und Farbe gewann!
Everything, everything tone and color gained!

Im Sonnenschein!
In the sunshine!

Blum' und Vogel, gross und klein!
Flower and bird, large and small!

Guten Tag!
Good day!

Ist's nicht eine schöne Welt?
Is it not a beautiful world?

Ei, du!   Gelt?
Hey, you!   What do you think?

Schöne Welt!
(A) beautiful world!

Nun fängt auch mein Glück wohl an?!
Now starts too my happiness perhaps [-]?!
(Perhaps now starts my happiness too)

Nein!   Nein!   Das ich mein',
No!   No!   That (one) I mean,
                    (think of)

mir nimmer, nimmer blühen kann!
(for) me never, never bloom can!
(can never bloom for me)

Mahler   Lieder eines fahrenden Gesellen
      Songs of a wayfarer

     3) Ich hab' ein glühend Messer
      I have a burning knife

Ich hab' ein glühend Messer,
I have a burning knife,

ein Messer in meiner Brust,
a knife in my breast,

o weh! o weh!
oh woe! oh woe!

Das schneid't so tief
That cuts so deep

in jede Freud' und jede Lust,
into every delight and every joy,

so tief!
so deep!

Es schneid't so weh und tief!
It cuts so painfully and deep!

Ach, was ist das für ein böser Gast!
Ah, what is that (one) but a wicked guest!

Nimmer hält er Ruh',
Never gives it repose,

nimmer hält er Rast!
never gives it rest!

Nicht bei Tag, nicht bei Nacht,
Not by day, not by night,

wenn ich schlief! O weh!
when I slept! Oh woe!

Wenn ich in den Himmel seh,
When I to the sky look,

seh' ich zwei blaue Augen steh'n!
see I two blue eyes [stand]!

O weh!
Oh woe!

Wenn ich im gelben Felde geh',
When I in the yellow field go,

seh' ich von Fern das blonde Haar
see I from afar the blonde hair

im Winde weh'n!
in the wind blow!

O weh!
Oh woe!

Wenn ich aus dem Traum auffahr'
When I from the dream awake

und höre klingen ihr silbern Lachen,
and hear ring her silvery laughter,

o weh!
oh woe!

Ich wollt' ich läg' auf der schwarzen Bahr',
I wished I lay on the black bier,

könnt' nimmer, nimmer die Augen aufmachen!
could never, never the eyes open!
(never to open the eyes again)

Mahler   Lieder eines fahrenden Gesellen
                Songs of a wayfarer

                4) Die zwei blauen Augen von meinem Schatz
                The two blue eyes of my darling

Die zwei blauen Augen von meinem Schatz,
The two blue eyes of my darling,

die haben mich in die weite Welt geschickt.
they have me into the wide world sent.

Da musst' ich Abschied nehmen
Then must I leave take

vom allerliebsten Platz!
from the much beloved place!

O Augen blau, warum habt ihr mich angeblickt!?
Oh eyes blue, why have you (at) me looked!?

Nun hab' ich ewig Leid und Grämen!
Now have I everlasting grief and sorrow!

Ich bin ausgegangen in stiller Nacht,
I am gone out into the quiet night,
 (have)

in stiller Nacht wohl über die dunkle Haide;
in the quiet night [well] over the dark heath;

hat mir Niemand Ade gesagt.
has to me nobody farewell said.

Ade! Mein Gesell' war Lieb' und Leide!
Farewell! My companion was love and grief!

Auf der Strasse steht ein Lindenbaum,
In the street stands a linden tree,

da hab' ich zum ersten Mal im Schlaf geruht!
there have I for the first time in sleep rested!

Unter dem Lindenbaum!
Under the linden tree!

Der hat seine Blüthen über mich geschneit -
That has its blossoms over me snowed -

da wusst' ich nicht, wie das Leben thut -
then knew I not, how [the] life does -

war Alles wieder gut!
was everything again good!

Ach, Alles wieder gut!
Ah, everything again good!

Alles! Alles! Lieb' und Leid,
Everything! Everything! Love and grief,

und Welt, und Traum!
and world, and dream!

Mahler   Rheinlegendchen
                    Rhine legend

Bald gras' ich am Neckar,
Now mow I at the Neckar,

bald gras' ich am Rhein,
now mow I at the Rhine,

bald hab' ich ein Schätzel,
now have I a sweetheart,

bald bin ich allein!
now am I alone!

Was hilft mir das Grasen,
What helps me the mowing,

wenn d'Sichel nicht schneid't,
if the sickle not cuts,

was hilft mir ein Schätzel,
what helps me a sweetheart,
    (good is to me a)

wenn's bei mir nicht bleibt!
if she with me not stays!

So soll ich denn grasen
So shall I then mow

am Neckar, am Rhein,
at the Neckar, at the Rhine,

so werf' ich mein goldenes
so throw I my golden

Ringlein hinein!
little ring in (the waters)!

Es fliesset im Neckar
It flows in the Neckar

und fliesset im Rhein,
and flows in the Rhine,

soll schwimmen hinunter
shall swim down

ins Meer tief hinein!
to the sea deep in!
(into the deep sea)

Und schwimmt es, das Ringlein,
And swims it, the little ring,

so frisst es ein Fisch!
so gulps it a fish!

Das Fischlein soll kommen
The little fish shall come

auf's Königs sein Tisch!
to the king's [his] table!

Der König tät fragen,
The king would ask,

wem's Ringlein sollt' sein?
whose the little ring should be?

Da tät mein Schatz sagen:
Then would my sweetheart say:

"Das Ringlein g'hört mein!"
"The little ring belongs (to) me!"

Mein Schätzlein tät springen
My little darling would jump

bergauf und bergein,
uphill and downhill,

tät mir wied'rum bringen
would to me again bring

das Goldringlein fein!
the little golden ring fine!

Kannst grasen am Neckar,
(You) may mow at the Neckar,

kannst grasen am Rhein!
(you) may mow at the Rhine!

Mahler   Rheinlegendchen   (Continued)

Wirf du mir nur immer
Throw you (for) me [but] always

dein Ringlein hinein!
your little ring into (the waters)!

Mahler   Um Mitternacht
                At midnight

Um Mitternacht hab' ich gewacht
At midnight have I (been) awake
       (I was awake)

und aufgeblickt zum Himmel;
and looked up at the sky;

kein Stern vom Sterngewimmel
no star of the star-throng
        (throng of stars)

hat mir gelacht um Mitternacht.
has (to) me smiled at midnight.

Um Mitternacht hab' ich gedacht
At midnight have I thought
        (my thoughts)

hinaus in dunkle Schranken.
out into dark distances.
(wandered into dark distances)

Es hat kein Lichtgedanken
[It] has no clear thought

mir Trost gebracht um Mitternacht.
(to) me consolation brought at midnight.

Um Mitternacht nahm ich in acht
At midnight took I care (of)
        (paid I attention to)

die Schläge meines Herzens;
the beats of my heart;

ein einz'ger Puls des Schmerzens
one only pulse of grief

war angefacht um Mitternacht.
was kindled at midnight.

Um Mitternacht kämpft' ich die Schlacht,
At midnight fought I the battle,

o Menschheit, deiner Leiden;
oh mankind, of your sufferings;

nicht konnt' ich sie entscheiden
not could I it solve

mit meiner Macht um Mitternacht.
with my strength at midnight.

Um Mitternacht hab' ich die Macht
At midnight have I the power

in Deine Hand gegeben;
into Thy hand given;

Herr!   Herr über Tod und Leben,
Lord!   Master over death and life,

Du hältst die Wacht
Thou keepest [the] watch

um Mitternacht!
at midnight!

Mahler   Wer hat dies Liedlein erdacht?
                    Who has this little song conceived?

Dort oben am Berg in dem hohen Haus!
There above on the mountain in the high house!

Da gucket ein fein's lieb's Mädel heraus!
There looks a fine lovely maiden out!

Es ist nicht dort daheime!
She is not there at home!

Es ist des Wirts sein Töchterlein!
She is the innkeeper's [his] little daughter!

Es wohnet auf grüner Heide!
She dwells on (the) green heath!

Mein Herzle ist wund!
My heart is sore!

Komm, Schätzle, mach's g'sund!
Come, darling, make it healthy!

Dein' schwarzbraune Äuglein,
Your black-brown little eyes,

die hab'n mich verwund't!
they have me wounded!

Dein rosiger Mund macht Herzen gesund.
Your rosy mouth makes hearts healthy.
           (lips make)

Macht Jugend verständig,
Makes youth sensible,

macht Tote lebendig,
makes dead ones alive,

macht Kranke gesund, ja gesund.
makes sick ones healthy, yes healthy.

Wer hat denn das schöne Liedlein erdacht?
Who has then the beautiful little song conceived?

Mahler   Wer hat dies... (Continued)

Es haben's drei Gäns' über's Wasser gebracht.
It have (it) three geese over the water brought.
(Three geese have brought it over the water)

Zwei graue und eine weisse!
Two grey ones and one white one!

Und wer das Liedlein nicht singen kann,
And who the little song not sing can,
(And who is not able to sing the little song)

dem wollen sie es pfeifen! Ja!
to that one will they it whistle!   Yes!
(to that one they will whistle it!   Yes)

Martini   Plaisir d'amour
               Pleasure of love

Plaisir d'amour ne dure qu'un moment
Pleasure of love lasts but a moment

Chagrin d'amour dure toute la vie.
Sorrow of love lasts all (one's) life.

J'ai tout quitté pour l'ingrate Silvie
I have all left for the ingrate Silvie
(I left all for the ungrateful Silvie)

Elle me quitte et prend un autre amant.
She me leaves and takes another lover.

Plaisir d'amour ne dure qu'un moment
Pleasure of love lasts but a moment

Chagrin d'amour dure toute la vie.
Sorrow of love lasts all (one's) life.

Tant que cette eau coulera doucement
As long as this water flows softly

Vers ce ruisseau qui borde la prairie,
Toward this brook which borders the prairie,

Je t'aimerai, me répétait Silvie.
I you will love, to me repeated Silvie.

L'eau coule encor, elle a changé pourtant.
The water flows still, she has changed, however.

Massenet   Ah! fuyez, douce image, from "Manon"
                    Ah! flee, sweet image

Je suis seul! Seul enfin! c'est le moment suprême!
I am alone! Alone at last! it is the moment supreme!

Il n'est plus rien que j'aime
There is no longer anything that I love

Que le repos sacré que m'apporte la foi!
But the rest sacred that to me brings faith!

Oui, j'ai voulu mettre Dieu même
Yes, I wanted to put God himself

Entre le monde et moi!
Between the world and me!

Ah! fuyez, douce image à mon âme trop chère;
Ah! flee, sweet image to my soul too dear;
(Ah! flee, sweet image too dear to my heart)

Respectez un repos cruellement gagné,
Respect a repose cruelly earned,
(Respect a dearly bought rest)

Et songez, si j'ai bu dans une coupe amère,
And think, if I have drunk in a cup bitter,
(And remember, if I have drunk from a bitter cup)

Que mon coeur l'emplirait de ce qu'il a saigné!
That my heart it would fill with what it has bled!
(That my heart could fill it up with what it has bled)

Ah, fuyez! loin de moi!
Ah, flee! far from me!

Que m'importe la vie et ce semblant de gloire?
What to me matters the life and this vision of glory?

Je ne veux que chasser du fond de ma mémoire
I want only to chase from the depths of my memory

Un nom maudit! ce nom qui m'obsède et pourquoi?
A name damned! this name which me obsesses and why?
(A damned name! this name that obsesses me, and why)

Massenet   Ah! fuyez... (Continued)

Mon Dieu! De votre flamme
My God! With your flame

Purifiez mon âme, Et dissipez à sa lueur
Purge my soul, And dissipate with its brightness

L'ombre qui passe encor dans le fond de mon coeur!
The shadow which passes yet in the depths of my heart!

Massenet   Il est doux, il est bon, from "Hérodiade"
            He is gentle, he is good

Celui dont la parole efface toutes peines,
He whose word erases all pains,

Le Prophète est ici! c'est vers lui que je vais!
(The Prophet is here! it is toward him that I go!
(The Prophet is here! I go to him)

Il est doux, il est bon, sa parole est sereine:
He is gentle, he is good, his word is calm:

Il parle, tout se tait.   Plus léger sur la plaine,
He speaks, all is quiet.   More light on the plain,

L'air attentif, passe sans bruit.   Il parle!
Looking attentive, (he) passes without noise.   He speaks!

Ah! quand reviendra-t-il? quand pourrai-je l'entendre?
Ah! when will return he? when can I him hear?
(Ah! when will he return! when can I hear him)

Je souffrais, j'étais seule et mon coeur s'est calmé
I suffered, I was alone and my heart was calmed

En écoutant sa voix mélodieuse tendre,
By listening to his voice melodious and tender,

Mon coeur s'est calmé!
My heart was calmed!

Prophète bien aimé, puis-je vivre sans toi!
Prophet well-loved, can I live without you!
(Beloved prophet, could I live without you)

C'est là! dans ce désert où la foule étonée
It is there! in that desert where the crowd surprised

Avait suivi ses pas, Qu'il m'accueillit un jour,
Had followed his steps, That he me welcomed one day,
(Followed his footsteps, That he received me one day)

enfant abandonnée!   Et qu'il m'ouvrit ses bras!
child abandoned!   And where he to me opened his arms!
(an abandoned child!   And where he opened to me his arms)

251

Massenet   Le rêve, from "Manon"
            The dream

Instant charmant Où la crainte fait trève,
Instant charming when fear makes truce,
(Precious moment when my fears are quelled)

Où nous sommes deux seulement! Tiens, Manon,
Where we are two only! Wait, Manon,
(When the two of us are alone! Yes, Manon)

en marchant Je viens de faire un rêve!
while walking I just had a dream!

En fermant les yeux je vois
By closing the eyes I see
(I close my eyes and see)

Là-bas une humble retraite
Over there a humble retreat

Une maisonnette Toute blanche au fond des bois!
A little house All white in the depths of the woods!

Sous ces tranquilles ombrages
Beneath those quiet shades

Les clairs et joyeux ruisseaux
The clear and happy streams

Où se mirent les feuillages, Chantent avec les oiseaux!
Where are mirrored the foliage, Sing with the birds!
(Reflecting leaves, sing with the birds)

C'est le paradis! Oh! non!
It is paradise! Oh! no!

Tout est là triste et morose,
All is there sad and morose,

Car il y manque une chose, Il y faut encor Manon!
For there lacks one thing, It there needs yet Manon!
(Because one thing is lacking. . . Manon must be there)

Viens! Là sera notre vie,
Come! There will be our life,
Si tu le veux, ô Manon!
If you so desire, oh Manon!

252

Massenet   Obéissons, quand leur voix appelle, from "Manon"
Let's obey, when their voice calls

Obéissons, quand leur voix appelle,
Let's obey, when their voice calls,
(Let's always obey the voice of tender love)

Aux tendres amours toujours!
To tender loves always!
(When it beckons us)

Tant que vous êtes belle, usez sans les compter
As long as you are beautiful, use without them counting
(As long as your beauty lasts, use up without counting them)

vos jours!   tous vos jours!
your days!   all your days!

Profitons bien de la jeunesse,
Let us profit well from the youth,
(Let's take advantage of our youth)

Des jours qu'amène le printemps;
From the days that brings the spring;
(Of the days that the spring brings)

Aimons, chantons, rions sans cesse.
Let's love, let's sing, let's laugh without stopping,

Nous n'avons encor que vingt ans! Ah!
We have yet but twenty years! Ah!
(We are still only twenty years old! Ah)

Le coeur, hélas! le plus fidèle,
The heart, alas! the most faithful,
(The most faithful heart, alas)

Oublie en un jour l'amour,
Forgets in one day love,
(Forgets love in one day)

Et la jeunesse ouvrant son aile A disparu sans retour.
And youth opening its wing Has disappeared without return.

Bien court, hélas, est le printemps!
So short, alas, is the spring!

Massenet   Ouvre tes yeux bleus
                    Open your blue eyes

Ouvre tes yeux bleus, ma mignonne:
Open your eyes blue, my darling:

Voici le jour.
Here is the day.

Déjà la fauvette fredonne
Already the warbler sings

Un chant d'amour.
A song of love.

L'aurore épanouit la rose:
The dawn brings forth the rose:

Viens avec moi Cueillir la marguerite éclose.
Come with me To pick the daisy blossomed.
(Come with me and pick the blooming daisy)

Réveille-toi!
Awake!

A quoi bon contempler la terre Et sa beauté?
To what good to contemplate the earth And its beauty?
(What good is it to contemplate the earth in all its splendor)

L'amour est un plus doux mystère
Love is a more sweet mystery

Qu'un jour d'été;
Than a day of summer;

C'est en moi que l'oiseau module
It is in me that the bird modulates
(In me the bird is singing)

Un chant vainqueur,
A song conqueror,
(His triumphant song)

Et le grand soleil qui nous brûle
And the great sun that us burns

Est dans mon coeur!
Is in my heart!

Massenet   Pleurez! pleurez, mes yeux!, from "Le Cid"
                 Weep! weep, my eyes!, from "The Cid"

De cet affreux combat je sors l'âme brisée!
From this frightful combat I come out the soul broken!
(I leave this frightful battle with a broken heart)

Mais enfin je suis libre et je pourrai du moins
But finally I am free and I can at least

Soupirer sans contrainte et souffrir sans témoins.
Sigh without restraint and suffer without witnesses.

Pleurez, mes yeux! Tombez, triste rosée
Weep, my eyes! Fall, sad dew

Qu'un rayon de soleil ne doit jamais tarir!
That a ray of sun should never dry up!

S'il me reste un espoir, c'est de bientôt mourir!
If there to me remains a hope, it is to soon die!
(If there is any hope left for me, it is that I may soon die)

Pleurez, mes yeux, pleures toutes vos larmes!
Weep, my eyes, weep all your tears!

Mais qui donc a voulu l'éternité des pleurs?
But who then wanted the eternity of tears?

O chers ensevelis, trouvez-vous tant de charmes
Oh dear enshrouded (ones), find you so much charm
(Oh dear departed ones, is it so pleasing to you)

A léguer aux vivants d'implacables douleurs?
To give to living (people) implacable sadnesses?

Hélas! je me souviens, il me disait:
Alas, I remember he to me said:
(Alas, I remember him telling me)

"Avec ton doux sourire
"With your sweet smile

Tu ne saurais jamais conduire
You would know never to lead
(You would only know how to lead (someone)

255

Massenet   Pleurez! pleurez... (Continued)

Qu'aux chemins glorieux ou qu'aux sentiers bénis!"
But to roads glorious or to paths blessed!"
(To the glorious road or the blessed path)

Ah! mon père! Hélas!
Ah! my father! Alas!

Massenet   Vision fugitive, from "Hérodiade"
            Fleeting vision

Ce breuvage pourrait me donner un tel rêve!
This beverage could to me give such a dream!

Je pourrais la revoir . . . Contempler sa beauté!
I could her see again . . . Contemplate her beauty!

Divine volupté à mes regards promise!
Divine delight to my glances promised!
(Divine delight promised to my gaze)

Espérance trop brève qui viens bercer mon coeur
Hope too brief that comes to rock my heart
(Hope too brief that attempts to comfort my heart)

et troubler ma raison . . .
and trouble my senses . . .

Ah! ne t'enfuis pas, douce illusion!
Ah! don't fly away, sweet illusion!

Vision fugitive et toujours poursuivie,
Vision fugitive and always pursued,
(Ever pursued and fleeting vision)

Ange mystérieux qui prends toute ma vie . . .
Angel mysterious who takes all my life . . .

Ah! c'est toi que je veux voir,
Ah! it is you whom I want to see,

O mon amour! ô mon espoir!
Oh my love! oh my hope!

Te presser dans mes bras!
You to press in my arms!
(To hold you in my arms)

Sentir battre ton coeur
To feel beating your heart
(And feel your heart beat)

D'une amoureuse ardeur!
With a loving ardor!

Puis, mourir enlacés
Then, to die entwined

dans une même ivresse,
in the same intoxication,

Pour ces transports, pour cette flamme.
For these passions, for this flame.

Ah! sans remords et sans plainte
Ah! without remorse and without complaint

Je donnerais mon âme pour toi,
I would give my soul for you,

mon amour! mon espoir!
my love! my hope!

Mendelssohn   Auf Flügeln des Gesanges
               On wings of song

Auf Flügeln des Gesanges,
On wings of song,

Herzliebchen, trag' ich dich fort,
Sweetheart, carry I you away,

fort nach den Fluren des Ganges,
away to the fields of the Ganges,

dort weiss ich den schönsten Ort;
there know I the most beautiful place;

da liegt ein rothblühender Garten
there lies a red-blooming garden

im stillen Mondenschein,
in the quiet moon shine,

die Lotosblumen erwarten
the lotus-flowers await

ihr trautes Schwesterlein.
their charming little sister.

Die Veilchen kiechern und kosen,
The violets titter and caress,

und schau'n nach den Sternen empor,
and look to the stars up,

heimlich erzählen die Rosen
secretly relate the roses

sich duftende Märchen in's Ohr.
[themselves] fragrant fairy-tales in the ear(s).

Es hüpfen herbei und lauschen
There hop near and listen

die frommen, klugen Gazell'n,
the gentle, clever gazelles,

und in der Ferne rauschen
and in the distance roar

des heil'gen Stromes Well'n.
the sacred river's waves.

Dort wollen wir niedersinken
There will we sink down

unter dem Palmenbaum,
beneath the palm tree,

und Lieb' und Ruhe trinken,
and love and rest drink,

und träumen seligen Traum.
and dream (a) blissful dream.

Mendelssohn   Frühlingslied
Spring—song

Durch den Wald, den dunk'len, geht
Through the forest, the dark one, goes

holde Frühlingsmorgenstunde,
gentle Spring's morning-hour,

durch den Wald vom Himmel weht
through the forest from heaven blows

eine leise Liebeskunde.
a soft message of love.

Selig lauscht der grüne Baum,
Blissful listens the green tree,

und er taucht mit allen Zweigen
and it dives with all branches

in den schönen Flühlingstraum,
into the beautiful Spring-dream,

in den vollen Lebensreigen.
into the full life's round-dance.

Blüht ein Blümlein irgendwo,
Blooms a little blossom somewhere,

wird's vom hellen Thau getränket,
will it by the clear dew (be) watered,

das Versteckte zittert froh,
the hidden one trembles joyfully,

dass der Himmel sein gedenket.
that [the] heaven of it thinks.

In geheimer Laubesnacht
In secret foliage's night

wird des Vogels Herz getroffen
will be the bird's heart hit
(will the bird's heart be hit)

von der Liebe Zaubermacht,
by [the] love's magic power,

261

Mendelssohn   Frühlingslied   (Continued)

und er singt ein süsses Hoffen.
and it sings a sweet hope.
        (of)

All' das frohe Lenzgeschick
All [the] joyful Spring's fate
(Heaven does not proclaim)

nicht ein Wort des Himmels kündet;
not one word of heaven proclaims;
(one word of joyful Spring's fate)

nur sein stummer, warmer Blick
only its mute, warm glance

hat die Seligkeit entzündet.
has the blissfulness kindled.

Also in den Winterharm,
Even in [the] Winter's grief,

der die Seele hielt bezwungen,
which the soul held enclosed,

ist dein Blick mir, still und warm,
is your glance to me, quietly and warmly,
(Quietly and warmly your glance has penetrated)

frühlingsmächtig eingedrungen.
(with) Spring-like power penetrated.
(me with Spring-like power)

Mendelssohn   Suleika

(See Schubert - Suleikas zweiter Gesang)

Mendelssohn   Venetianisches Gondellied
                   Venetian Gondola song

Wenn durch die Piazetta
When through the piazetta
         (little square)

die Abendluft weht,
the evening breeze blows,

dann weisst du, Ninetta,
then know you, Ninetta,

wer wartend hier steht;
who waiting here stands;

du weisst, wer trotz Schleier
you know, who in spite of veil

und Maske dich kennt,
and mask you recognizes,

du weisst, wie die Sehnsucht
you know, how [the] longing

im Herzen mir brennt.
in the heart (of) me burns.
(in my heart burns)

Ein Schifferkleid trag' ich
A sailor's suit wear I

zur selbigen Zeit,
at the same time,

und zitternd dir sag' ich:
and trembling to you say I:

das Boot ist bereit!
the boat is ready!

O komm jetzt, wo Lunen
O come now, as around Luna
            (the moon)

noch Wolken umzieh'n!
still clouds hover!
(clouds still hover)

lass durch die Lagunen,
let through the lagoons,

Geliebte, uns flieh'n!
beloved, us flee!

Wenn durch die Piazetta
When through the piazetta

die Abendluft weht,
the evening breeze blows,

dann weisst du, Ninetta,
then know you, Ninetta,

wer wartend hier steht.
who waiting here stands.

Meyerbeer   Ah! mon fils, from "Le Prophète"
                 Ah! my son, from "The Prophet"

Ah!   mon fils, sois béni!
Ah!   my son, be blessed!

Ta pauvre mère te fut plus chère
Your poor mother to you was more dear

que ta Bertha, que ton amour!
than your Bertha, than your love!

Ah!   mon fils!   tu viens, hélas!
Ah!   my son!   you come, alas!
(Ah!   my son!   you have just, alas)

de donner pour ta mère plus que la vie,
from giving for your mother more than the life,
(given for your mother more than your life)

en donnant ton bonheur!
by giving your happiness!

Ah!   mon fils!   que vers le ciel
Ah!   my son!   let (up) to heaven

s'élève ma prière,
rise my prayer,

et sois béni dans le Seigneur!   Jean!   ah!
and be blessed in the Lord!   John!   ah!

Mozart   Abendempfindung
              Evening impression

Abend ist's, die Sonne ist verschwunden,
Evening it is, the sun is disappeared,
                        (has)

und der Mond strahlt Silberglanz;
and the moon radiates silver-shine;

so entflieh'n des Lebens schönste Stunden,
thus escape [the] life's most beautiful hours,

flieh'n vorüber wie im Tanz.
fly by as in the dance.

Bald entflieht des Lebens bunte Szene,
Soon escapes [the] life's colorful scene,

und der Vorhang rollt herab;
and the curtain rolls down;

aus ist unser Spiel, des Freundes Träne
out is our play, the friend's tear
(ended has our play)

fliesset schon auf unser Grab.
flows already upon our grave.

Bald vielleicht, mir weht, wie Westwind leise,
Soon perhaps, to me blows, like Westwind softly,
                        (a gentle Westwind blows to me)

eine stille Ahnung zu,
a silent foreboding [-],

schliess ich dieses Lebens Pilgerreise,
end I this life's pilgrimage,

fliege in das Land der Ruh!
fly into the land of rest!

Werd't ihr dann an meinem Grabe weinen,
Will you then at my grave cry,

trauernd meine Asche sehn,
mournful (at) my ashes look,

dann, o Freunde, will ich euch erscheinen
then, oh friends, will I (to) you appear

und will Himmel auf euch wehn.
and will heaven upon you blow.
(and will send heaven to you)

Schenk' auch du ein Tränchen mir
Give also you a little tear to me

und pflücke mir ein Veilchen auf mein Grab,
and pick [me] a violet for my grave,

und mit deinem seelenvollen Blicke
and with your soulful glance

sieh' dann sanft auf mich herab.
look then gently at me down.

Weih' mir eine Träne, und ach!
Dedicate to me a tear, and ah!

schäme dich nur nicht, sie mir zu weih'n,
shame you but not, it to me to dedicate,
(but be not ashamed to dedicate it to me)

o, sie wird in meinem Diademe
oh, it will in my tiara

dann die schönste Perle sein.
then the most beautiful pearl be.

Mozart   Ach, ich fühl's (from "Die Zauberflöte")
              Ah, I feel it, "The Magic Flute"

Ach, ich fühl's, es ist verschwunden,
Ah, I feel it, it is disappeared,
          (has)

ewig hin der Liebe Glück!
eternally gone [the] love's happiness!

Nimmer kommt ihr, Wonnestunden,
Never come you, hours of bliss,
(You hours of bliss will)

meinem Herzen mehr zurück.
to my heart more back.
(nevermore return to my heart)

Sieh' Tamino, diese Tränen
Look, Tamino, these tears

fliessen, Trauter, dir allein.
flow, beloved, (for) you alone.

Fühlst du nicht der Liebe Sehnen,
Feel you not [the] love's longing,
(If you do not feel love's longing)

so wird Ruh' im Tode sein.
so will rest in death be.
(then rest will come only in death)

Mozart   Als Luise...

Als Luise die Briefe ihres ungetreuen Liebhabers
   verbrannte*
When Luise the letters of her unfaithful lover burned

Erzeugt von heisser Phantasie,
Produced by hot imagination,

in einer schwärmerischen Stunde
in a passionate hour
(brought to the world)

zur Welt gebrachte, geht zu Grunde,
to the world brought, go to the bottom,
(in a passionate hour, perish)

ihr Kinder der Melancholie!
you children of melancholy!

Ihr danket Flammen euer Sein,
You owe flames your existence,
(You owe your existence to flames in the heart)

ich geb euch nun den Flammen wieder,
I give you now to the flames back,

und all' die schwärmerischen Lieder,
and all the passionate songs,

denn ach! er sang nicht mir allein.
for oh! he sang not (for) me alone.

Ihr brennet nun, und bald, ihr Lieben,
You burn now, and soon, you dear(s) (letters),

ist keine Spur von euch mehr hier.
is no trace of you [more] here.
(there is no trace of you left)

Doch ach! der Mann, der euch geschrieben,
But oh! the man, who you wrote,
                (who wrote you)

brennt lange noch vielleicht in mir.
burns long [yet] perhaps in me.
                (it seems)

*known also as: Unglückliche Liebe
                Unhappy love

270

Mozart   An Chloe
             To Chloe

Wenn die Lieb' aus deinen blauen,
When [the] love from your blue,

hellen, offnen Augen sieht,
bright, open eyes glances,

und vor Lust hinein zu schauen
and of joy into(them) to look
(and for joy to look into them)

mir's im Herzen klopft und glüht;
me it in the heart beats and glows;
(my heart beats and glows)

und ich halte dich und küsse
and I hold you and kiss

deine Rosenwangen warm,
your rosy cheeks warm,

liebes Mädchen, und ich schliesse
beloved maiden, and I clasp

zitternd dich in meinen Arm!
trembling you in my arm!

Mädchen, und ich drücke
Maiden and I press

dich an meinen Busen fest,
you to my bosom firmly,

der im letzten Augenblicke
which in the last moment
(which releases you only in the)

sterbend nur dich von sich lässt;
dying only you from itself leaves;
(last moment when dying)

den berauschten Blick umschattet
the raving view shades
(this wonderful feeling is shaded)

271

eine düstre Wolke mir,
a dark cloud me,
(by a dark cloud)

und ich sitze dann ermattet,
and I sit [then] faint,

aber selig neben dir.
but happy near you.

Mozart   Das Veilchen
           The violet

Ein Veilchen auf der Wiese stand,
A violet in the meadow stood,
                    (grew)

gebückt in sich und unbekannt:
stooped [in itself] and unknown:

es war ein herzig's Veilchen.
it was a sweet violet.

Da kam ein' junge Schäferin
There came a young shepherdess

mit leichtem Schritt und muntern Sinn
with light step and lively spirit

daher, die Wiese her und sang.
hither, the meadow along and sang.

Ach! denkt das Veilchen, wär ich nur
Ah! thinks the violet, were I only

die schönste Blume der Natur,
the most beautiful flower of nature,

ach, nur ein kleines Weilchen,
ah, only a little while,

bis mich das Liebchen abgepflückt
till me the darling plucked
(till the darling plucked me)

und an dem Busen matt gedrückt,
and at the bosom [drowsy] pressed,
(and pressed me to her bosom)

ach nur ein Viertelstündchen lang.
ah! only a quarter-hour long.

Ach, aber ach! das Mädchen kam
ah, but ah! the maiden approached

und nicht in Acht das Veilchen nahm,
and no attention (to) the violet paid,

ertrat das arme Veilchen.
trampled the poor violet.

Es sank und starb und freut' sich noch:
It sank and died and delights itself yet:
           (and yet is delighted)

und sterb' ich denn, so sterb' ich doch durch sie,
and die I then, so die I [but] through her,

zu ihren Füssen doch.
to her feet nevertheless.

Das arme Veilchen! es war ein herzig's Veilchen.
the poor violet! it was a sweet violet.

Mozart   Der Hölle...

Der Hölle Rache kocht in meinem Herzen, from "Die
  Zauberflöte"
[The] Hell's revenge boils in my heart, "The Magic Flute"

Der Hölle Rache kocht in meinem Herzen;
[The] Hell's revenge boils in my heart;

Tod und Verzweiflung flammen um mich her!
death and despair flame around me!

Fühlt nicht durch dich Sarastro Todesschmerzen,
Feels not through you Sarastro pains of death,
(if Sarastro does not feel pains of death through you)

so bist du meine Tochter nimmermehr.
then are you my daughter nevermore.

Verstossen sei auf ewig, verlassen sei auf ewig,
Expelled be [at] eternally, deserted be [at] eternally,

zertrümmert sein auf ewig alle Bande der Natur,
destroyed be [at] eternally all ties of nature,
                    (all natural ties)

wenn nicht durch dich Sarastro wird erblassen!
if not through you Sarastro will turn pale!

Hört! Rachegötter! hört der Mutter Schwur!
Hear! Gods of revenge! hear the mother's oath!

Mozart   Dies Bildnis...

Dies Bildnis ist bezaubernd schön, from "Die Zauberflöte"
This image is charmingly beautiful, "The Magic Flute"

Dies Bildnis ist bezaubernd schön,
This image is charmingly beautiful,

wie noch kein Auge je geseh'n!
as yet no eye ever (has) seen!

Ich fühl' es, wie dies Götterbild
I feel it, how this image of God

mein Herz mit neuer Regung füllt.
my heart with new impulse fills.

Dies Etwas kann ich zwar nicht nennen,
This something can I though not name,
(Though I can not name this "something")

doch fühl' ich's hier wie Feuer brennen.
yet feel I it here like fire burn.
(I feel it here burn like fire)

Soll die Empfindung Liebe sein?
Should the feeling love be?

Ja, ja, die Liebe ist's allein.
Yes, yes, [the] love is it alone.

O, wenn ich sie nur finden könnte!
Oh, if I her only find could!
(Oh, if I only could find her)

O, wenn sie doch schon vor mir stände!
Oh, if she but already before me stood!
(Oh, if she already stood before me)

Ich würde, warm und rein,
I would, warm and pure,

was würde ich? Ich würde sie voll Entzücken
what would I? I would her full(of) delight

an diesen heissen Busen drücken,
to this warm bosom press,

276

Mozart   Dies Bildnis... (Continued)

und ewig wäre sie dann mein!
and eternally were she then mine!
               (would she be mine)

Mozart   In diesen heil'gen Hallen, from "Die Zauberflöte"
              In these sacred halls, "The Magic Flute"

In diesen heil'gen Hallen
In these sacred halls

kennt man die Rache nicht,
knows one [the] revenge not,
(one does not know revenge)

und ist der Mensch gefallen,
and is [the] man fallen,

führt Liebe ihn zur Pflicht.
guides love him to(his) duty.

Dann wandelt er an Freundes Hand
Then goes he on (his) friend's hand

vergnügt und froh in's bess're Land!
delighted and glad into the better land!

In diesen heil'gen Mauern,
Within these sacred walls,

wo Mensch den Menschen liebt,
where man [the] man loves,
(where man loves man)

kann kein Verräther lauern,
can no traitor lurk,

weil man dem Feind vergiebt.
since one the foe pardons.
(since one pardons the foe)

Wen solche Lehren nicht erfreu'n,
Whom such teachings not please,

verdienet nicht, ein Mensch zu sein.
deserves not, a man to be.

Mozart   O Iris und Osiris, from "Die Zauberflöte"
               Oh Isis and Osiris, "The Magic Flute"

O Isis und Osiris, schenket
Oh Isis and Osiris, present

der Weisheit Geist dem neuen Paar!
[the] wisdom's spirit to the new pair!

Die ihr der Wanderer Schritte lenket,
Who you the wanderer's steps guide,
(You who guide the steps of the wanderer)

stärkt mit Geduld sie in Gefahr.
strengthen with patience them in danger.
(in danger strengthen them with patience)

Lasst sie der Prüfung Früchte sehen;
Let them the test's fruits see;
(Let them see the results of the test)

doch sollten sie zu Grabe gehen,
but should they to the grave go,
(but should they go to their graves)

so lohnt der Tugend kühnen Lauf,
then reward [the] virtue's daring course,

nehmt sie in euren Wohnsitz auf.
admit them into your dwelling [-].

Mozart   Warnung
              Warning

Männer suchen stets zu naschen,
Men seek always to nibble,

lässt man sie allein;
leaves one them alone;
(if one leaves them alone)

leicht sind Mädchen zu erhaschen,
easily are maidens to catch,

weiss man sie zu überraschen.
knows one them to surprise.

Soll das zu verwundern sein?
Should this [to] astonishing be?
(Should this be astonishing)

Mädchen haben frisches Blut,
Maidens have fresh blood,

und das Naschen schmeckt so gut!
and the nibbling tastes so good!

Doch das Naschen vor dem Essen
But the nibbling before the meal

nimmt den Appetit.
takes(away) the appetite.

Manche kam, die das vergessen,
Many a maiden lost, who this forgot,
              (who has forgotten this)

um den Schatz, den sie besessen,
the lover, whom she possessed,

und um ihren Liebsten mit.
and(lost) her beloved one with(him).
              (at the same time)

Väter, lasst euch's Warnung sein,
Fathers, let you it warning be,
(Fathers, let it be a warning to you)

sperrt die Zuckerplätzchen ein,
lock the sugar-cookies up,

sperrt die jungen Mädchen, die Zuckerplätzchen ein!
lock the young maidens, the sugar-cookies up!

Mozart   Wiegenlied*
               Cradle-song

Schlafe, mein Prinzchen, schlaf' ein,
Sleep, my little prince, fall asleep,

es ruhen die Vögelein,
[it] rest the little birds,

Garten und Wiese verstummt,
garden and meadow grow silent,

auch nicht ein Bienchen mehr summt,
also not a little bee anymore buzzes,

Luna mit silbernen Schein
(The) moon with silvery shine

gucket zum Fenster herein.
peeps through the window [in].

Schlafe beim silbernen Schein,
Sleep during the silvery shine,

schlafe, mein Prinzchen, schlaf' ein!
sleep, my little prince, fall asleep!

Alles im Schlosse schon liegt,
Everyone in the castle already lies,
                                   (rests)

alles in Schlummer gewiegt;
everyone in slumber cradled;

reget kein Mäuschen sich mehr,
moves no little mouse [itself] anymore,

Keller und Küche sind leer,
cellar and kitchen are empty,

nur in der Zofe Gemach
only in the maid's room

tönet ein schmachtendes Ach!
sounds a languishing "Ah"!

Was für ein Ach mag dies sein?
What for an "Ah" may this be?

Mozart   Wiegenlied   (Continued)

schlafe, mein Prinzchen, schlaf' ein!
sleep, my little prince, fall asleep!

Wer ist beglückter als du?
Who is happier than you?

Nichts als Vergnügen und Ruh'!
Nothing but pleasure and rest!

Spielwerk und Zucker vollauf
Toys and sugar abundantly
            (candies)

und noch Karossen im Lauf,
and also carriages in readiness,

alles besorgt und bereit,
everyone(is) worried and ready,

dass nur mein Prinzchen nicht schreit.
that only my little prince(should) not cry.

Was wird da künftig erst sein?
What will there in(the) future then be?

schlafe, mein Prinzchen, schlaf' ein!
sleep, my little prince, fall asleep!

*This song is by Bernhard Flies and is not, as often
referred to, by Mozart.

Offenbach   Les oiseaux...

Les oiseaux dans la charmille, from "Les Contes
 d'Hoffmann"
The birds in the arbor, from "The Tales of Hoffmann"

Les oiseaux dans la charmille,
The birds in the arbor,

Dans les cieux l'astre du jour,
In the heavens the star of the day,
(The sun in the sky)

Tout parle à la jeune fille D'amour!   Ah!
All speaks to the young girl Of love!   Ah!

tout parle d'amour!   Ah!
all speaks of love!   Ah!

Voilà la chanson gentille,
Here is the song gentle,
(It is the pleasing song)

La chanson d'Olympia!
The song of Olympia!

Tout ce qui chante et résonne
All that which sings and resounds

Et soupire, tour à tour,
And sighs, one by one,

Emeut son coeur qui frissonne D'amour!
Moves her heart that trembles With love!

Voilà la chanson mignonne, la chanson d'Olympia!
Here is the song darling, the song of Olympia!

Offenbach   Scintille...

Scintille, diamant, from "Les Contes d'Hoffmann"
Sparkle, diamond, from "The Tales of Hoffmann"

Scintille, diamant, Miroir où se prend l'alouette,
Sparkle, diamond, Mirror where is taken the lark,
(Sparkle, diamond, Mirror that catches the lark)

Scintille, diamant, fascine, attire-la;
Sparkle, diamond, fascinate, draw her;

L'alouette ou la femme A cet appas vainqueur
The lark or the woman To this charm conquering

Vont de l'aile ou du coeur;
Goes by wing or by the heart;

L'une y laisse la vie Et l'autre y perd son âme!
The one there leaves the life And the other there loses her
    soul!
(One to relinquish life and the other to give up her soul)

Beau diamant, attire-la!
Beautiful diamond, draw her!

Paladilhe   Psyché
                   Psyche

Je suis jaloux, Psyché, de toute la nature!
I am jealous, Psyche, of all of nature!

Les rayons du soleil vous baisent trop souvent,
The rays of sun you kiss too often,
(The rays of sun kiss you too often)

Vos cheveux souffrent trop les caresses du vent.
Your hair suffers too much the caresses of the wind.
(The wind caresses your hair too much)

Quand il les flatte, j'en murmure!
When it them flatters, I about it grumble!
(When it flatters your hair thus, I get moody)

L'air même que vous respirez
The air itself that you breathe
(Even the air that you breathe)

Avec trop de plaisir passe sur votre bouche.
With too much pleasure passes over your mouth.
(Passes with too much delight between your lips)

Votre habit de trop près vous touche!
Your clothing of too close you touches!
(Your clothes too closely touch you)

Et sitôt que vous soupirez
And as soon as you sigh

Je ne sais quoi qui m'effarouche
I don't know what that me startles
(Something that startles me, I know not what)

Craint, parmi vos soupirs, des soupirs égarés!
Fears, among your sighs, (some) sighs gone astray!

Reger   Maria Wiegenlied
                   Maria's cradle-song

Maria sitzt am Rosenhag und wiegt ihr Jesuskind,
Maria sits by the rosebush and cradles her Jesus-child,

durch die Blätter leise weht der warme Sommerwind.
through the leaves gently blows the warm summerwind.

Zu ihren Füssen singt ein buntes Vögelein:
At her feet sings a colored little bird:

Schlaf', Kindlein, süsses, schlaf' nun ein!
Sleep, little child, sweet one, sleep now!

Hold ist dein Lächeln, holder deines Schlummers Lust,
Lovely is your smile, lovelier your slumbers delight,

leg dein müdes Köpfchen fest an deiner Mutter Brust!
put your tired little head securely on your mother's breast!

Schlaf', Kindlein, süsses, schlaf' nun ein.
Sleep, little child, sweet one, sleep now!

Saint-Saëns   Amour, viens aider, from "Samson et Dalila"
Love, come to the aid

Samson recherchant ma présence,
Samson seeking my presence,
(Samson looking for me)

Ce soir doit venir en ces lieux.
Tonight is supposed to come in these places.
(Should come here tonight)

Voici l'heure de la vengeance
Here is the hour of the vengeance
(Now is the time for revenge)

Qui doit satisfaire nos Dieux!
That should satisfy our Gods!

Amour! viens aider ma faiblesse!
Love! Come to aid my weakness!

Verse le poison dans son sein!
Pour the poison in his breast!

Fais que, vaincu par mon adresse,
Make that, conquered by my skill,
(Permit that, conquered by my skill)

Samson soit enchaîné demain!
Samson be chained tomorrow!

Il voudrait en vain de son âme
He would like in vain from his soul
(In vain he would like, from his heart)

Pouvoir me chasser me bannir!
To be able me to chase, me banish!
(To chase me, to banish me)

Pourrait-il éteindre la flamme
Could he extinguish the flame

Qu'alimente le souvenir?
That nourishes the memory?
(Which memory nourishes)

Il est à moi!   c'est mon esclave!
He is to me!   He is my slave!
(He is mine!   He is my slave)

Mes frères craignent son courroux;
My brothers fear his wrath;

Moi, seule entre tous, je le brave,
Me, alone among all, I him brave,
(I alone, of all of them, can stand up to him)

Et le retiens à mes genoux!
And him hold at my knees!
(And keep him before me at my knees)

Amour!   viens aider ma faiblesse!
Love!   come to aid my weakness!

Contre l'amour sa force est vaine;
Against love his strength is (in) vain;

Et lui, le fort parmi les forts,
And he, the strong among the strong (men),
(And he, the paragon of strength)

Lui, qui d'un peuple rompt la chaîne,
He, who of a people breaks the chain,
(He who leads a people out of bondage)

Succombera sous mes efforts!
Will succumb under my efforts!
(Will succumb to my efforts)

Saint-Saëns   Mon coeur...

Mon coeur s'ouvre à ta voix, from "Samson et Dalila"
My heart opens to your voice

Mon coeur s'ouvre à ta voix comme s'ouvrent les fleurs
My heart opens to your voice as open the flowers
(My heart opens to your voice as flowers open)

Aux baisers de l'aurore!
To the kisses of the dawn!

Mais, ô mon bien-aimé, pour mieux sécher mes pleurs,
But, oh my beloved, to better dry my tears,
(But, oh my beloved, to dry my tears completely)

Que ta voix parle encore!
Let your voice speak again!

Dis-moi qu'à Dalila tu reviens pour jamais,
Tell me that to Dalila you return for ever,

Redis à ma tendresse Les serments d'autrefois,
Repeat to my tenderness The oaths of old times,

ces serments que j'aimais!
these promises that I loved!

Ah! réponds à ma tendresse,
Ah! reply to my tenderness,
(Ah! answer my tenderness)

Verse-moi, verse-moi l'ivresse!
Pour me, pour me the drunkeness!

Réponds à ma tendresse!
Answer my tenderness!

Ainsi qu'on voit des blés les épis onduler
As one sees of the wheat the blades undulate
(Like blades of wheat that bend)

Sous la brise légère,
Under the breeze light,
(In the light wind)

Ainsi frémit mon coeur, prêt à se consoler,
Thus trembles my heart, ready to be consoled,

Saint-Saëns   Mon coeur... (Continued)

A ta voix qui m'est chère!
At your voice which to me is dear!
(By your voice so dear to me)

La flèche est moins rapide à porter le trépas,
The arrow is less rapid to carry the death,
(The arrow is less rapid in bringing death)

Que ne l'est ton amante à voler dans tes bras!
Than is your lover to fly into your arms!

Samson! je t'aime!
Samson! I you love!

Saint-Saëns   Printemps...

Printemps qui commence, from "Samson et Dalila"
Spring which begins

Printemps qui commence, Portant l'espérance
Spring which begins, carrying hope

Aux coeurs amoureux, Ton souffle qui passe,
To hearts in love, Your breeze that passes,

De la terre efface Les jours malheureux.
From the earth effaces the days unhappy.
(Erases from the earth unhappy days)

Tout brûle en notre âme Et ta douce flamme
Everything burns in our soul(s) And your soft flame

Vient sécher nos pleurs;
Comes to dry our tears;

Tu rends à la terre, Par un doux mystère,
You give to the earth, By a sweet mystery,

Les fruits et les fleurs.
The fruits and the flowers.

En vain je suis belle! Mon coeur plein d'amour,
In vain I am beautiful! My heart full of love,

Pleurant l'infidèle, Attend son retour!
Weeping the infidel, Awaits his return!

Vivant d'espérance, Mon coeur désolé
Living on hope, My heart desolate

Garde souvenance Du bonheur passé.
Keeps remembrance Of happiness past.
(Remembers past happiness)

A la nuit tombante J'irai triste amante
At the night falling I will go sad lover
(At nightfall, like a sad lover I shall go)

M'asseoir au torrent, L'attendre en pleurant!
To sit at the torrent, Him to await while weeping!
(Sit by the river, wait for him and weep)

292

Chassant ma tristesse, S'il revient un jour,
Chasing my sadness, If he comes back one day,

à lui ma tendresse Et la douce ivresse
to him my tenderness And the sweet intoxication

Qu'un brûlant amour Garde à son retour.
That a burning love Keeps for his return.

Chassant ma tristesse,
Chasing my sadness,

S'il revient un jour, à lui ma tendresse!
If he comes back one day, to him my tenderness!

Et la douce ivresse
And the sweet intoxication

Qu'un brûlant amour Garde à son retour!
That a burning love Keeps for his return!

Schubert   Am Grabe Anselmo's
               At the grave of Anselmo

Dass ich dich verloren habe,
That I you lost have,
(That I have lost you)

dass du nicht mehr bist,
that you no more are,
(that you live no longer)

ach, dass hier in diesem Grabe
ah, that here in this grave

mein Anselmo ist,
my Anselmo is,

das ist mein Schmerz!
that is my sorrow!

Seht, wie liebten wir uns beide,
See, how loved we each other,
(See, how much we loved each other)

und, so lang' ich bin, kommt Freude
and, as long as I am, comes joy
(and, as long as I live, returns joy)

niemals wieder in mein Herz.
never again into my heart.

Schubert   Am Meer
            At the sea

Das Meer erglänzte weit hinaus
The sea shone far out

im letzten Abendscheine;
in the last evening-glow;

wir sassen am einsamen Fischerhaus,
we sat at the solitary fisher-house,

wir sassen stumm und alleine.
we sat silently and alone.

Der Nebel stieg, das Wasser schwoll,
The mist rose, the waters swelled,

die Möve flog hin und wieder;
the seagull flew back and forth;

aus deinen Augen liebevoll
from your eyes loving
            (loving eyes)

fielen die Thränen nieder.
dropped the tears [down].

Ich sah sie fallen auf deine Hand
I saw them drop upon your hand

und bin auf's Knie gesunken;
and am on the knee sunken;
(and I sank to my knees)

ich hab von deiner weissen Hand
I have from your white hand

die Thränen fortgetrunken.
the tears drunk away.

Seit jener Stunde verzehrt sich mein Leib,
Since that hour consumed itself my body,
                    (is)

die Seele stirbt vor Sehnen;
the soul dies of longing;

Schubert   Am Meer   (Continued)

mich hat das unglücksel'ge Weib
me has the unfortunate woman

vergiftet mit ihren Thränen.
poisoned with her tears.

Schubert   An die Leier
             To the lyre

Ich will von Atreus' Söhnen,
I will(sing) of Atreus' sons,

von Kadmus will ich singen!
of Cadmus will I sing!

Doch meine Saiten tönen
But my strings sound

nur Liebe im Erklingen.
only love [in the ringing].

Ich tauschte um die Saiten,
I exchanged [-] the strings,

die Leier möcht ich tauschen!
the lyre wish I (to) exchange!

Alcidens Siegesschreiten
Alciden's victory-march

sollt' ihrer Macht entrauschen!
should of their force ring out!

Doch auch die Saiten tönen
But also those strings sound

nur Liebe im Erklingen.
only love [in the ringing].

So lebt denn wohl, Heroen!
So farewell then [-], heros!

denn meine Saiten tönen,
for my strings sound,

statt Heldensang zu drohen,
instead(of a) hero's song [to boom],

nur Liebe im Erklingen.
only love [in the ringing].

Schubert   An die Musik
            To [the] music

Du holde Kunst, in wie viel grauen Stunden,
You noble art, in how many grey hours,

wo mich des Lebens wilder Kreis umstrickt,
when me [the] life's wild sphere ensnared,

hast du mein Herz zu warmer Lieb entzunden,
have you my heart to warm love kindled,

hast mich in eine bessre Welt entrückt.
have me into a better world transferred.

Oft hat ein Seufzer, deiner Harf entflossen,
Often has a sigh, from your harp flowed,
                (flowed from your harp)

ein süsser, heiliger Akkord von dir
a sweet, holy chord from you

den Himmel bessrer Zeiten mir erschlossen,
the heaven of better times me opened,
(opened up for me the heaven of better times)

du holde Kunst, ich danke dir dafür.
you noble art, I thank you for it.

Schubert   An die Nachtigall
               To the nightingale

Er liegt und schläft an meinem Herzen,
He lies and sleeps at my heart,

mein guter Schutzgeist sang ihn ein,
my good guardian spirit sang him [in] (to sleep),
        (guardian angel)

und ich kann fröhlich sein und scherzen,
and I can cheerful be and jest,

kann jeder Blum und jedes Blatts mich freun.
can (of) each flower and each leaf [me] rejoice.

Nachtigall, ach!   Nachtigall, ach!
Nightingale, ah!   nightingale, ah!

sing mir den Amor nicht wach!
sing (me the) Cupid not awake!
(do not awaken Cupid with your song)

Schubert   An Silvia
               To Sylvia

Was ist Silvia, saget an,
Who is Sylvia, say it,

dass sie die weite Flur preist?
that she the wide field praises?
(that all nature praises her)

Schön und zart seh ich sie nahn,
Beautiful and tender see I her approach,

auf Himmels Gunst und Spur weist,
[to] heaven's grace and symbol show,

dass ihr alles untertan.
that (to) her all (are) devoted.

Ist sie schön und gut dazu?
Is she beautiful and good also?

Reiz labt wie milde Kindheit;
Charm refreshes like gentle childhood;

ihrem Aug eilt Amor zu,
to her eye rushes Amor [-].

dort heilt er seine Blindheit,
there heals he his blindness,

und verweilt in süsser Ruh.
and stays in sweet rest.

Darum Silvia, tön, o Sang,
Therefore (to) Sylvia, sound, oh song,

der holden Silvia Ehren;
[the] lovely Sylvia's honor;

jeden Reiz besiegt sie lang,
every charm excells she long,
                        (by far)

den Erde kann gewähren:
which earth can give:

Kränze ihr und Saitenklang!
garlands (to) her and sounds of strings!

Schubert   Auf dem Wasser zu singen
               On the water to sing

Mitten im Schimmer der spiegelnden Wellen
Midst the glitter of the reflecting waves

gleitet, wie Schwäne, der wankende Kahn;
glides, like swans, the rocking boat;

ach, auf der Freude sanft schimmernden Wellen
ah, on [the] joy's gentle glittering waves

gleitet die Seele dahin wie der Kahn;
glides the soul [on] like the boat;

denn von dem Himmel herab auf die Wellen
for from [the] heaven down upon the waves

tanzet das Abendroth rund um den Kahn.
dances the evening-glow around the boat.

Über den Wipfeln des westlichen Haines
Above the tree-tops of the western grove

winket uns freundlich der rötliche Schein,
beckons us friendly the reddish glow,

unter den Zweigen des östlichen Haines
below the branches of the eastern grove

säuselt der Kalmus im rötlichen Schein;
whispers [the] calamus in the reddish glow;

Freude des Himmels und Ruhe des Haines
joy of [the] heaven and calmness of the grove

atmet die Seel im errötenden Schein.
breathes the soul in the reddening glow.

Ach, es entschwindet mit tauigem Flügel
Ah, [it] vanishes with dewy wing
(Ah, time vanishes from me with dewy wing)

mir auf den wiegenden Wellen die Zeit.
[me] on the rocking waves [the] time.
(on the rocking waves)

Schubert   Auf dem... (Continued)

Morgen entschwinde mit schimmerndem Flügel
Tomorrow vanishes with glittering wing

wieder wie gestern und heute die Zeit,
again as yesterday and today [the] time,

bis ich auf höherem, strahlenden Flügel
till I on higher, radiant wing

selber entschwinde der wechselnden Zeit.
myself vanish from the changing time.

Schubert   Aufenthalt
             (My) Abode

Rauschender Strom, brausender Wald,
Roaring river, rustling forest,

starrender Fels mein Aufenthalt.
rigid rock my abode.

Wie sich die Welle an Welle reiht,
As [itself the] wave to wave follows,

fliessen die Tränen mir ewig erneut.
flow the tears [me] eternally renewed.

Hoch in den Kronen wogend sich's regt,
(As) high in the crowns billowing [itself] it moves,
                  (tree tops)

so unaufhörlich mein Herze schlägt.
so unending my heart beats.

Und wie des Felsen uraltes Erz,
And as the rock's very old ore,

ewig derselbe bleibet mein Schmerz.
eternally the same remains my grief.

Schubert   Ave Maria
                Ave Maria

Ave Maria!   Jungfrau mild,
Ave Maria!   Virgin gentle,

erhöre einer Jungfrau Flehen,
listen to a virgin's supplication,

aus diesem Felsen starr und wild
from this rock rigid and wild

soll mein Gebet zu dir hin wehen.
shall my prayer to you [towards] drift.

Wir schlafen sicher bis zum Morgen,
We sleep securely till the morning,

ob Menschen noch so grausam sind.
though men [yet] so cruel are.

O Jungfrau, sieh der Jungfrau Sorgen,
Oh Virgin, see the virgin's troubles,

o Mutter, hör ein bittend Kind!
oh, mother, hear a praying child!

Ave Maria!
Ave Maria!

Ave Maria!   Unbefleckt!
Ave Maria!   Immaculate!

Wenn wir auf diesen Fels hinsinken zum Schlaf,
When we on this rock sink down to sleep,

zum Schlaf, und uns dein Schutz bedeckt,
to sleep and us your protection covers,

wird weich der harte Fels uns dünken.
will soft the hard rock us seem.
(will the hard rock seem soft to us)

Du lächelst, Rosendüfte wehen
You smile, rose's scents drift

in dieser dumpfen Felsenkluft.
in this damp chasm.

Schubert   Ave Maria   (Continued)

O Mutter, höre Kindes Flehen,
Oh mother, hear (the) child's begging,

o Jungfrau, eine Jungfrau ruft!
oh Virgin, a virgin calls!

Ave Maria!   Reine Magd!
Ave Maria!   Pure maid!

Der Erde und der Luft Dämonen,
The earth's and the air's demons,

von deines Auges Huld verjagt,
by your eye's grace driven away,

sie können hier nicht bei uns wohnen.
they can here not with us dwell.

Wir wolln uns still dem Schicksal beugen,
We will [us] quietly to fate bow,
(We will bow ourselves quietly to fate)

da uns dein heilger Trost anweht;
as (to) us your holy comfort drifts;

der Jungrau wolle hold dich neigen,
to the virgin will kindly yourself bend,
(kindly bend yourself to the virgin)

dem Kind, das für den Vater fleht!
to the child, that [to] the father implores!

Ave Maria!
Ave Maria!

Schubert   Das Fischermädchen
                 The fisher-maiden

Du schönes Fischermädchen,
You beautiful fisher-maiden,

treibe den Kahn ans Land,
drive the boat to the land,
            (to the shore)

komm zu mir und setz dich nieder,
come to me and sit [yourself] down,

wir kosen Hand in Hand.
we flirt hand in hand.

Leg an mein Herz dein Köpfchen
Put on my heart your little head

und fürchte dich nicht zu sehr;
and fear [yourself] not too much;

vertraust du dich doch sorglos
entrust you yourself [but] without worries

täglich dem wilden Meer!
daily to the wild sea!

Mein Herz gleicht ganz dem Meere,
My heart equals wholly the sea,
           (is like)

hat Sturm und Ebb und Flut,
has storm and ebb-tide and high tide,

und manche schöne Perle
and many a beautiful pearl

in seiner Tiefe ruht.
in its depth rests.

Schubert   Dem Unendlichen
                To the Eternal

Wie erhebt sich das Herz,
How uplifts [itself] the heart,

wenn es dich, Unendlicher, denkt!
when it (of) Thee, Eternal, thinks!

Wie sinkt es, wenn es auf sich herunterschaut!
How sinks it, when it at itself looks down!

Elend schauts wehklagend dann und Nacht und Tod!
Misery sees it lamenting then and night and death!

Allein du rufst mich aus meiner Nacht,
Alone Thou callest me from my night,

der im Elend, der im Tode hilft!
who in misery, who in death helpest!

Dann denk' ich es ganz, dass du ewig mich schufst,
Then think I it wholly, that Thou eternal me created,
(Then I truly know, that Thou hast created me immortal)

Herrlicher, den kein Preis, unten am Grab,
Glorious one, to whom no praise, below at the grave,
(Glorious Lord, God, no praise)

oben am Thron, Herr, Gott, den, dankend entflammt,
above at the throne, Lord, God, to whom, thankful inflamed,
(no jubilation, heightened by thankfulness, is chanted)

kein Jubel genug besingt!
no jubilation enough chanted!
(enough to Thee, be it below at the grave or above at the
   throne)

Weht, Bäume des Lebens, in's Harfengetön!
Rustle, trees of life, into the harp-sounds!

Rausche mit ihnen in's Harfengetön, krystallner Strom!
Roar with them into the harp-chords, crystalline stream!

Ihr lispelt und rauscht, und, Harfen, ihr tönt nie es ganz!
You lisp and roar, and, harps, you sound never it enough!

Gott ist es, den ihr preist.
God is it, whom you praise.

Welten, donnert im feierlichen Gang!
Worlds, thunder into the solemn march!

Welten, donnert in der Posaunen Chor!
Worlds, thunder into the trombone's choir!

Tönt, all' ihr Sonnen, auf der Strasse voll Glanz,
Sound, all you suns, on the road full (of) shine,

in der Posaunen Chor!
into the trombone's choir!

Ihr Welten, ihr donnert,
You worlds, you thunder (never it enough),

du, der Posaunen Chor, hallest nie es ganz!
you, the trombone's choir, sound never it enough!

Gott, nie es ganz!
God, never it enough!

Gott ist es, den ihr preist!
God is it, whom you praise!

Schubert   Der Atlas
              [The] Atlas

Ich unglücksel'ger Atlas!
I unhappy Atlas!

Eine Welt, die ganze Welt der Schmerzen,
A world, the whole world of sorrows,

muss ich tragen;
must I carry;

ich trage Unerträgliches,
I carry (the) intolerable,

und brechen will mir das Herz im Leibe.
and break will [me] the heart in the body.

Du stolzes Herz, du hast es ja gewollt!
You proud heart, you have it so intended!

Du wolltest glücklich sein,
You wanted happy (to) be,

unendlich glücklich, oder unendlich elend,
unendingly happy, or unendingly miserable,

stolzes Herz, und jetzo bist du elend.
proud heart, and now are you miserable.

Ich unglücksel'ger Atlas!
I unhappy Atlas!

Die ganze Welt der Schmerzen muss ich tragen!
The whole world of sorrows must I carry!

Schubert   Der Doppelgänger
                The double

Still ist die Nacht, es ruhen die Gassen,
Quiet is the night, [it] silent the alleys,

in diesem Hause wohnte mein Schatz;
in this house dwelled my beloved;

sie hat schon längst die Stadt verlassen,
she has [already] long ago the town left,

doch steht noch das Haus auf demselben Platz.
but stands yet the house on the same place.

Da steht auch ein Mensch und starrt in die Höhe,
There stands also a man and stares into the high,
                                        (upwards)

und ringt die Hände vor Schmerzensgewalt;
and wrings the hands in grief's force;

mir graust es, wenn ich sein Antlitz sehe,
me shudders [it], when I his face see,

der Mond zeigt mir meine eigne Gestalt.
the moon shows me my own figure.

Du Doppelgänger, du bleicher Geselle!
You double, you pale fellow!

Was äffst du nach mein Liebesleid,
What imitates you my love-suffering,
(Why do you imitate)

das mich gequält auf dieser Stelle
that me tormented at this spot

so manche Nacht, in alter Zeit?
so many a night, in old time?
                        (bygone times)

Schubert   Der Erlkönig
                The Erlking

Wer reitet so spät durch Nacht und Wind?
Who rides so late through night and wind?

Es ist der Vater mit seinem Kind;
It is the father with his child;

er hat den Knaben wohl in dem Arm,
he has the boy well in the arm,

er fasst ihn sicher, er hält ihn warm.
he holds him securely, he holds him warm.
                            (keeps)

Mein Sohn, was birgst du so bang dein Gesicht?
My son, what hide you so fearful your face?
           (why do you hide your face so fearfully)

Siehst, Vater, du den Erlkönig nicht?
See, father, you the Erlking not?
(Don't you see the Erlking, father)

Den Erlenkönig mit Kron und Schweif?
The Erlking with crown and train?
                            (mantle)

Mein Sohn, es ist ein Nebelstreif.
My son, it is a streak of mist.

"Du liebes Kind, komm, geh mit mir!
"You dear child, come, go with me!

gar schöne Spiele spiel ich mit dir;
many nice games play I with you;

manch bunte Blumen sind an dem Strand,
many colorful flowers are at the beach,

meine Mutter hat manch gülden Gewand. "
my mother has many a golden dress. "

Mein Vater, mein Vater, und hörest du nicht,
My father, my father, and hear you not,

was Erlenkönig mir leise verspricht?
what Erlking me softly promises?

311

Sei ruhig, bleibe ruhig, mein Kind:
Be quiet, remain quiet, my child:

in dürren Blättern säuselt der Wind.
in dry leaves rustles the wind.

"Willst, feiner Knabe, du mit mir gehn?
"Will, fine boy, you with me go?

meine Töchter sollen dich warten schön;
my daughters shall you attend well;
                    (shall attend you well)

meine Töchter führen den nächtlichen Reihn
my daughters lead the nightly round-dance

und wiegen und tanzen und singen dich ein. "
and cradle and dance and sing you into (sleep). "
                    (to)

Mein Vater, mein Vater, und siehst du nicht dort
My father, my father, and see you not there

Erlkönigs Töchter am düstern Ort?
Erlking's daughters at the dark place?

Mein Sohn, mein Sohn, ich seh es genau,
My son, my son, I see it clearly,

es scheinen die alten Weiden so grau.
there shine the old willows so grey.

"Ich liebe dich, mich reizt deine schöne Gestalt,
"I love you, me incites your beautiful figure,
                    (your beautiful figure incites me)

und bist du nicht willig, so brauch ich Gewalt. "
and (if) are you not willing, so use I force. "

"Mein Vater, mein Vater, jetzt fasst er mich an!
"My father, my father, now grasps he me!

Erlkönig hat mir ein Leids getan."
Erlking has me a harm done!"

Schubert   Der Erlkönig   (Continued)

Dem Vater grauset's, er reitet geschwind,
The father shudders [it], he rides fast,

er hält in Armen das ächzende Kind,
he holds in the arms the groaning child,

erreicht den Hof mit Müh und Not;
reaches the hearth in trouble and distress;

in seinen Armen das Kind war tot.
in his arms the child was dead.

Schubert   Der Hirt auf dem Felsen
                   The shepherd on the rock

Wenn auf dem höchsten Fels ich steh',
When on the highest rock I stand,

in's tiefe Thal hernioderseh',
into the deep valley down look,

und singe,
and sing,

fern aus dem tiefen dunkeln Thal
afar from the deep dark valley

schwingt sich empor der Widerhall,
swings [itself] up the echo,

der Widerhall der Klüfte.
the echo of the cliffs.

Je weiter meine Stimme dringt,
The further my voice penetrates,

je heller sie mir wiederklingt
the brighter it (to) me sounds back

von unten.
from below.

Mein Liebchen wohnt so weit von mir,
My sweetheart dwells so far from me,

drum sehn' ich mich so heiss nach ihr
therefore long I [myself] so warmly for her

hinüber!
yonder!

In tiefem Gram verzehr' ich mich,
In deep sorrow consume I myself,

mir ist die Freude hin,
(from) me is [the] joy gone,

auf Erden mir die Hoffnung wich,
on earth (for) me [the] hope vanished,

ich hier so einsam bin.
I here so lonely am.

So sehnend klang im Wald das Lied,
So longing sounded in the forest the song,

so sehnend klang es durch die Nacht,
so longing sounded it through the night,

die Herzen es zum Himmel zieht
[the] hearts it to heaven draws

mit wunderbarer Macht.
with wondrous might.

Der Frühling will kommen,
[The] Spring will come,

der Frühling meine Freud',
[the] Spring my joy,

nun mach' ich mich fertig,
now make I myself ready,

zum Wandern bereit.
for wandering prepared.

Je weiter meine Stimme dringt,
The further my voice penetrates,

je heller sie mir wiederklingt.
the brighter it (to) me sounds back.

Schubert   Der Jüngling an der Quelle
            The young lad at the spring

Leise rieselnder Quell!
Softly murmuring spring!

ihr wallenden flispernden Pappeln!
you flowing whispering poplars!

euer Schlummergeräusch
your sleepy cadences

wecket die Liebe nur auf.
arouse [the] love only.

Linderung sucht' ich bei euch,
Alleviation (of love) sought I near you,

und sie zu vergessen, die Spröde, ach,
and her to forget, the coy one, ah,

und Blätter und Bach
and leaves and brook

seufzen, Louise, dir nach.
sigh, Louise, you for.
            (for you)

Schubert   Der Musensohn
                  The son of the muses

Durch Feld und Wald zu schweifen,
Through field and forest to rove,

mein Liedchen weg zu pfeifen,
my little song [off] to whistle,

so geht's von Ort zu Ort!
so goes it from place to place!
(so go I from one place to another)

Und nach den Takte reget
And to the rhythm stirs

und nach dem Mass beweget
and to the measure moves

sich alles an mir fort.
every thing [on] me on.

Ich kann sie kaum erwarten,
I can [it] hardly await,

die erste Blum im Garten,
the first flower in the garden,

die erste Blüt am Baum.
the first bud on the tree.

Sie grüssen meine Lieder,
They greet my songs,

und kommt der Winter wieder,
and comes [the] winter again,

sing ich noch jenen Traum.
sing I still that dream.

Ich sing ihn in der Weite,
I sing it in the distance,

auf Eises Läng und Breite,
on the ice's length and width,

da blüht der Winter schön!
there blooms the winter fine!

317

Auch diese Blüte schwindet,
Also this bud disappears,

und neue Freude findet
and new joy presents

sich auf bebauten Höhn.
itself on tilled hillsides.

Denn wie ich bei der Linde
Then as I at the linden (tree)

das junge Völkchen finde,
the young people find,

sogleich erreg ich sie.
immediately excite I them.

Der stumpfe Bursche bläht sich,
The dull lad swells himself,

das steife Mädchen dreht sich
the stiff maiden turns [herself]

nach meiner Melodie.
to my melody.

Ihr gebt den Sohlen Flügel
You give to the soles wings
            (wings to the footsteps)

und treibt durch Tal und Hügel
and drive through valley and hill

den Liebling weit von Haus.
the darling far from house.

Ihr lieben, holden Musen,
You dear, gentle muses,

wann ruh ich ihr am Busen
when rest I her on the bosom
(when do I rest on her bosom)

auch endlich aus?
[also finally] again?

Schubert   Der Schiffer
                 The boatman

Im Winde, im Sturme befahr' ich den Fluss,
In wind, in storm navigate I the river,

die Kleider durchweichet der Regen im Guss;
the clothes drenches the rain in the downpour;
        (are drenched by)

ich peitsche die Wellen mit mächtigem Schlag,
I whip the waves with forceful stroke,

erhoffend mir heiteren Tag.
hoping (for) myself (a) clear day.

Die Wellen, sie jagen das ächzende Schiff,
The waves, they hunt the groaning boat,

es drohet der Strudel, es drohet das Riff,
it threatens the whirlpool, it threatens the reef,

Gesteine entkollern den felsigen Höh'n,
stones tumble (from) the rocky heights,

und Tannen erseufzen wie Geistergestöhn.
and fir trees sigh like ghosts' groan.

So musste es kommen, ich hab' es gewollt,
So must it come, I have it wanted,
(So it had to happen)

ich hasse ein Leben behaglich entrollt;
I hate a life (which) leisurely unfolds;

und schlängen die Wellen den ächzenden Kahn,
and would swallow the waves the groaning boat,
(and if the waves threaten to swallow the groaning boat)

ich priese doch immer die eigene Bahn.
I would praise but always the own way.
(I would not alter my course)

Drum tose des Wassers ohnmächtiger Zorn,
Therefore (let) roar the waters feeble rage,

319

dem Herzen entquillet ein seliger Born,
from the heart springs a blissful fountain,

die Nerven erfrischend: o himmlische Lust!
the nerves refreshing: oh heavenly joy!

dem Sturme zu trotzen mit männlicher Brust.
the storm to defy with manly breast.

Schubert   Der Tod und das Mädchen
                     (The) Death and the maiden

Vorüber, ach! vorüber
Onward, ah! onward

geh, wilder Knochenmann!
go, wild man of bones!

Ich bin noch jung, geh, Lieber!
I am still young, pass, dear!

und rühre mich nicht an.
and touch me not [-].

Gieb deine Hand, du schön und zart Gebild!
Give your hand, you fine and delicate creature!

bin Freund und komme nicht zu strafen.
am friend and come not to punish.

Sei gutes Muts! ich bin nicht wild,
Be of good courage! I am not fierce,
(Be confident)

sollst sanft in meinen Armen schlafen!
(you) shall gently in my arms sleep!

Schubert   Der Wanderer
                   The wanderer

Ich komme vom Gebirge her,
I descend from the mountain-range,

es dampft das Tal, es braust das Meer.
[it] steams the valley, [it] roars the sea.

Ich wandle still, bin wenig froh,
I walk quietly, am scarcely happy,

und immer fragt der Seufzer: wo? immer wo?
and always asks the sigh: where? always where?

Die Sonne dünkt mich hier so kalt,
The sun seems (to) me here so cold,

die Blüte welk, das Leben alt,
the bud withered, the life old,

und was sie reden, leerer Schall,
and what they talk, (is) empty sound,

ich bin ein Fremdling überall.
I am a stranger everywhere.

Wo bist du, mein geliebtes Land?
Where are you, my beloved land?

gesucht, geahnt, und nie gekannt!
looked for, imagined and never known!

Das Land so hoffnungsgrün,
The land so hopefully green,

das Land, wo meine Rosen blühn,
the land, where my roses bloom,

wo meine Freunde wandelnd gehn,
where my friends walking go,
                   (go walking)

wo meine Toten auferstehn,
where my dead ones resurrect,
                   (are unforgotten)

Schubert   Der Wanderer   (Continued)

das Land, das meine Sprache spricht,
the land, which my language speaks,
          (where my language is spoken)

o Land, wo bist du?
oh land, where are you?

Ich wandle still, bin wenig froh,
I walk quietly, am scarcely happy,

und immer fragt der Seufzer: wo?   immer wo?
and always asks the sigh: where?   always where?

Im Geisterhauch tönt's mir zurück:
In the breath of the spirits sounds it to me back:

"Dort, wo du nicht bist, dort ist das Glück!"
"There, where you not are, there is [the] happiness!"

Schubert   Der Wanderer an den Mond
            The wanderer to the moon

Ich auf der Erd', am Himmel du,
I on the earth, in the sky you,

wir wandern beide rüstig zu:
we wander both vigorously onward:

Ich ernst und trüb, du mild und rein,
I serene and troubled, you mild and pure,

was mag der Unterschied wohl sein?
what may the difference then be?

Ich wandre fremd von Land zu Land,
I wander unknown from land to land,

so heimathlos, so unbekannt;
so homeless, so unknown;

Berg auf, Berg ab, Wald ein, Wald aus,
mountain up, mountain down, forest in, forest out,

doch bin ich nirgend, ach! zu Haus.
but am I nowhere, ah! at home.

Du aber wanderst auf und ab
You [but] wander up and down

aus Westens Wieg' in Ostens Grab,
from the west's cradle to the east's grave,

wallst Länder ein und Länder aus,
drifts lands in and lands out,
(drift into lands and out of lands)

und bist doch, wo du bist, zu Haus.
and are yet, where you are, at home.

Der Himmel, endlos ausgespannt,
The sky, endlessly outstretched,

ist dein geliebtes Heimathland:
is your dear homeland:

324

Schubert   Der Wanderer... (Continued)

o glücklich, wer, wohin er geht,
oh happy (the one) who, where he goes,

doch auf der Heimath Boden steht!
yet on the homeland's ground stands!

Schubert   Die Allmacht
             The Omnipotence

Gross ist Jehova, der Herr!
Great is Jehovah, the Lord!

denn Himmel und Erde verkünden seine Macht.
for heaven and earth proclaim His power.

Du hörst sie im brausenden Sturm,
you hear it in the raging storm,

in des Waldstroms laut aufrauschenden Ruf;
in the forest-stream's loud roaring call;

gross ist Jehova, der Herr, gross ist seine Macht.
great is Jehovah, the Lord, great is His power.

Du hörst sie in des grünenden Waldes Gesäusel,
You hear it in the greening woods rustling,

siehst sie in wogender Saaten Gold,
see it in waving field's gold,

in lieblicher Blumen glühendem Schmelz,
in lovely flowers glowing sweetness,

im Glanz des sternebesäeten Himmels.
in the glow of the star-studded heaven.

Furchtbar tönt sie im Donnergeroll
Fearful sounds it in the roll of thunder

und flammt in des Blitzes
and flames in the lightning's

schnell hinzuckendem Flug,
fast quivering flash,

doch kündet das pochende Herz
but proclaims the beating heart
(but the beating heart proclaims)

dir fühlbarer noch Jehovas Macht,
(to) you more impressive still Jehovah's power,
(Jehovah's, the eternal God's power)

des ewigen Gottes,
the eternal God's,
(still more impressive to you)

blickst du flehend empor
look you imploring up
(if you look up imploring)

und hoffst auf Huld und Erbarmen.
and hope for grace and mercy.

Gross ist Jehova, der Herr!
Great is Jehovah, the Lord!

Schubert   Die Forelle
                The trout

In einem Bächlein helle,
In a brooklet clear
(In a clear brooklet),

da schoss in froher Eil
there shot in joyful haste
(in joyful haste)

die launische Forelle
the moody trout
(the moody trout)

vorüber wie ein Pfeil.
by like an arrow.
(shot by like an arrow)

Ich stand an dem Gestade
I stood on the bank

und sah in süsser Ruh
and looked in sweet repose

des muntern Fischlein's Bade
(at) the lively little fish's bath

im klaren Bächlein zu.
in the clear brooklet.

Ein Fischer mit der Rute
A fisher with the rod

wohl an dem Ufer stand,
also at the bank stood,

und sah's mit kaltem Blute,
and saw it with cold blood,

wie sich das Fischlein wand.
how [itself] the little fish twisted.

So lang' dem Wasser Helle,
As long (as) the water's brightness,

Schubert   Die Forelle   (Continued)

so dacht ich, nicht gebricht,
so thought I, not breaks,
            (is not meddled with)

so fängt er die Forelle
[so] catches he the trout
(he does not catch the trout)

mit seiner Angel nicht.
with his rod not.
(with his rod)

Doch endlich ward dem Diebe
But finally grew (for) the thief
(But finally time did not pass)

die Zeit zu lang.
the time too long.
(fast enough for the thief)

Er macht das Bächlein tückisch trübe,
He makes the brooklet slyly muddy,
(He slyly muddies the brooklet)

und eh ich es gedacht,
and before I [it] thought,

so zuckte seine Rute,
so jerked his rod,

das Fischlein zappelt dran,
the little fish struggles on it,

und ich mit regem Blute
and I with excited blood
(and I with angry blood)

sah die Betrogne an.
looked the deceived at.
(looked at the deceived)

Schubert   Die junge Nonne
                  The young nun

Wie braust durch die Wipfel der heulende Sturm!
How rustles through the tree-tops the howling storm!

Es klirren die Balken, es zittert das Haus!
[It] creak the beams, [it] trembles the house!

es rollet der Donner, es leuchtet der Blitz,
[It] rolls the thunder, [it] flashes the lightning,

und finster die Nacht, wie das Grab!
and dark the night, as the tomb!

Immerhin, so tobt' es auch jüngst noch in mir!
Similarly, so raged it also recently [still] in me!

Es brauste das Leben, wie jetzo der Sturm,
[It] roared [the] life, as now the storm,

es bebten die Glieder, wie jetzo der Blitz,
[it] tremble the limbs, as now the lightning,

und finster die Brust, wie das Grab.
and dark the bosom, as the tomb.

Nun tobe, du wilder, gewaltger Sturm,
Now rage, you wild, powerful storm,

im Herzen ist Friede, im Herzen ist Ruh,
in the heart is peace, in the heart is rest,

des Bräutigams harret die liebende Braut,
for the bridegroom waits the loving bride,

gereinigt in prüfender Glut der ewigen Liebe getraut.
purified in testing heat to the eternal love wedded.
                         (wedded to eternal love)

Ich harre, mein Heiland!   mit sehnendem Blick!
I wait, my Lord!   with longing glance!

komm, himmlischer Bräutigam, hole die Braut,
come, heavenly bridegroom, take the bride,

erlöse die Seele von irdischer Haft!
free the soul from worldly confinement!

Schubert   Die junge Nonne   (Continued)

Horch, friedlich ertönet das Glöcklein vom Turm!
Listen, peacefully sounds the little bell from the tower!

Es lockt mich das süsse Getön
[it] calls me the sweet peeling

allmächtig zu ewigen Höhn!
powerfully to eternal heights!

Alleluja!
Alleluja!

Schubert   Die Liebe hat gelogen
               [The] Love has lied

Die Liebe hat gelogen,
[The] love has lied,

die Sorge lastet schwer,
[the] sorrow weighs heavily,

betrogen, ach! betrogen
deceived, ah! deceived
(everyone around has)

hat alles mich umher!
have all me around!
(deceived me)

Es fliessen heisse Tropfen
[it] flow hot drops
(Hot drops flow always)

die Wange stets herab,
the cheeks always down,
(down the cheeks)

lass ab, mein Herz, zu klopfen,
let off, my heart, to beat,
(stop)

du armes Herz, lass ab!
you poor heart, let off!
               (stop)

Schubert   Die Schöne Müllerin
                The Beautiful Miller's Daughter

                1) Das Wandern
                (The) wandering

Das wandern ist des Müllers Lust, das Wandern!
[The] wandering is the miller's joy, [the] wandering!

Das muss ein schlechter Müller sein,
That must a bad miller be,

dem niemals fiel das Wandern ein,
who never thought of [the] wandering [-],

das Wandern, das Wandern.
[the] wandering, [the] wandering.

Vom Wasser haben wir's gelernt, vom Wasser!
From the waters have we it learned, from the waters!

Das hat nicht Rast bei Tag und Nacht,
They have no rest at day and night,

ist stets auf Wanderschaft bedacht,
are always of wandering thinking,

das Wasser, das Wasser.
the waters, the waters.

Das sehn wir auch den Rädern ab, den Rädern!
That perceive we also from the wheels [-], the wheels!

Die gar nicht gerne stille stehn,
They not at all like motionless (to) stand,
(They do not like to stand motionless)

die sich mein Tag nicht müde drehn,
they themselves my day not tired turn,
(untiring they turn all day)

die Räder, die Räder.
the wheels, the wheels.

Die Steine selbst, so schwer sie sind, die Steine!
The (mill-)stones themselves, so heavy they are, the
    stones!

Schubert   Das Wandern (Continued)

Sie tanzen mit den muntern Reih'n
They dance [with them] the joyful round-dance
            (the wheels)

und wollen gar noch schneller sein,
and want quite still faster (to) be,
(and want to be still faster)

die Steine, die Steine.
the stones, the stones.

O Wandern, Wandern, meine Lust, o Wandern!
Oh wandering, wandering, my joy, oh wandering!

Herr Meister und Frau Meisterin,
Mr. master and Mrs. master,

lasst mich in Frieden weiterzieh'n
let me in peace move on

und wandern, und wandern.
and wander, and wander.

Schubert   Die Schöne Müllerin
                The Beautiful Miller's Daughter

                2) Wohin?
                    Where to?

Ich hört ein Bächlein rauschen wohl aus dem Felsenquell,
I heard a brooklet rush [right] from the rock's spring,

hinab zum Tale rauschen so frisch und wunderhell.
down to the valley rush so crisp and wondrously clear.

Ich weiss nicht, wie mir wurde, nicht, wer den Rat mir gab,
I know not, what I felt, not, who the advice me gave,

ich musste auch hinunter mit meinem Wanderstab.
I must (go) also down with my traveller's-staff.
(I also must go down with my traveller's-staff)

Hinunter und immer weiter, und immer dem Bache nach,
Down and always on, and always the brook after,
                                        (following)

und immer frischer rauschte und immer heller der Bach.
and always crisper rushed and always clearer the brook.
(and always crisper and always clearer rushed the brook)

Ist das denn meine Strasse? O Bächlein, sprich, wohin?
Is this then my road? Oh, brooklet, speak, where to?

du hast mit deinem Rauschen mir ganz berauscht den Sinn.
you have with your rushing me wholly intoxicated the mind.

Was sag ich denn vom Rauschen? das kann kein Rauschen
    sein:
Why speak I then of rushing? that can no rushing be;

Es singen wohl die Nixen tief unten ihren Reihn.
[It] sing maybe the water-nymphs deep down their round-
    dance.
(Maybe the water-nymphs deep down are singing their
    round-dance)

Lass singen, Gesell, lass rauschen, und wandre fröhlich nach!
Let (it) sing, fellow, let (it) rush, and wander joyously with
    (the brook)!
Es gehn ja Mühlenräder in jedem klaren Bach.
[It] turn [yes] mill-wheels in each clear brook.
335

Schubert   Die Schöne Müllerin
                The Beautiful Miller's Daughter

     3)   Halt
         Stay

Eine Mühle seh' ich blicken
A mill see I looking

aus den Erlen heraus,
from the alders out,
(out from the alders)

durch Rauschen und Singen
through roaring and singing

bricht Rädergebraus.
bursts (the) wheels' clatter.

Ei, willkommen,
Hey, welcome,

süsser Mühlengesang!
sweet mill-song!

Und das Haus, wie so traulich,
And the house, [how] so cosy,

und die Fenster, wie blank,
and the windows, how bright,

und die Sonne, wie helle
and the sun, how clearly

vom Himmel sie scheint!
from heaven she shines!

Ei, Bächlein, liebes Bächlein,
Hey, brooklet, dear brooklet,

war es also gemeint?
was it thus meant (to be)?

336

Schubert Die Schöne Müllerin
The Beautiful Miller's Daughter

4) Danksagung an den Bach
Thanks to the brook

War es also gemeint,
Was it thus meant (to be),

mein rauschender Freund,
my rushing friend,

dein Singen, dein Klingen,
your singing, your rustling,

war es also gemeint?
was it thus meant (to be)?

Zur Müllerin hin,
To the miller's daughter [on],

so lautet der Sinn,
so sounds the meaning,
(is that the meaning of your rustling)

gelt, hab' ich's verstanden,
isn't it, have I [it] understood,

zur Müllerin hin!
to the miller's daughter [on]!

Hat sie dich geschickt,
Has she you sent,

oder hast mich berückt;
or have (you) me bewitched;

das möcht' ich noch wissen,
that want I still (to) know,

ob sie dich geschickt?
if she (has) you sent?

Nun wie's auch mag sein,
Now as [it] also may be,
(whatever the case may be)

ich gebe mich d'rein,
I give [myself] in,

was ich such', hab' ich funden,
what I search (for), have I found,

wie's immer mag sein.
as it always may be.

Nach Arbeit ich frug,
For work I asked,

nun hab' ich genug
now have I enough

für die Hände, für's Herze
for the hands, for the heart

vollauf genug.
plenty enough.

Schubert   Die Schöne Müllerin
                  The Beautiful Miller's Daughter

        5)   Am Feierabend
           At the restful evening

Hätt ich tausend Arme zu rühren!
Had I thousand arms to move!

könnt ich brausend die Räder führen!
could I loudly the wheels drive!

könnt ich wehen durch alle Haine!
could I blow through all groves!

könnt ich drehen alle Steine!
could I turn all stones!

dass die schöne Müllerin
that the beautiful miller's daughter

merkte meinen treuen Sinn!
noticed my faithful mind!
               (thoughts)

Ach, wie ist mein Arm so schwach!
Ah, how is my arm so weak!

was ich hebe, was ich trage,
what I lift, what I carry,

was ich schneide, was ich schlage,
what I cut, what I beat,

jeder Knappe tut mir's nach.
every lad does me it like.
           (does it like me)

Und da sitz ich in der grossen Runde,
And there sit I in the [great] gathering,

in der stillen, kühlen Feierstunde,
in the calm, cool hour of rest,

und der Meister spricht zu allen:
and the master speaks to all:

339

Schubert   Am Feierabend (Continued)

euer Werk hat mir gefallen;
your work has me pleased;

und das liebe Mädchen sagt
and the dear maiden says (to)

allen eine gute Nacht.
all a good night.

Schubert   Die Schöne Müllerin
      The Beautiful Miller's Daughter

    6) Der Neugierige
    The inquisitive (one)

Ich frage keine Blume,
I ask no flower,

ich frage keinen Stern;
I ask no star;

sie können mir alle nicht sagen,
they can me all not say,
(they all can not tell me)

was ich erführ so gern.
what I want to know so eagerly.
(what I would like to know)

Ich bin ja auch kein Gärtner,
I am surely [also] not a gardener,

die Sterne stehn zu hoch;
the stars stand too high;

mein Bächlein will ich fragen,
my brooklet will I ask,

ob mich mein Herz belog.
if (to) me my heart lied.

O Bächlein meiner Liebe,
Oh, brooklet, of my love,

wie bist du heut so stumm!
how are you today so mute!

Will ja nur eines wissen,
Want but only one (thing to) know,

ein Wörtchen um und um.
one little word again and again.

"Ja," heisst das eine Wörtchen,
"Yes," is called the one little word,

das andre heisset "nein,"
the other one is called "no,"

die beiden Wörtchen
[the] both little words

schliessen die ganze Welt mir ein.
enclose the whole world for me.

O Bächlein meiner Liebe,
Oh brooklet of my love,

was bist du wunderlich!
why are you (so) strange!

Will's ja nicht weiter sagen,
Will it surely not repeat,
(I will surely tell no one)

sag, Bächlein, liebt sie mich?
say, brooklet, loves she me?

Schubert   Die Schöne Müllerin
                The Beautiful Miller's Daughter

        7) Ungeduld
            Impatience

Ich schnitt' es gern in alle Rinden ein,
I would carve it fondly into all barks (of trees),

ich grüb es gern in jeden Kieselstein,
I would chisel it willingly into each pebble,

ich möcht es sä'n auf jedes frische Beet
I like it to sow upon each new flower-bed

mit Kressensamen, der es schnell verrät,
with water-cress seeds, which it quickly discloses,

auf jeden weissen Zettel möcht ich's schreiben:
upon each white slip of paper wish I it to write:

Dein ist mein Herz, dein ist mein Herz
Yours is my heart, yours is my heart

und soll es ewig, ewig bleiben!
and shall it eternally, eternally remain!

Ich möcht mir ziehen einen jungen Star,
I like [me] to raise a young starling,

bis dass er spräch die Worte rein und klar,
till [that] he would speak the words pure and clear,

bis er sie spräch mit meines Mundes Klang,
till he them would speak with my mouth's sound,
                                        (lips)

mit meines Herzen's vollem, heissem Drang;
with my heart's full, warm urge;

dann säng er hell durch ihre Fensterscheiben:
then would sing he brightly through her windowpanes:

Dein ist mein Herz, dein ist mein Herz
Yours is my heart, yours is my heart

und soll es ewig, ewig bleiben!
and shall it eternally, eternally, remain!

Den Morgenwinden möcht ich's hauchen ein,
Into the morning breezes like I it (to) breathe,
(I like to breathe it into the morning breezes)

ich möcht es säuseln durch den regen Hain;
I like it (to) whisper through the brisk grove;

o leuchtet' es aus jedem Blumenstern!
oh, would shine it from each flower-star!

trüg es der Duft zu ihr von nah und fern!
would carry it the scent to her from near and far!

ihr Wogen, könnt ihr nichts als Räder treiben?
you waves, can you nothing but wheels drive?

Ich meint, es müsst in meinen Augen stehn,
I thought, it must in my eyes stand,
        (one must see it in my eyes)

auf meinen Wangen müsst man's brennen sehn,
on my cheeks must one it burn see,
(one must see it burn on my cheeks)

zu lesen wär's auf meinem stummen Mund,
to read were it on my mute mouth,
        (lips)

ein jeder Atemzug gäb's laut ihr kund;
every breath would make it loudly to her known;
(every breath loudly would make it known to her)

und sie merkt nichts von all dem bangen Treiben:
and she notices nothing of all the yearning activities:

Dein ist mein Herz,
Yours is my heart,

und soll es ewig, ewig bleiben!
and shall it eternally, eternally remain!

Schubert   Die Schöne Müllerin
                 The Beautiful Miller's Daughter

        8) Morgengruss
            Greeting in the morning

Guten Morgen, schöne Müllerin!
Good morning, beautiful miller's daughter!

wo steckst du gleich das Köpfchen hin,
where turn you promptly the little head to,
(why do you turn your little head)

als wär' dir was geschehen?
as had to you something happened?
(as if something had happened to you)

Verdriesst dich denn mein Gruss so schwer?
Dislike you [then] my greeting so profoundly?

verstört dich denn mein Blick so sehr?
disturbs you [then] my glance so much?

So muss ich wieder gehen.
So must I again go.

O lass mich nur von ferne steh'n,
Oh let me   only from afar [stand],

nach deinem lieben Fenster seh'n
at your dear window look

von ferne, ganz von ferne!
from afar, quite from afar!

Du blondes Köpfchen, komm hervor!
You blonde little head, come out!

hervor aus eurem runden Tor,
out from your round gate,

ihr blauen Morgensterne.
you blue morning-stars.

Ihr schlummertrunk'nen Äugelein,
You slumber-drunk little eyes,

ihr taubetrübten Blümelein,
you dewey-sad little flowers,

was scheuet ihr die Sonne?
why shun you the sun?

Hat es die Nacht so gut gemeint,
Has [it] the night so well meant,
(Was the night so good to you)

dass ihr euch schliesst und bückt und weint
that you [yourselves] close and bend and weep

nach ihrer stillen Wonne?
for its quiet joy?

Nun schüttelt ab der Träume Flor,
Now shake off the dreams' veil,

und hebt euch frisch und frei empor
and lift yourselves refreshed and free up

in Gottes hellen Morgen!
into God's bright morning!

Die Lerche wirbelt in der Luft,
the lark circles in the air,

und aus dem tiefen Herzen ruft
and from the deep heart calls

der Liebe Leid und Sorgen.
[the] love's grief and sorrow.

Schubert   Die Schöne Müllerin
                The Beautiful Miller's Daughter

                9)   Des Müllers Blumen
                     The miller's flowers

Am Bach viel kleine Blumen steh'n,
At the brook many little flowers stand,

aus hellen blauen Augen seh'n;
from clear blue eyes (they) look;

der Bach, der ist des Müllers Freund
the brook [that] is the miller's friend

und hellblau Liebchen's Auge scheint,
and light blue sweetheart's eye(s) shine[s],

d'rum sind es meine Blumen.
therefore are they my flowers.

Dicht unter ihrem Fensterlein,
Right under her little window,

da pflanz' ich meine Blumen ein;
there plant I my flowers [-];

da ruft ihr zu, wenn alles schweigt,
then call her to, when everything silences,
              (to her)

wenn sich ihr Haupt zum Schlummer neigt,
when [itself] her head for slumber inclines,

ihr wisst ja, was ich meine.
you know well, what I mean.

Und wenn sie tut die Äuglein zu,
And when she closes the little eyes [-],

und schläft in süsser, süsser Ruh,
and sleeps in sweet, sweet repose,

dann lispelt als ein Traumgesicht
then whisper like a dream-face
(then little flowers, like a dream-face, whisper)

347

ihr zu: Vergiss mein nicht!
her to: Forget me not!
(to her)

Das ist es, was ich meine.
That is it, what I mean.

Und schliesst sie früh die Läden auf,
And opens she in the morning the shutters [-],

dann schaut mit Liebesblick hinauf;
then look with love's glance up;

der Tau in euren Äugelein,
the dew in your little eyes,

das sollen meine Tränen sein,
[that] shall my tears be,

die will ich auf euch weinen.
they will I upon you weep.
(which I will weep upon you)

Schubert   Die Schöne Müllerin
                  The Beautiful Miller's Daughter

                  10)   Tränenregen
                        Rain of tears

Wir sassen so traulich beisammen
We sat so intimately together

im kühlen Erlendach,
in the cool roof of alders,
(under the cool roof of alders)

wir schauten so traulich zusammen
we looked so intimately together

hinab in den rieselnden Bach.
down into the murmuring brook.

Der Mond war auch gekommen,
The moon was also appeared,
            (had)

die Sternlein hinterdrein,
the little stars after (her),

und schauten so traulich zusammen
and (they) looked so intimately together

in den silbernen Spiegel hinein.
into the silvery mirror [in].

Ich sah nach keinem Monde,
I looked for no moon,

nach keinem Sternenschein,
for no stars' lustre,

ich schaute nach ihrem Bilde,
I looked for her image,

nach ihren Augen allein.
for her eyes solely.

Und sahe sie nicken und blicken
And saw her (reflection) nod and glance

349

herauf aus dem seligen Bach,
up from the blissful brook,

die Blümlein am Ufer, die blauen,
the little flowers at the bank, the blue ones,

sie nickten und blickten ihr nach.
they nodded and glanced her after.
　　　　　　　　　　　(after her)

Und in den Bach versunken
And into the brook sunken
(The whole heaven seemed sunken)

der ganze Himmel schien,
the whole heaven seemed,
(into the brook)

und wollte mich mit hinunter
and wanted me with down
(and wanted to pull me down)

in seine Tiefe ziehn.
into its depth to pull.
(also into its depth)

Und über den Wolken und Sternen,
And above the clouds and stars,

da rieselte munter der Bach
there murmured sprightly the brook

und rief mit Singen und Klingen:
and called with singing and ringing:

Geselle, Geselle, mir nach!
fellow, fellow, me follow!

Da gingen die Augen mir über,
There ran the eyes of mine over,
(Then my eyes filled with tears)

da ward es im Spiegel so kraus;
then got [it in] the mirror so rippled;

sie sprach: es kommt ein Regen,
she said: it comes a rain,
            (it will rain)

ade! ich geh nach Haus.
farewell! I go [to] home.

Schubert   Die Schöne Müllerin
               The Beautiful Miller's Daughter

11)   Mein!
      Mine!

Bächlein lass dein Rauschen sein!
Little brook, let your murmuring be!
      (stop your murmuring)

Räder, stellt eur Brausen ein!
Wheels, cease your roaring!

all ihr muntern Waldvögelein,
all you lively little forest birds,

gross und klein,
large and small,

endet eure Melodein!
end your melodies!

Durch den Hain aus und ein
Through the grove out and in

schalle heut ein Reim allein:
sound today one rhyme only:

die geliebte Müllerin
the beloved miller's daughter

ist mein, ist mein!
is mine, is mine!

Frühling, sind das alle deine Blümelein?
Spring, are those all (of) your little flowers?

Sonne, hast du keinen hellern Schein?
Sun, have you no brighter shine?

Ach! so muss ich ganz allein,
Ah! then must I completely alone,

mit dem seligen Worte mein,
with the blissful word (of) mine,

unverstanden in der weiten Schöpfung sein!
misunderstood in the wide creation be!
(remain in this wide world without being understood)

Schubert   Die Schöne Müllerin
                    The Beautiful Miller's Daughter

              12)   Pause
              Intermission

Meine Laute hab' ich gehängt an die Wand,
My lute have I hung on the wall,

hab' sie umschlungen mit einem grünen Band;
have it entwined with a green ribbon;

ich kann nicht mehr singen, mein Herz ist zu voll,
I can no more sing, my heart is too full,

weiss nicht, wie ich's in Reime zwingen soll;
know not, how I it into rhymes force shall;
            (how to force it into rhymes)

meiner Sehnsucht allerheissesten Schmerz
my longing's [very] burning pain

durft' ich aushauchen in Liederscherz,
could I exhale into songs' pleasantry,
      (was I permitted to exhale into songs' pleasantry)

und wie ich klagte, so süss und fein,
and as I lamented, so sweetly and gently,

glaubt' ich doch, mein Leiden wär' nicht klein.
thought I [however], my sorrow had been not small.

Ei, wie gross ist wohl meines Glückes Last,
Oh, how enormous is now my joy's weight,

dass kein Klang auf Erden es in sich fasst!
that no sound on earth it in itself holds!
            (can contain it)

Nun, liebe Laute, ruh' an dem Nagel hier,
Now, dear lute, rest on the nail here,

und weht ein Lüftchen über die Saiten dir,
and blows a little breeze over the strings [of you],

und streift eine Biene mit ihren Flügeln dich,
and brushes a bee with her wings you,
      (and if a bee brushes you with her wings)

353

da wird mir so bange und es durchschauert mich.
then gets me so fearful and it shudders me.
(then become I so fearful and I shudder)

Warum liess ich das Band auch hängen so lang?
Why let I the ribbon [then] hang so long?

Oft fliegt's um die Saiten mit seufzendem Klang.
Often flies it around the strings with sighing sound.

Ist es der Nachklang meiner Liebespein?
Is it the echo of my love's pain?

Soll es das Vorspiel neuer Lieder sein?
Shall it the prelude of new songs be?

Schubert   Die Schöne Müllerin
                The Beautiful Miller's Daughter

                13) Mit dem grünen Lautenbande
                     With the green lute-ribbon

"Schad' um das schöne grüne Band,
"What a pity for the nice green ribbon,

dass es verbleicht hier an der Wand,
that it fades here on the wall,

ich hab' das Grün so gern. "
I like [the] green so much. "

So sprachst du, Liebchen, heut' zu mir;
Thus spoke you, sweetheart, today to me;

gleich knüpf' ich's ab und send' es dir.
at once untie I it [-] and send it to you.

Nun hab' das Grüne gern.
Now be fond (of) [the] green [-].

Ist auch dein ganzer Liebster weiss,
Is even your entire lover white,
(Even though your lover is entirely white with flour)

soll Grün doch haben seinen Preis,
shall green yet have its praise,

und ich auch hab' es gern;
and I too am fond of it;

weil unsre Lieb' ist immergrün,
since our love is evergreen,

weil grün der Hoffnung Fernen blüh'n,
since green the hope's far reaches bloom,
(since hope's far reaches are green)

drum haben wir es gern.
therefore are we fond of it.

Nun schlinge in die Locken dein
Now twine into the locks (of) yours

355

das grüne Band gefällig ein,
the green ribbon charmingly [-],

du hast ja's Grün so gern.
you are but (of) [the] green so fond.

Dann weiss ich, wo die Hoffnung wohnt,
Then know I, where [the] hope dwells,

dann weiss ich, wo die Liebe thront,
then know I, where [the] love (is) enthroned,

dann hab' ich's Grün erst gern.
then am I (of) [the] green really fond.

Schubert   Die Schöne Müllerin
                  The Beautiful Miller's Daughter

                  14) Der Jäger
                       The hunter

Was sucht denn der Jäger am Mühlbach hier?
What seeks [then] the hunter at the mill-brook here?

Bleib', trotziger Jäger, in deinem Revier!
Stay, obstinate hunter, in your hunting-ground!

Hier gibt es kein Wild zu jagen für dich,
Here gives it no game to hunt for you,
(Here is no game for you to hunt)

hier wohnt nur ein Rehlein, ein zahmes, für mich.
here dwells only a little doe, a tame one, for me.

Und willst du das zärtliche Rehlein seh'n,
And want you the tender little doe (to) see,

so lass deine Büchsen im Walde steh'n,
then let your guns in the woods stay,

und lass deine klaffenden Hunde zu Haus,
and leave your barking dogs at home,

und lass auf dem Horne den Saus und Braus,
and stop on the horn the tooting and blowing,

und scheere vom Kinne das struppige Haar,
and clip from the chin the shabby hair,

sonst scheut sich im Garten das Rehlein fürwahr.
else shies [itself] in the garden the little doe [surely].

Doch besser, du bliebest im Walde dazu,
Yet better, you remained in the forest also,

und liessest die Mühlen und Müller in Ruh'.
and would leave the mills and (the) miller in peace.

Was taugen die Fischlein im grünen Gezweig?
What good (are) the little fish in the green branches?

Was will denn das Eichhorn im bläulichen Teich?
What wants [then] the squirrel in the blueish pond?

D'rum bleibe, du trotziger Jäger, im Hain,
Therefore stay, you obstinate hunter, in the meadow,

und lass mich mit meinen drei Rädern allein;
and leave me with my three wheels alone;

und willst meinem Schätzchen dich machen beliebt,
and want (by) my sweetheart you make (yourself) liked,
(and if you want to be liked by my sweetheart)

so wisse, mein Freund, was ihr Herzchen betrübt.
then know, my friend, what her little heart saddens.

Die Eber, die kommen zu Nacht aus dem Hain,
The boars, they come at night from the grove,

und brechen in ihren Kohlgarten ein,
and break into her cabbage-garden [-],

und treten und wühlen herum in dem Feld,
and tread and wallow around in the field,

die Eber, die schiesse, du Jägerheld.
the boars, them shoot, you hunter-hero.

Schubert   Die Schöne Müllerin
                  The Beautiful Miller's Daughter

                  15) Eifersucht und Stolz
                       Jealousy and pride

Wohin so schnell, so kraus und wild, mein lieber Bach?
Whereto so fast, so crisp and wild, my dear brook?

eilst du voll Zorn dem frechen Bruder Jäger nach?
haste you full (of) anger the insolent brother hunter after?
(Do you haste full of anger after the arrogant brother
    hunter)

Kehr um und schilt erst deine Müllerin
Turn around and scold first your miller's daughter

für ihren leichten, losen, kleinen Flattersinn,
for her light, loose, little flirtatious mind,

kehr um! Sahst du sie gestern Abend nicht am Tore stehn,
turn around! Saw you her yesterday evening not at the gate
    stand,
(Did you not see her last evening standing at the gate)

mit langem Halse nach der grossen Strasse sehn?
with long neck at the big street look?
(with long neck looking towards the main street)

Wenn von dem Fang der Jäger lustig zieht nach Haus,
When from the catch the hunter gayly marches [towards]
    home,

da steckt kein sittsam Kind den Kopf zum Fenster 'naus.
then puts no decent child the head from the window out.

Geh, Bächlein, hin und sag ihr das; doch sag ihr nicht,
Go, brooklet, there and tell her that; but tell her not,

hörst du, kein Wort, von meinem traurigen Gesicht;
hear you, no word, of my sad face;

sag ihr: er schnitzt bei mir sich eine Pfeif aus Rohr
tell her: he carves near me [himself] a pipe of cane

                       359

und bläst den Kindern schöne Tänz und Lieder vor,
and blows (for) the children beautiful dances and tunes,
   (plays)

sag ihr's!
tell her this!

Schubert   Die Schöne Müllerin
                The Beautiful Miller's Daughter

                16) Die liebe Farbe
                The beloved color

In Grün will ich mich kleiden,
In green will I myself clothe,

in grüne Tränenweiden:
in green tearful willows:

mein Schatz hat's Grün so gern.
my darling is (of) [the] green so fond.

Will suchen einen Cypressenhain,
Will seek a cypress grove,

eine Heide voll grünen Rosmarein.
a heath full (of) green rosemary.

Mein Schatz hat's Grün so gern.
My darling is (of) [the] green so fond.

Wohlauf zum fröhlichen Jagen,
Now on to jolly hunting,

wohlauf durch Heid' und Hagen,
now on through heath and brush,

mein Schatz hat's Jagen so gern.
my darling is (of) the hunt so fond.

Das Wild, das ich jage, das ist der Tod,
The game, that I hunt, that is [the] death,

die Heide, die heiss' ich die Liebesnoth.
the heath, [-] call I [the] love's distress.

Mein Schatz hat's Jagen so gern.
My darling is (of) the hunt so fond.

Grabt mir ein Grab im Wasen,
Dig me a grave in the meadow,

deckt mich mit grünen Rasen:
cover me with green turf:

361

mein Schatz hat's Grün so gern.
my darling is (of) [the] green so fond.

Kein Kreuzlein schwarz, kein Blümlein bunt,
No little cross black, no little flower colored,
                              (no colored little flower)

grün, alles grün so rings und rund.
green, everything green so round about.

Mein Schatz hat's Grün so gern.
My darling is (of) [the] green so fond.

Schubert	Die Schöne Müllerin
The Beautiful Miller's Daughter

17) Die böse Farbe
The hateful color

Ich möchte zieh'n in die Welt hinaus,
I want (to) wander into the world [out],

hinaus in die weite Welt;
[out] into the wide world;

wenn's nur so grün, so grün nicht wär',
if it only so green, so green not were,

da draussen in Wald und Feld!
there outside in forest and field!

Ich möchte die grünen Blätter all'
I want the green leaves all

pflücken von jedem Zweig,
to pluck from every branch,

ich möchte die grünen Gräser all'
I want the green grasses all
(I want to weep on the green)

weinen ganz totenbleich.
to weep (on) [quite] deathly-pale.
(grasses till they are deathly-pale)

Ach Grün, du böse Farbe du,
Ah, green, you hateful color you,

was siehst mich immer an
why look (you at) me always [-]

so stolz, so keck, so schadenfroh,
so proudly, so boldly, so (with) malicious joy,

mich armen weissen Mann?
(at) me poor white man (flour-covered miller)?

Ich möchte liegen vor ihrer Tür
I want (to) lie at her door

363

in Sturm und Regen und Schnee,
in storm and rain and snow,

und singen ganz leise bei Tag und bei Nacht
and sing quite softly by day and by night

das eine Wörtchen "Ade. "
the one little word "Good-bye. "

Horch, wenn im Wald ein Jagdhorn schallt,
Listen, when in the forest a hunting-horn sounds,

da klingt ihr Fensterlein,
[there] vibrates her little window,

und schaut sie auch nach mir nicht aus,
and looks she also for me not out,
(and as she does not look out for me)

darf ich doch schauen hinein.
may I but look into (it).

O binde von der Stirn dir ab
Oh take from the forehead [you off]

das grüne, grüne Band.
the green, green ribbon.

Ade, ade, und reiche mir
Good-bye, good-bye, and give me

zum Abschied deine Hand.
in farewell your hand.

Schubert   Die Schöne Müllerin
        The Beautiful Miller's Daughter

      18) Trock'ne Blumen
        Dry flowers

Ihr Blümlein alle, die sie mir gab,
You little flowers all, which she me gave,

euch soll man legen mit mir in's Grab.
you shall one lay with me in the grave.

Wie seht ihr alle mich an so weh,
How look you all (at) me [-] so sadly,
(Why do you look at me so sadly)

als ob ihr wüsstet, wie mir gescheh'?
as if you knew, what to me happened?

Ihr Blümlein alle, wie welk, wie blass?
You little flowers all, how wilted, how pale?

ihr Blümlein alle, wovon so nass?
you little flowers all, of what so moist?

Ach, Tränen machen nicht maiengrün,
Ah, tears make not May-green,
        (green as in May)

machen tote Liebe nicht wieder blüh'n,
make dead love not again bloom,

und Lenz wird kommen, und Winter wird geh'n,
and Spring will come, and Winter will pass,

und Blümlein werden im Grase steh'n;
and little flowers will in the grass stand;

und Blümlein liegen in meinem Grab,
and little flowers lie in my grave,

die Blümlein alle, die sie mir gab.
the little flowers all, which she me gave.

Und wenn sie wandelt am Hügel vorbei
And when she walks at the mound past
        (past the mound)

und denkt im Herzen: der meint' es treu!
and thinks in the heart: he meant it faithfully!

dann Blümlein alle heraus, heraus!
then little flowers all come out, come out!

der Mai ist kommen, der Winter ist aus.
[the] May has come, [the] winter is gone.

Schubert   Die Schöne Müllerin
                          The Beautiful Miller's Daughter

                    19)   Der Müller und der Bach
                         The miller and the brook

(Der Müller)
(The miller)
Wo ein treues Herze in Liebe vergeht,
Where a faithful heart in love fades,

da welken die Lilien auf jedem Beet;
there wither the lilies upon each bed;

da muss in die Wolken der Vollmond gehn,
there must into the clouds the full moon go,

damit seine Tränen die Menschen nicht sehn;
in order that her tears [the] men (should) not see;

da halten die Englein die Augen sich zu
there keep the little angels the eyes [themselves] closed

und schluchzen und singen die Seele zur Ruh.
and sob and sing the soul to rest.

(Der Bach)
(The brook)
Und wenn sich die Liebe dem Schmerz entringt,
And when itself [the] love of [the] grief frees,
(And when love frees itself of grief)

ein Sternlein, ein neues am Himmel erblinkt;
a little star, a new one in heaven blinks;

da springen drei Rosen, halb rot und halb weiss,
there spring up three roses, half red and half white,
(There spring up from the thorny sprigs three roses)

die welken nicht wieder, aus Dornenreis;
they wither not again, from the sprigs of thorns;
(half red and half white, which will wither no more)

und die Engelein schneiden die Flügel sich ab
and the little angels cut the wings [themselves] off

und gehn alle Morgen zur Erde herab.
and go every morning to the earth down.

(Der Müller)
(The miller)
Ach Bächlein, liebes Bächlein, du meinst es so gut;
Ah brooklet, dear brooklet, you mean [it] so well;

ach Bächlein, aber weisst du, wie Liebe tut?
ah brooklet, but know you, how love does?
          (but do you know what love does)

Ach unten, da unten die kühle Ruh!
Ah below, there below the cool rest!

ach Bächlein, liebes Bächlein, so singe nur zu.
ah brooklet, dear brooklet, [so] sing just on.

Schubert   Die Schöne Müllerin
                The Beautiful Miller's Daughter

          20)   Des Baches Wiegenlied
                The brook's lullaby

Gute Ruh', gute Ruh',
Good rest, good rest,

tu die Augen zu!
close the eyes [-]!

Wandrer, du müder, du bist zu Haus.
Wanderer, you tired one, you are at home.

Die Treu ist hier,
[The] faith is here,

sollst liegen bei mir,
(you) shall lie with me,

bis das Meer will trinken die Bächlein aus.
till the sea will drink the brooklets [out].

Will betten dich kühl
(I) will cover you cool

auf weichem Pfühl
on soft pillow

in dem blauen kristallenen Kämmerlein.
in the blue crystal little chamber.
                            (grotto)

Heran, heran,
Come one, come on,

was wiegen kann,
who cradle can,

woget und wieget den Knaben mir ein!
rock and cradle the boy [me in]!
                            (to sleep)

Wenn ein Jagdhorn schallt
When a hunting-horn sounds

aus dem grünen Wald,
from the green forest,

will ich sausen und brausen wohl um dich her.
will I rush and rustle [well] around you [-].

Blickt nicht herein,
Look not in,

blaue Blümelein!
blue little flowers!

Ihr macht meinem Schläfer die Träume so schwer.
You make my slumbering one's [the] dreams so heavy.

Hinweg, hinweg,
Away, away,

von dem Mühlensteg,
from the mill's bridge.

böses Mägdelein,
bad little maiden,

dass ihn dein Schatten nicht weckt!
that [him] your shadow not wakes!

Wirf mir herein
Throw to me [in]

dein Tüchlein fein,
your little scarf fine,

dass ich die Augen ihm halte bedeckt.
that I the eyes (of) him keep covered.

Gute Nacht, gute Nacht!
Good night, good night!

Bis alles wacht,
Till all (are) awake,

schlaf aus deine Freude,
sleep out your joy,

schlaf aus dein Leid!
sleep out your grief!

Der Vollmond steigt,
The full moon climbs,

der Nebel weicht,
the mist fades,

und der Himmel da oben,
and [the] heaven there up,
                    (up there)

wie ist er so weit!
how is it so far!

Schubert   Du bist die Ruh
               You are the repose

Du bist die Ruh,
You are the repose,

der Friede mild,
the peace gentle,
(the gentle peace)

die Sehnsucht du,
the longing you,

und was sie stillt.
and what it quiets.

Ich weihe dir
I dedicate to you

voll Lust und Schmerz
full (of) joy and pain

zur Wohnung hier
as dwelling here

mein Aug und Herz.
my eye and heart.

Kehr ein bei mir,
Stay here with me,
(Dwell at my place)

und schliesse du
and close [you]
(and behind you)

still hinter dir
quietly behind you
(quietly close tight)

die Pforten zu.
the doors tight.
(the doors)

Treib andern Schmerz
Drive other pain

aus dieser Brust!
from this bosom!

voll sei dies Herz
full be this heart

von deiner Lust.
of your joy.

Dies Augenzelt,
This [tent of my] eye,

von deinem Glanz
by your glow

allein erhellt,
alone illuminated,

o füll es ganz!
oh fill it entirely!

Schubert   Fischerweise
                  Fisherman's tune

Den Fischer fechten Sorgen
(With) the fisher fight troubles
(Troubles and grief and sorrow)

und Gram und Leid nicht an,
and grief and sorrow not,
(do not worry the fisher)

er löst am frühen Morgen
he unties in the early morning
(in the early morning with buoyant mind)

mit leichtem Sinn den Kahn.
with light mind the boat.
(he unties the boat)

Da lagert rings noch Friede
There settles around [yet] peace

auf Wald und Flur und Bach,
on forest and field and brook,

er ruft mit seinem Liede
he calls with his song

die goldne Sonne wach.
the golden sun awake.

Er singt zu seinem Werke
He sings to his work

aus voller, frischer Brust,
from the full, young chest,

die Arbeit gibt ihm Stärke,
the work gives him strength,

die Stärke Lebenslust.
the strength (gives him) joy of life.

Bald wird ein bunt Gewimmel
Soon will a colorful school (of fish)

in allen Tiefen laut,
in all depths form,

und plätschert durch den Himmel,
and splashes through the heaven,

der sich im Wasser baut.
which itself in the water builds.
                              (reflects)

Doch wer ein Netz will stellen,
But who a net will place,

braucht Augen, klar und gut,
needs eyes, clear and good,

muss heiter gleich den Wellen
must (be) cheerful like the waves

und frei sein wie die Flut;
and free be like the flood;

dort angelt auf der Brücke
there fishes from the bridge

die Hirtin, schlauer Wicht!
the shepherdess, sly wretch (you fisherman)!

gib auf nur deine Tücke,
give up now your malice,

den Fisch betrügst du nicht!
that fish deceives you not!
(that fish (the shepherdess) you do not deceive)

Schubert   Frühlingsglaube
                    Faith in Spring

Die linden Lüfte sind erwacht,
The gentle breezes are awakened,

sie säuseln und wehen Tag und Nacht,
they rustle and blow day and night,

sie schaffen an allen Enden.
they work on all ends.
         (in all directions)

O frischer Duft, o neuer Klang!
Oh fresch scent,   oh new sound!

Nun, armes Herze, sei nicht bang!
Now, poor heart, be not afraid!

nun muss sich alles wenden.
now must [itself] everything change.

Die Welt wird schöner mit jedem Tag,
The world grows more beautiful with each day,

man weiss nicht, was noch werden mag,
one knows not, what still become may,
         (what still may happen)

das Blühen will nicht enden, es will nicht enden;
the flowering will not end, it will not end;

es blüht das fernste, tiefste Thal:
[it] blooms the most distant, deepest valley:

Nun, armes Herz, vergiss der Qual!
Now, poor heart, forget the agony!

Nun muss sich alles wenden.
Now must [itself] everything change.

Schubert   Ganymed
                Ganymed

Wie im Morgenglanze du rings mich anglühst,
How in the morning splendor you all around me glow,
(How you glow all around me in the morning splendor)

Frühling, Geliebter!
Spring, beloved!

Mit tausendfacher Liebeswonne sich an mein Herze drängt
With thousandfold joy of love [itself] to my heart urges

deiner ewigen Wärme heilig Gefühl,
your eternal warmth sacred feeling,
(the sacred feeling of your eternal warmth)

unendliche Schöne!
unending beauty!

Dass ich dich fassen möcht in diesen Arm!
That I you hold may in this arm!
(That I may hold you in my arm)

Ach, an deinem Busen lieg ich und schmachte,
Ah, at your bosom lie I and languish,

und deine Blumen, dein Gras drängen sich an mein Herz.
and your flowers, your grass urge themselves to my heart.

Du kühlst den brennenden Durst meines Busens,
You cool the burning thirst of my bosom,

lieblicher Morgenwind,
lovely morning-breeze,

ruft drein die Nachtigall liebend nach mir aus dem Nebeltal.
into which the nightingale calls lovingly for me from the
    misty valley.

Ich komm! ich komme! ach! wohin?
I come! I come! ah! where to?

Hinauf strebt's hinauf!
Upward draws it, upward!

Es schweben die Wolken abwärts,
[It] glide the clouds down,
(the clouds glide down)

die Wolken neigen sich der sehnenden Liebe.
the clouds descend [themselves] to the longing love.

Mir! in eurem Schosse aufwärts! umfangend umfangen!
To me! in your lap upward! embracing embrace!

aufwärts an deinen Busen, alliebender Vater!
upward to your bosom, all-loving Father!

Schubert   Gretchen am Spinnrade
               Margaret at the spinning-wheel

Meine Ruh ist hin, mein Herz ist schwer;
My rest is gone, my heart is heavy;

ich finde sie nimmer und nimmermehr.
I find it never and nevermore.

Wo ich ihn nicht hab, ist mir das Grab,
As I him not have, (it) is to me the grave,

die ganze Welt ist mir vergällt.
the whole world is to me embittered.

Mein armer Kopf ist mir verrückt,
My poor head is [me] confused,

mein armer Sinn ist mir zerstückt.
my poor mind is [me] shattered.

Meine Ruh ist hin, mein Herz ist schwer;
My rest is gone, my heart is heavy;

ich finde sie nimmer und nimmermehr.
I find it never and nevermore.

Nach ihm nur schau ich zum Fenster hinaus,
For him only look I [from] the window out,

nach ihm nur geh ich aus dem Haus.
for him only go I out from the house.

Sein hoher Gang, sein' edle Gestalt,
His proud bearing, his noble figure,

seines Mundes Lächeln, seiner Augen Gewalt,
his lips' smile, his eyes' power,

und seiner Rede Zauberfluss,
and his speech's magic flow,

sein Händedruck, und ach! sein Kuss!
his handclasp, and ah! his kiss!

Meine Ruh ist hin, mein Herz ist schwer;
My rest is gone, my heart is heavy;

ich finde sie nimmer und nimmermehr.
I find it never and nevermore.

Mein Busen drängt sich nach ihm hin.
My bosom urges [itself] to him.

Ach! dürft ich fassen und halten ihn!
Ah! could I touch and hold him!

und küssen ihn, so wie ich wollt,
and kiss him, so as I wanted,

an seinen Küssen vergehen sollt!
with his kisses perish could!
(oh, could I perish with his kisses)

o könnt ich ihn küssen, so wie ich wollt,
oh could I him kiss, [so] as I wanted,

an seinen Küssen vergehen sollt!
with his kisses perish could!

Schubert   Heiden - Röslein
                 Sweetbriar

Sah ein Knab ein Röslein stehn,
Saw a boy a little rose standing,

Röslein auf der Heiden,
little rose on the heath,

war so jung und morgenschön,
(it) was so young and morning-fresh,

lief er schnell, es nah zu sehn,
ran he fast, it near to see,
(he ran fast, to look at it from near by)

sah's mit vielen Freuden.
saw it with many joys.

Röslein, Röslein, Röslein rot,
Little rose, little rose, little rose red,

Röslein auf der Heiden.
little rose on the heath.

Röslein sprach: ich steche dich,
Little rose spoke: I prick you,

dass du ewig denkst an mich,
that you eternally think of me,

und ich will's nicht leiden.
and I will it not tolerate.

Und der wilde Knabe brach's
And the wild boy broke the

Röslein auf der Heiden;
little rose on the heath;

Röslein wehrte sich und stach,
little rose defended itself and pricked,

half ihr doch kein Weh und Ach,
helped it [but] no wailing,

musst es eben leiden.
had it just (to) endure.

381

Schubert   Ihr Bild
                Her image

Ich stand in dunkeln Träumen
I stood in somber dreams

und starrt' ihr Bildnis an,
and gazed her image at,
(and gazed at her image)

und das geliebte Antlitz
and the beloved face

heimlich zu leben begann.
mysteriously to live began.
(mysteriously came alive)

Um ihre Lippen zog sich
Around her lips showed [itself]

ein Lächeln wunderbar,
a smile wonderful,

und wie von Wehmuthsтränen
and as of tears of sorrow

erglänzte ihr Augenpaar.
glistened her pair of eyes.

Auch meine Thränen flossen
Also my tears flowed
(My tears also flowed)

mir von den Wangen herab -
me from the cheeks down -
(down my cheeks)

und ach! ich kann es nicht glauben,
and ah! I can it not believe,

dass ich dich verloren hab!
that I you lost have!
(that I have lost you)

382

Schubert   Im Abendrot
              In the evening glow

O, wie schön ist deine Welt,
Oh, how beautiful is Thy world,

Vater, wenn sie golden strahlet!
Father, when it golden shines!

wenn dein Glanz hernieder fällt,
when Thy splendour down falls,
               (descends)

und den Staub mit Schimmer malet,
and the dust with glitter paints,

wenn das Rot, das in der Wolke blinkt,
when the red, that in the cloud glows,

in mein stilles Fenster sinkt!
in my quiet window sinks!

Könnt' ich klagen, könnt' ich zagen?
Could I complain, could I hesitate?

irre sein an dir und mir?
doubtful be in Thee and me?

Nein, ich will im Busen tragen
No, I will in the bosom carry

deinen Himmel schon allhier.
Thy heaven already here.

Und dies Herz, eh' es zusammenbricht,
And this heart, before it collapses,

trinkt noch Glut und schlürft noch Licht.
drinks still glow and sips still light.

Schubert   Im Frühling
                  In Spring

Still sitz' ich an des Hügels Hang,
Quietly sit I by the hill's slope,

der Himmel ist so klar,
the sky is so clear,

das Lüftchen spielt im grünen Tal,
the little breeze plays in the green valley,

wo ich beim ersten Frühlingsstrahl
where I at the first beam of Spring

einst, ach, so glücklich war;
once, ah, so happy was;

wo ich an ihrer Seite ging
where I at her side walked

so traulich und so nah',
so intimately and so near,

und tief im dunkeln Felsenquell
and deep in the dark rock's spring

den schönen Himmel blau und hell,
the beautiful sky blue and bright,
(I saw the beautiful bright blue sky)

und sie im Himmel sah.
and her in heaven saw.
(and her in that sky)

Sieh', wie der bunte Frühling
Look, how the colorful spring

schon aus Knosp' und Blüte blickt!
already from bud and blossom peeps!

Nicht alle Blüten sind mir gleich,
Not all blossoms are to me the same,

am liebsten pflückt' ich von dem Zweig,
love best to pick [I] from the branch,
(I love best)

von welchem sie gepflückt!
from which she picked!

Denn alles ist wie damals noch,
For all is as then still,
(Everything is now as it used to be)

die Blumen, das Gefild;
the flowers, the fields;

die Sonne scheint nicht minder hell,
the sun shines not less bright,

nicht minder freundlich schwimmt im Quell
not less friendly swims in the fountain

das blaue Himmelsbild.
the blue heaven's image.

Es wandeln nur sich Will' und Wahn,
[It] change only [themselves] will and illusion,
(Will and illusion only change)

es wechseln Lust und Streit;
[it] change joy and struggle;
(and joy and struggle change)

vorüber flieht der Liebe Glück,
[by] flees [the] love's happiness,

und nur die Liebe bleibt zurück,
and only [the] love remains [back],

die Lieb' und ach, das Leid!
[the] love and ah, [the] grief!

O wär' ich doch ein Vöglein nur
Oh would be I but a little bird only
(Oh would I only be a little bird)

dort an dem Wiesenhang,
there by the meadow's slope,

dann blieb' ich auf den Zweigen hier,
then remained I on the branches here,
(then would I remain on the branches here)

und säng' ein süsses Lied von ihr
and sang a sweet song of her

den ganzen Sommer lang.
the whole summer long.

Schubert   Jägers Abendlied
                  Hunter's Evening-song

Im Felde schleich ich still und wild,
In the field creep I quietly and fiercely,

gespannt mein Feuerrohr,
cocked my gun,

da schwebt so licht dein liebes Bild,
there hovers so light your dear image,

dein süsses Bild mir vor.
your sweet image me before.
                    (before my eyes)

Du wandelst jetzt wohl still und mild
You walk now [probably] quietly and gently

durch Feld und liebes Thal,
through field and charming valley,

und, ach, mein schnell verrauschend Bild,
and, ah, my fast dying away image,

stellt sich dir's nicht einmal?
appears [itself] to you it not once?
(does it not once appear to you)

Mir ist es, denk ich nur an dich,
To me is it, think I only of you,

als in den Mond zu sehn,
as at the moon to look,
(as looking at the moon)

ein stiller Friede kommt auf mich,
a silent peace comes to me,

weiss nicht, wie mir geschehn.
(I) know not, what to me (has) happened.

Schubert   Lachen und Weinen
             Laughing and weeping

Lachen und Weinen zu jeglicher Stunde
Laughing and weeping at every hour

ruht bei der Lieb auf so mancherlei Grunde.
depends in matters of love upon so many a reason.

Morgens lacht' ich vor Lust,
In the morning laughed I for joy,

und warum ich nun weine
and why I now weep

bei des Abendes Scheine,
in the evening's shine,

ist mir selb' nicht bewusst.
is to me [myself] not known.

Weinen und Lachen zu jeglicher Stunde
Weeping and laughing at every hour

ruht bei der Lieb auf so mancherlei Grunde.
depends in matters of love upon so many a reason.

Abends weint' ich vor Schmerz;
In the evening wept I for grief;

und warum du erwachen
and why you awake
                    (can)

kannst am Morgen mit Lachen,
can in the morning with laughter,
(awake)

muss ich dich fragen, o Herz.
must I you ask, oh heart.

Schubert   Liebesbotschaft
                    Love's message

Rauschendes Bächlein, so silbern und hell,
Rushing brooklet, so silvery and clear,

eilst zur Geliebten so munter und schnell?
hurries to the beloved so sprightly and quick?

ach, trautes Bächlein, mein Bote sei du;
ah, charming brooklet, my messenger be you;

bringe die Grüsse des Fernen ihr zu.
bring the greetings of the distant one her to.
                              (to her)

All ihre Blumen im Garten gepflegt,
All her flowers in the garden cared for,
                      (which she cared for and)

die sie so lieblich am Busen trägt,
which she so charmingly on the bosom carries,

und ihre Rosen in purpurner Glut,
and her roses in purple glow,

Bächlein erquicke mit kühlender Flut.
brooklet refresh with cooling waters.

Wenn sie am Ufer, in Träume versenkt,
When she at the bank, in dreams (is) lost,

meiner gedenkend, das Köpfchen hängt,
of me thinking, the little head droops,

tröste die Süsse mit freundlichem Blick,
console the sweet one with friendly glance,

denn der Geliebte kehrt bald zurück.
for the lover comes soon back.

Neigt sich die Sonne mit röthlichem Schein,
Sets [itself] the sun with reddish shine,

wiege das Liebchen in Schlummer ein.
cradle the darling into slumber.

Rausche sie murmelnd in süsse Ruh,
Rush her murmuring into sweet rest,
(Carry my beloved)

flüstre ihr Träume der Liebe zu.
whisper to her dreams of love [-].

Schubert   Lied der Mignon
                  Song of Mignon

Nur wer die Sehnsucht kennt,
Only who [the] longing knows,

weiss, was ich leide!
realizes, what I suffer!

Allein und abgetrennt
Alone and separated

von aller Freude,
from all joy,

seh ich ans Firmament
look I to the firmament

nach jener Seite.
to that side.
          (direction where my beloved is)

Ach! der mich liebt und kennt,
Ah! who me loves and knows,

ist in der Weite.
is in the distance.

Es schwindelt mir, es brennt
It stuns me, it burns

mein Eingeweide.
my vital organs.

Nur wer die Sehnsucht kennt,
Only who [the] longing knows,

weiss, was ich leide!
realizes, what I suffer!

Schubert   Litanei
                  Litany

Ruhn in Frieden alle Seelen,
Rest in peace all souls,
(All souls rest in peace)

die vollbracht ein banges Quälen,
who overcame a fearful torment,

die vollendet süssen Traum,
who ended (a) sweet dream,

lebenssatt, geboren kaum,
weary of life, born scarcely,
(just born, already weary of life)

aus der Welt hinüber schieden:
from the world to over there depart:

alle Seelen ruhn in Frieden!
all souls rest in peace!

Liebevoller Mädchen Seelen,
Loving maiden's souls,

deren Thränen nicht zu zählen,
whose tears not to count,
(whose tears can not be counted)

die ein falscher Freund verliess,
who a faithless friend deserted,

und die blinde Welt verstiess:
and (who) the blind world expelled:

alle, die von hinnen schieden,
all, who from here departed,

alle Seelen ruhn in Frieden!
all souls rest in peace!

Und die nie der Sonne lachten,
And (they) who never at the sun smiled,

unterm Mond auf Dornen wachten,
(who) beneath the moon on thorns (stayed) awake,

Gott im reinen Himmelslicht
God in the pure light of heaven

einst zu sehn von Angesicht:
once to see by sight:

alle, die von hinnen schieden,
all, who from here departed,

alle Seelen ruhn in Frieden!
all souls rest in peace!

Schubert   Nacht und Träume
                         Night and dreams

Heilge Nacht, du sinkest nieder;
Blissful night, you descend [-];

nieder wallen auch die Träume,
down glide also the dreams,
(as your moonlight travels through space)

wie dein Mondlicht durch die Räume,
as your moonlight through the space
(so glide down the dreams),

durch der Menschen stille, stille Brust.
through [the] man's quiet, tranquil breast.
(into)

Die belauschen sie mit Lust;
They listen to them with joy;
(Men)   (dreams)

rufen, wenn der Tag erwacht:
exclaim, when the day awakes:

Kehre wieder, heilge Nacht!
Return, blissful night!

holde Träume, kehret wieder!
lovely dreams, return!

Schubert   Rastlose Liebe
                 Restless love

Dem Schnee, dem Regen,
The snow, the rain,
(Towards the snow)

dem Wind entgegen,
the wind against,
(the rain, the wind)

im Dampf der Klüfte,
in the vapor of the chasms,

durch Nebeldüfte
through scents of fog

immer zu!
always onward!

ohne Rast und Ruh!
without pause and rest!

Lieber durch Leiden
Rather through suffering

wollt ich mich schlagen,
would I [myself] fight,

als so viel Freuden
then so many joys

des Lebens ertragen.
of life endure.

Alle das Neigen
All the inclinations

von Herzen zu Herzen,
from heart to heart,

ach, wie so eigen
ah, how so peculiar

schaffet es Schmerzen!
creates it pains!

Wie, soll ich fliehn?
How, shall I flee?

Wälderwärts ziehn?
Forest-bound roam?

Alles vergebens!
All in vain!

Krone des Lebens,
Crown of life,

Glück ohne Ruh,
happiness without rest,

Liebe bist du,
love are you,

o Liebe bist du!
oh love are you!

Schubert   Schlummerlied
                Slumber song

Es mahnt der Wald, es ruft der Strom:
[It] beckons the forest, [it] calls the stream:

"Du liebes Bübchen, zu uns komm!"
"You dear little boy, to us come!"

Der Knabe kommt, und staunend weilt,
The boy approaches, and astonished lingers,

und ist von jedem Schmerz geheilt.
and is of each pain healed.

Aus Büschen flötet Wachtelschlag,
From bushes sounds (the) quail's warble,

mit ihren Farben spielt der Tag,
with its colors plays the day,

auf Blümchen rot, auf Blümchen blau
on little flowers red, on little flowers blue

erglänzt des Himmel's feuchter Tau.
shines [the] heaven's moist dew.

Ins frische Gras legt er sich hin:
In the fresh grass lies he [himself] down:

lässt über sich die Wolken zieh'n -
lets above him the clouds move -

an seine Mutter angeschmiegt
against his mother nestled

hat ihn der Traumgott eingewiegt.
has him the God of dreams cradled.

Schubert   Sei mir gegrüsst
                 Be [by me] greeted

O du Entrissne mir und meinem Kusse,
Oh you, torn from me and my kiss,

sei mir gegrüsst, sei mir geküsst!
be [by me] greeted, be [by me] kissed!

Erreichbar nur meinem Sehnsuchtsgrusse,
Attainable only by my longing's greeting,

sei mir gegrüsst, sei mir geküsst!
be [by me] greeted, be [by me] kissed!

Du von der Hand der Liebe diesem Herzen Gegebne,
You by the hand of love to this heart given,
(Love's hand has given you to my heart)

du von dieser Brust Genommne mir!
you from this bosom taken [-]!

mit diesem Tränengusse
with this shower of tears

sei mir gegrüsst, sei mir geküsst!
be [by me] greeted, be [by me] kissed!

Zum Trotz der Ferne, die sich, feindlich trennend,
In defiance of the distance, which itself, inimically
   separating,
(In defiance of the distance which, as a foe separating us)

hat zwischen mich und dich gestellt;
has between me and you placed;
(has itself placed between me and you)

dem Neid der Schicksalsmächte zum Verdrusse
to the envy of the powers of fate as displeasure
(to the envy and displeasure of the powers of fate)

sei mir gegrüsst, sei mir geküsst!
be [by me] greeted, be [by me] kissed!

Wie du mir je im schönsten Lenz der Liebe
As you me [then] in the most beautiful Spring of love

mit Gruss und Kuss entgegenkamst,
with greeting and kiss met,

mit meiner Seele glühendstem Ergusse
with my soul's most burning outpouring

sei mir gegrüsst, sei mir geküsst!
be [by me] greeted, be [by me] kissed!

Ein Hauch der Liebe tilget Räum' und Zeiten,
A breath of love annuls spaces and times,

ich bin bei dir, du bist bei mir,
I am with you, you are with me,

ich halte dich in dieses Arms Umschlusse,
I hold you in this arm's embrace,

sei mir gegrüsst, sei mir geküsst!
be [by me] greeted, be [by me] kissed!

Schubert   Ständchen
                Serenade

Leise flehen meine Lieder
Softly implore my songs

durch die Nacht zu dir;
through the night to you;

in den stillen Hain hernieder,
to the quiet grove below,

Liebchen, komm zu mir!
darling, descend to me!

Flüsternd schlanke Wipfel rauschen
Whispering slender tree-tops rustle

in des Mondes Licht,
in the moon's light,

des Verräters feindlich Lauschen
the traitor's hostile eavesdropping

fürchte, Holde, nicht.
fear, gentle one, not.
(fear not, gentle one)

Hörst die Nachtigallen schlagen?
Hear (you) the nightingales sing?

Ach! sie flehen dich,
Ah! they implore you,

mit der Töne süssen Klagen
with the tones sweet lament

flehen sie für mich.
implore they for me.

Sie verstehn des Busens Sehnen,
They understand the bosom's longing,

kennen Liebesschmerz,
(they) know love's sorrow,

rühren mit den Silbertönen
stir with the silvertones

jedes weiche Herz.
each tender heart.

Lass auch dir die Brust bewegen,
Let also you the bosom move,
(Let also your bosom be moved)

Liebchen, höre mich!
darling, hear me!

bebend harr' ich dir entgegen!
trembling wait I you to meet!

komm, beglücke mich!
come, make happy me!
(come, make me happy)

Schubert   Suleika

Was bedeuted die Bewegung?
What means the stir?

Bringt der Ost mir frohe Kunde?
Brings the east (wind) me glad news?

Seiner Schwingen frische Regung
Its wings fresh movement

kühlt des Herzens tiefe Wunde.
cools the heart's deep wound.

Kosend spielt er mit dem Staube,
Caressing plays it with the dust,

jagt ihn auf in leichten Wölkchen,
lifts it up in light little clouds,

treibt zur sichern Rebenlaube
drives to the safe arbor of vines

der Insekten frohes Völkchen.
the insects gay little swarm.

Lindert sanft der Sonne Glühen,
Softens gently the sun's glow,

kühlt auch mir die heissen Wangen,
cools also me the hot cheeks,

küsst die Reben noch im Fliehen,
kisses the vines still in the fleeing,
(while fleeing, kisses the vines)

die auf Feld und Hügel prangen.
which on fields and hills flourish.

Und mir bringt sein leises Flüstern
And to me brings its soft whisper

von dem Freunde tausend Grüsse;
from the friend (a) thousand greetings;

eh' noch diese Hügel düstern,
before yet these hills darken,

grüssen mich wohl tausend Küsse.
greet me certainly (a) thousand kisses.

Und so kannst du weiter ziehen!
And thus can you onward move!

Diene Freunden und Betrübten.
Serve friends and sorrowful ones.

Dort, wo hohe Mauern glühen,
There, where high walls glow,

dort find ich bald den Vielgeliebten.
there find I soon the much loved one.

Ach, die wahre Herzenskunde,
Ah, the true heart's message,

Liebeshauch, erfrischtes Leben
love's breath, refreshed life

wird mir nur aus seinem Munde,
comes to me only from his mouth,
                              (lips)

kann mir nur sein Atem geben.
can me only his breath give.
(can only his breath give me)

Schubert   Suleikas zweiter Gesang
                    Suleika's second song

Ach, um deine feuchten Schwingen,
Ah, for your moist wings,

West, wie sehr ich dich beneide,
west (wind), how much I you envy,

denn du kannst ihm Kunde bringen,
for you can (to) him message bring,

was ich in der Trennung leide!
what I in [the] separation suffer!

Die Bewegung deiner Flügel
The movement of your wings

weckt im Busen stilles Sehnen,
arouses in the bosom silent longing,

Blumen, Auen, Wald und Hügel
flowers, fields, forest and hills

steh'n bei deinem Hauch in Tränen.
stand in your breeze in tears.

Doch dein mildes, sanftes Wehen
But your mild, soft blowing

kühlt die wunden Augenlider;
cools the sore eyelids;

ach, für Leid müsst' ich vergehen,
ah, for grief must I pass away,

hofft' ich nicht zu seh'n ihn wieder.
hoped I not to see him again.

Eile denn zu meinem Lieben,
Hurry then to my beloved,

spreche sanft zu seinem Herzen;
speak gently to his heart;

doch vermeid', ihn zu betrüben
but avoid, him to sadden

und verbirg ihm meine Schmerzen!
and hide (from) him my pains!

Sag' ihm, aber sag's bescheiden:
Tell him, but tell it discreetly:

seine Liebe sei mein Leben;
his love (will) be my life;

freudiges Gefühl von beiden
joyful feeling of both

wird mir seine Nähe geben;
will me his nearness give;

sag' ihm, aber bescheiden:
tell him, but discreetly:

seine Liebe sei mein Leben.
his love (will) be my life.

Schubert   Wanderers Nachtlied
                  Wanderer's night-song

Über allen Gipfeln ist Ruh,
Above all hill-tops is rest,

in allen Wipfeln spürest du
in all tree-tops feel you

kaum einen Hauch;
hardly a breath;

die Vöglein schweigen,
the little birds (are) silent,

schweigen im Walde.
silent in the woods.

Warte nur, balde
Wait now, soon

ruhest du auch.
rest you also.

Schubert   Wiegenlied
                Lullaby

Schlafe, schlafe, holder, süsser Knabe,
Sleep, sleep, lovely, sweet boy,

leise wiegt dich deiner Mutter Hand;
softly rocks you your mother's hand;

sanfte Ruhe, milde Labe
gentle rest, mild comfort

bringt dir schwebend dieses Wiegenband.
brings you gliding this cradleband. *

Schlafe, schlafe in dem süssen Grabe,
Sleep, sleep in the sweet grave,

noch beschützt dich deiner Mutter Arm;
still protects you your mother's arm;

alle Wünsche, alle Habe
all desires, all things

fasst sie liebend, alle liebewarm.
understands she lovingly, all warm of love.

Schlafe, schlafe in der Flaumen Schosse,
Sleep, sleep in the down's lap,

noch umtönt dich lauter Liebeston,
still sounds (to) you pure love's sound,

eine Lilie, eine Rose,
a lily, a rose,

nach dem Schlafe werd' sie dir zum Lohn.
after the sleep get [it] you as reward.
                (you get)

* cradleband - is a string by which a cradle is rocked.

407

Schubert   Winterreise
            Winter Journey

            1) Gute Nacht
            Good night

Fremd bin ich eingezogen,
Strange am I entered,
(As a stranger I entered)

fremd zieh ich wieder aus.
strange wander I [again] out.
(as a stranger I wander out)

Der Mai war mir gewogen
[The] May was to me kind

mit manchem Blumenstrauss.
with many a flower-bouquet.

Das Mädchen sprach von Liebe,
The maiden spoke of love,

die Mutter gar von Eh'.
the mother even of marriage.

Nun ist die Welt so trübe,
Now is the world so gloomy,

der Weg gehüllt in Schnee.
the path covered in snow.

Ich kann zu meiner Reisen
I can for my travels

nicht wählen mir die Zeit,
not choose [me] the time,

muss selbst den Weg mir weisen
must myself the path me show
(I must find myself the path)

in dieser Dunkelheit.
in this darkness.

Es zieht ein Mondenschatten
[It] moves a moon-shadow
(A moon-shadow moves)

408

als mein Gefährte mit,
as my companion with (me),

und auf den weissen Matten
and on the white fields

such ich des Wildes Tritt.
seek I the games' footprint.
                (footprint of game)

Was soll ich länger weilen,
Why shall I longer stay,

dass man mich trieb' hinaus?
that one me drives out?
(until someone drives me out)

Lass irre Hunde heulen
Let mad dogs howl

vor ihres Vater's Haus.
at her father's house.

Die Liebe liebt das Wandern,
[The] love loves [the] wandering,

Gott hat sie so gemacht,
God has it so made,

von Einem zu dem Andern,
from one to the other,

Gott hat sie so gemacht.
God has it so made.

Die Liebe liebt das Wandern,
[The] love loves [the] wandering,

fein Liebchen, gute Nacht,
fine sweetheart, good night,

von Einem zu dem Andern,
from one to the other,

fein Liebchen, gute Nacht.
fine sweetheart, good night.

Will dich im Traum nicht stören,
Will you in (your) dream not bother,

wär' schad um deine Ruh,
would be a pity for your rest,

sollst meinen Tritt nicht hören,
(you) should my step not hear,

sacht, sacht die Türe zu.
softly, softly the door (I) close.

Schreib' im Vorübergehen
(I) write in passing by

an's Tor dir: gute Nacht,
on the gate (for) you: good night,

damit du mögest sehen,
that you may see,

an dich hab' ich gedacht.
of you have I thought.

Schubert   Winterreise
                      Winter Journey

          2) Die Wetterfahne
             The weather-vane

Der Wind spielt mit der Wetterfahne
The wind plays with the weather-vane

auf meines schönen Liebchens Haus.
on my fair sweetheart's house.

Da dacht' ich schon in meinem Wahne,
There thought I [already] in my illusion,

sie pfiff den armen Flüchtling aus.
it whistles the poor fugitive out.
(it wanted to expel the poor fugitive)

Er hätt' es eher bemerken sollen,
He should have [it] sooner noticed [-],
(The fugitive)

des Hauses aufgestecktes Schild,
the house's upraised sign,

so hätt' er nimmer suchen wollen
then had he never looked [wanted]

im Haus ein treues Frauenbild.
in the house (for) a faithful woman.

Der Wind spielt drinnen mit den Herzen
The wind plays inside with the hearts

wie auf dem Dach, nur nicht so laut.
as on the roof, but not so loud.

Was fragen sie nach meinen Schmerzen?
What ask they for my pains?
(They do not care about my grief)

Ihr Kind ist eine reiche Braut.
Their child is a wealthy bride.

Schubert   Winterreise
                        Winter Journey

                    3) Gefror'ne Tränen
                        Frozen tears

Gefror'ne Tropfen fallen
Frozen drops fall

von meinen Wangen ab;
from my cheeks [down];

ob es mir denn entgangen,
if it me then escaped,
(did it escape me)

dass ich geweinet hab'?
that I wept [have]?

Ei Tränen, meine Tränen,
O tears, my tears,

und seid ihr gar so lau,
and are you [even] so tepid,

dass ihr erstarrt zu Eise,
that you freeze to ice,

wie kühler Morgentau?
like cool morning-dew?

Und dringt doch aus der Quelle
And spring yet from the source
(And yet you started out from)

der Brust so glühend heiss,
of the breast so glowing hot,
(the breast so glowing hot)

als wolltet ihr zerschmelzen
as wanted you (to) melt
(as though you wanted to melt)

des ganzen Winters Eis.
the whole winter's ice.

Schubert   Winterreise
      Winter Journey

    4) Erstarrung
    Numbness

Ich such' im Schnee vergebens
I seek in the snow in vain

nach ihrer Tritte Spur,
for her steps' trace,

wo sie an meinem Arme
where she at my arm

durchstrich die grüne Flur.
roved (through) the green plain.

Ich will den Boden küssen,
I will the ground kiss,

durchdringen Eis und Schnee
pierce ice and snow

mit meinen heissen Tränen,
with my hot tears,

bis ich die Erde seh'.
till I the earth see.

Wo find' ich eine Blüte?
Where find I a blossom?

Wo find' ich grünes Gras?
Where find I green grass?

Die Blumen sind erstorben,
The flowers have perished,

der Rasen sieht so blass.
the turf looks so pale.

Soll denn kein Angedenken
Shall then no souvenir

ich nehmen mit von hier?
I take with (me) from here?

Wenn meine Schmerzen schweigen,
When my pains silence,
                    (become silent)

wer sagt mir dann von ihr?
who tells me then of her?

Mein Herz ist wie erstorben,
My heart is almost dead,

kalt starrt ihr Bild darin;
cold stares her image in it;

schmilzt je das Herz mir wieder,
thaws ever the heart [me] again,

fliesst auch ihr Bild dahin.
flows [also] her image away.

Schubert   Winterreise
                  Winter Journey

                  5) Der Lindenbaum
                  The linden tree

Am Brunnen vor dem Tore
At the well in front of the gate

da steht ein Lindenbaum;
there stands a linden tree;

ich träumt' in seinem Schatten
I dreamt in its shade

so manchen süssen Traum.
so many a sweet dream.

Ich schnitt in seine Rinde
I cut into its bark

so manches liebe Wort;
so many a dear word;

es zog in Freud und Leide
it drew in joy and grief
(in joy and grief it drew)

zu ihm mich immerfort.
to him me continually.
(me continually to him)

Ich musst auch heute wandern
I must also today wander
(I had to wander also today)

vorbei in tiefer Nacht,
past it in deep night,

da hab ich noch im Dunkel
there have I [yet] in the darkness

die Augen zugemacht.
the eyes closed.

Und seine Zweige rauschten,
And his branches rustled,

als riefen sie mir zu:
as call they me at:
(as if they called to me)

komm her zu mir, Geselle,
come here to me, fellow,

hier findst du deine Ruh!
here find you your rest!

Die kalten Winde bliesen
The cold winds blew

mir grad ins Angesicht,
me straight into the face,

der Hut flog mir vom Kopfe,
the hat flew me from the head,
(the hat flew from my head)

ich wendete mich nicht.
I turned [myself] not.

Nun bin ich manche Stunde
Now am I many an hour

entfernt von jenem Ort,
remote from that place,

und immer hör ich's rauschen:
and always hear I it rustle:

du fändest Ruhe dort!
you would find rest there!

Schubert   Winterreise
            Winter Journey

6) Wasserflut
   High water

Manche Trän aus meinen Augen
Many a tear from my eyes

ist gefallen in den Schnee;
is fallen in the snow;

seine kalten Flocken saugen
its cold flakes suck
            (absorb)

durstig ein das heisse Weh.
thirstily [in] the hot pain.
            (burning)

Wenn die Gräser sprossen wollen,
When the grasses sprout want,
            (want to sprout)

weht daher ein lauer Wind,
blows around a mild wind,

und das Eis zerspringt in Schollen
and the ice bursts into blocks

und der weiche Schnee zerrinnt.
and the soft snow melts.

Schnee, du weisst von meinem Sehnen,
Snow, you know of my longing,

sag, wohin doch geht dein Lauf?
say, whither [but] goes your course?

Folge nach nur meinen Tränen,
Follow [-] just my tears,

nimmt dich bald das Bächlein auf.
(then) takes you soon the little brook [-].

Wirst mit ihm die Stadt durchziehen,
(You) will with it the town cross,
(With it you will pass through the town)

Schubert   Wasserflut   (Continued)

muntre Strassen ein und aus;
(pass through) lively streets in and out;

fühlst du meine Tränen glühen,
feel you my tears glow,
                    (burn)

da ist meiner Liebsten Haus.
there is my beloved's house.

Schubert   Winterreise
                Winter Journey

            7)   Auf dem Flusse
                 On the river

Der du so lustig rauschtest,
Who you so gaily rippled,
(You who)

du heller, wilder Fluss,
you clear, wild river,

wie still bist du geworden,
how silent have you become,

gibst keinen Scheidegruss!
(you) give no farewell-greeting!

Mit harter, starrer Rinde
With hard, rigid crust
                    (ice)

hast du dich überdeckt,
have you yourself covered,

liegst kalt und unbeweglich
(you) lie cold and motionless

im Sande ausgestreckt.
in the sand outstretched.

In deine Decke grab' ich
Into your (frozen) surface carve I

mit einem spitzen Stein
with a pointed stone

den Namen meiner Liebsten
the name of my beloved

und Stund' und Tag hinein.
and hour and day [-].

Den Tag des ersten Grusses,
The day of the first greeting,

419

den Tag an dem ich ging;
the day on which I left;

um Nam' und Zahlen windet
around name and figures twines

sich ein zerbroch'ner Ring.
[itself] a broken ring.

Mein Herz, in diesem Bache
My heart, in this stream

erkennst du wohl dein Bild?
recognize you now your likeness?

Ob's unter seiner Rinde
If it under its crust
                    (ice)

wohl auch so reissend schwillt?
[then] also so rapidly swells?

Schubert   Winterreise
                 Winter Journey

          8)   Rückblick
              Backward glance

Es brennt mir unter beiden Sohlen,
It burns me under both soles,

tret' ich auch schon auf Eis und Schnee,
tread I even [yet] on ice and snow,

ich möcht' nicht wieder Atem holen,
I wish not again breath take,
         (to breathe again)

bis ich nicht mehr die Türme seh.
till I no more the towers see.

Hab' mich an jedem Stein gestossen,
Have myself on every stone knocked,
                     (bruised)

so eilt' ich aus der Stadt hinaus;
thus hurried I from the town [out];

die Krähen warfen Bäll' und Schlossen
the crows threw balls and hailstones

auf meinen Hut von jedem Haus.
upon my hat from every house.

Wie anders hast du mich empfangen,
How differently have you me received,

du Stadt der Unbeständigkeit!
you town of inconstancy!

An deinen blanken Fenstern sangen
At your bright windows sang

die Lerch' und Nachtigall im Streit.
the lark and nightingale in competition.

Die runden Lindenbäume blühten,
The round linden trees blossomed,

die klaren Rinnen rauschten hell,
the clear streamlets rushed brightly,

und ach, zwei Mädchenaugen glühten,
and ah, two maiden eyes glowed,

da war's gescheh'n um dich, Gesell.
then was it done with you, fellow.
(then were you done for, fellow)

Kommt mir der Tag in die Gedanken,
Comes me the day in the thoughts,
(When that day returns to my thoughts)

möcht ich noch einmal rückwärts seh'n,
want I [still] once more backwards (to) look,

möcht' ich zurücke wieder wanken,
want I back again to stagger,

vor ihrem Hause stille steh'n.
at her house quietly stand.

Schubert   Winterreise
                Winter Journey

            9) Irrlicht
                Will-o'-the-wisp

In die tiefsten Felsengründe
Into the deepest gorges of the rocks

lockte mich ein Irrlicht hin.
lured me a will-o'-the-wisp [-].

Wie ich einen Ausgang finde,
How I a way out find,

liegt nicht schwer mir in dem Sinn.
lies not heavily me in the mind.
                (on my mind)

Bin gewohnt das Irregehen,
Am accustomed the going astray,

's führt ja jeder Weg zum Ziel:
[it] leads surely every path to the goal:

unsre Freuden, unsre Leiden,
our joys, our sufferings,

alles eines Irrlichts Spiel.
all (are) a will-o'-the-wisp's whim.

Durch des Bergstroms trock'ne Rinnen
Through the mountain-stream's dry ditches

wind' ich ruhig mich hinab;
climb I calmly [myself] down;

jeder Strom wird's Meer gewinnen,
every stream will the sea reach,

jedes Leiden auch sein Grab.
every suffering also its grave.

Schubert   Winterreise
               Winter Journey

           10) Rast
               Rest

Nun merk' ich erst, wie müd' ich bin,
Now feel I [only], how tired I am,

da ich zur Ruh' mich lege;
as I to rest myself lay;

das Wandern hielt mich munter hin,
[the] wandering kept me tireless [-],

auf unwirtbarem Wege.
on inhospitable road.

Die Füsse frugen nicht nach Rast,
The feet ask not for rest,

es war zu kalt zum Stehen;
it was too cold for standing (still);

der Rücken fühlte keine Last,
the back felt no burden.
(my)

der Sturm half fort mich wehen.
the storm helped on me blow.
                (to blow me on)

In eines Köhlers engem Haus
In a charcoal-burner's narrow house
                (tiny)

hab' Obdach ich gefunden,
have shelter I found,

doch meine Glieder ruh'n nicht aus,
but my limbs rest not [-],

so brennen ihre Wunden.
thus burn their wounds.

Auch du, mein Herz, in Kampf und Sturm
Also you, my heart, in struggle and storm

Schubert   Rast   (Continued)

so wild und so verwegen,
so wild and so daring,

fühlst in der Still' erst deinen Wurm
feel in [the] quietness only your worm
                                    (pain)

mit heissem Stich sich regen!
with (a) hot sting [itself] stirring!

Schubert   Winterreise
              Winter Journey

              11) Frühlingstraum
              Dream of spring

Ich träumte von bunten Blumen,
I dreamt of colored flowers,

so wie sie wohl blühen im Mai;
[so] as they [may] bloom in May;

ich träumte von grünen Wiesen,
I dreamt of green meadows,

von lustigem Vogelgeschrei.
of merry bird-calls.

Und als die Hähne krähten,
And when the cocks crowed,

da ward mein Auge wach,
there did my eye awake,

da war es kalt und finster,
there was it cold and dark,

es schrien die Raben vom Dach.
[it] cried the ravens from the roof.
(the ravens cried from the roof)

Doch an den Fensterscheiben,
But on the window-panes,

wer malte die Blätter da?
who painted the leaves there?

Ihr lacht wohl über den Träumer,
You laugh maybe about the dreamer,

der Blumen im Winter sah.
who flowers in winter saw.

Ich träumte von Lieb' um Liebe,
I dreamt of love for love,

von einer schönen Maid,
of a fair maiden,

von Herzen und von Küssen,
of caressing and of kissing,

von Wonne und Seligkeit.
of joy and blissfulness.

Und als die Hähne krähten,
And when the cocks crowed,

da ward mein Herze wach;
there did my heart awake;

nun sitz' ich hier alleine
now sit I here alone

und denke dem Traume nach.
and think of the dream [-].

Die Augen schliess' ich wieder,
The eyes close I again,

noch schlägt das Herz so warm;
still beats the heart so warmly;

wann grünt ihr Blätter am Fenster?
when green you leaves at the window?
        (bloom)

Wann halt' ich mein Liebchen im Arm?
When hold I my beloved in the arm?

Schubert   Winterreise
                    Winter Journey

              12)   Einsamkeit
                    Solitude

Wie eine trübe Wolke
As a dusky cloud

durch heit're Lüfte geht,
through serene winds moves,

wenn in der Tannen Wipfel
when in the fir's tops

ein mattes Lüftchen weht,
a feeble little breeze blows,

so zieh' ich meine Strasse
so walk I my road

dahin mit trägem Fuss,
along with dragging foot
                      (step)

durch helles, frohes Leben
through bright, joyful life

einsam und ohne Gruss.
alone and without greeting.

Ach! dass die Luft so ruhig,
Ah! [that] the air (is) so calm,

ach! dass die Welt so licht!
ah! [that] the world (is) so clear!

Als noch die Stürme tobten,
When once the storms raged,

war ich so elend nicht.
was I so miserable not.

Schubert   Winterreise
                  Winter Journey

              13) Die Post
                 The mail

Von der Strasse her ein Posthorn klingt.
From the street [there] a post-horn sounds.

Was hat es, dass es so hoch aufspringt,
What has it, that it so high jumps,

mein Herz?
my heart?

Die Post bringt keinen Brief für dich.
The mail brings no letter for you.

Was drängst du denn so wunderlich,
What urges you then so wondrously,

mein Herz?
my heart?

Nun ja, die Post kommt aus der Stadt,
Well yes, the mail comes from the town,

wo ich ein liebes Liebchen hatt,
where I a dear darling had,

mein Herz!
my heart!

Willst wohl einmal hinübersehn
Will (you) perhaps once look across
(You probably want to look across once)

und fragen, wie es dort mag gehn,
and ask, how it there may go,

mein Herz?
my heart?

Schubert   Winterreise
              Winter Journey

14) Der greise Kopf
     The hoary head

Der Reif hat einen weissen Schein
[The] frost has a white shine

mir über's Haupt gestreuet;
me over the head sprinkled;

da glaubt' ich schon ein Greis zu sein
then believed I already an old man to be

und hab' mich sehr gefreuet.
and was [myself] very pleased.

Doch bald ist er hinweg getaut,
But soon is it away melted,

hab' wieder schwarze Haare,
(I) have again black hair,

dass mir's vor meiner Jugend graut:
that I [it] at my youth shudder:

wie weit noch bis zur Bahre!
how far still to the bier!

Vom Abendrot zum Morgenlicht
From evening-red to morning-light

ward mancher Kopf zum Greise.
changed many a head into (an) old man.

Wer glaubt's? und meiner ward es nicht
Who believes it? [and] mine changed [it] not

auf dieser ganzen Reise!
on this whole journey!

Schubert   Winterreise
                Winter Journey

                15) Die Krähe
                     The crow

Eine Krähe war mit mir
A crow has with me

aus der Stadt gezogen,
from the town journeyed,

ist bis heute für und für
is till today again and again

um mein Haupt geflogen.
around my head flown.

Krähe, wunderliches Tier,
Crow, strange creature,

willst mich nicht verlassen?
will (you) me not leave?

Meinst wohl, bald als Beute hier
(You) think perhaps, soon as prey here

meinen Leib zu fassen?
my body to take?

Nun, es wird nicht weit mehr geh'n
Well, it will not (much) further [more] go

an dem Wanderstabe.
on the traveller's staff.

Krähe, lass' mich endlich seh'n
Crow, let me at last see

Treue bis zum Grabe.
fidelity until the grave.

Schubert   Winterreise
               Winter Journey

               16) Letzte Hoffnung
                    Last hope

Hie und da ist an den Bäumen
Here and there is on the trees

manches bunte Blatt zu seh'n,
many a colored leaf to see,

und ich bleibe vor den Bäumen
and I pause in front of the trees

oftmals in Gedanken steh'n.
often in thoughts [-].

Schaue nach dem einen Blatte,
Look for the one leaf,

hänge meine Hoffnung dran;
hang my hope on it;

spielt der Wind mit meinem Blatte,
plays (then) the wind with my leaf,

zittr' ich, was ich zittern kann.
tremble I, what I tremble can.
               (as much as I am able to tremble)

Ach, und fällt das Blatt zu Boden,
Ah, and falls the leaf to the ground,

fällt mit ihm die Hoffnung ab,
falls with it [the] hope [off],

fall' ich selber mit zu Boden,
fall I myself with (it) to the ground,

wein' auf meiner Hoffnung Grab.
weep on my hope's grave.

Schubert   Winterreise
                       Winter Journey

                 17)   Im Dorfe
                      In the village

Es bellen die Hunde, es rasseln die Ketten;
[It] bark the dogs, [it] rattle the chains;
(The dogs bark, the chains rattle)

es schlafen die Menschen in ihren Betten,
[it] sleep the people in their beds,
(the people sleep)

träumen sich Manches, was sie nicht haben,
dreaming [themselves] (of) something, which they (do) not
    have,

tun sich im Guten und Argen erlaben;
do themselves in good and wrong (things) refresh;

und morgen früh ist alles zerflossen.
and (in the) morrow early is all faded away.

Je nun, sie haben ihr Teil genossen,
As it is, they have their share enjoyed,
                        (dreams)

und hoffen, was sie noch übrig liessen,
and (they) hope, what [they] still remains,

doch wieder zu finden auf ihren Kissen.
[then] again to find on their pillows.

Bellt mich nur fort, ihr wachen Hunde,
Bark me [but] away, you watchful dogs,

lasst mich nicht ruh'n in der Schlummerstunde!
let me not rest in the slumber-hour!

Ich bin zu Ende mit allen Träumen,
I am at end with all dreams,

was will ich unter den Schläfern säumen?
why shall I among the sleepers tarry?

433

Schubert   Winterreise
                  Winter Journey

          18) Der stürmische Morgen
               The stormy morning

Wie hat der Sturm zerrissen
How has the storm torn

des Himmels graues Kleid;
the sky's grey attire;

die Wolkenfetzen flattern
the cloud-wisps flutter

umher in mattem Streit,
around in (a) feeble struggle,

und rote Feuerflammen
and red fire-flames

zieh'n zwischen ihnen hin:
move between them [-]:

das nenn' ich einen Morgen
that call I a morning
(that is what I call a morning)

so recht nach meinem Sinn.
just right to my mind.
(just to my liking)

Mein Herz sieht an dem Himmel
My heart sees in the sky

gemalt sein eig'nes Bild;
painted its own image;

es ist nichts als der Winter,
it is nothing but [the] winter,

der Winter kalt und wild.
[the] winter cold and wild.

Schubert   Winterreise
             Winter Journey

             19)   Täuschung
                   Delusion

Ein Licht tanzt freundlich vor mir her,
A light dances friendly before me [-],

ich folg' ihm gern, und seh's ihm an,
I follow it gladly and notice [it --],

dass es verlockt den Wandersmann.
that it lures the wanderer.

Ach! wer wie ich so elend ist,
Ah! who as myself so miserable is,
(Ah! who is miserable as I am)

gibt gern sich hin der bunten List,
gives willingly himself [-] to the colored delusion,

die hinter Eis und Nacht und Graus
which after ice and night and horror

ihm weist ein helles, warmes Haus
(to) him shows a bright, warm house

und eine liebe Seele drin.
and a dear soul in it.

Nur Täuschung ist für mich Gewinn.
Only delusion is for me gain.

Schubert   Winterreise
                  Winter Journey

                  20) Der Wegweiser
                       The guide-post

Was vermeid ich denn die Wege,
Why avoid I [then] the roads,

wo die andern Wanderer gehn,
where the other wanderers go,

suche mir versteckte Stege
seek (for) me hidden paths

durch verschneite Felsenhöhn?
through snow-covered rocky heights?

Habe ja doch nichts begangen,
Have yes but nothing done,
     (certainly)

dass ich Menschen sollte scheun,
that I men should shun,

welch ein törichtes Verlangen
what a stupid desire

treibt mich in die Wüstenein?
drives me into [the] deserted lands?

Weiser stehen auf den Wegen,
guide-posts stand on the roads,

weisen auf die Städte zu,
point to the towns [-],

und ich wandre sonder Massen,
and I walk without measure,

ohne Ruh, und suche Ruh.
without rest, and seek rest.
                  (but)

Einen Weiser seh ich stehen
One guide-post see I standing

unverrückt vor meinem Blick;
constantly before my view;
                    (eyes)

eine Strasse muss ich gehen,
one road must I go,

die noch keiner ging zurück.
which yet no one walked back.
(from which no one has yet returned)

Schubert   Winterreise
                  Winter Journey

              21) Das Wirtshaus
                   The inn

Auf einen Totenacker
To a cemetery

hat mich mein Weg gebracht.
has me my path brought.

Allhier will ich einkehren,
Here will I enter,

hab ich bei mir gedacht.
have I [to myself] thought.

Ihr grünen Totenkränze
Ye green wreaths

könnt wohl die Zeichen sein,
could well the signs be,

die müde Wanderer laden
which tired wanderers invite
(which invite tired wanderers)

ins kühle Wirtshaus ein.
into (the) cool inn [-].

Sind denn in diesem Hause
Are then in this house

die Kammern all besetzt?
the chambers all occupied?

Bin matt zum Niedersinken,
Am exhausted to (the point of) prostration,

bin tödlich schwer verletzt.
am deadly gravely wounded.

O unbarmherzge Schenke,
Oh cruel inn,

doch weisest du mich ab?
but refuses you me [-]?
(but do you refuse me)

Nun weiter denn, nur weiter,
Now ahead then, always ahead,

mein treuer Wanderstab!
my faithful staff!

Schubert   Winterreise
                  Winter Journey

                  22) Mut
                       Courage

Fliegt der Schnee mir in's Gesicht,
Flies the snow me into the face,

schüttl' ich ihn herunter;
shake I it off;

wenn mein Herz im Busen spricht,
when my heart in the bosom speaks,

sing' ich hell und munter.
sing I clearly and merrily.

Höre nicht, was es mir sagt,
Hear not, what it (to) me speaks,

habe keine Ohren;
have no ears;

fühle nicht, was es mir klagt,
feel not, what it to me complains,

Klagen ist für Toren.
complaining is for fools.

Lustig in die Welt hinein
(I go) gaily into the world [-]

gegen Wind und Wetter;
against wind and weather;

will kein Gott auf Erden sein,
want no God on earth (to) be,
(if no God wants to be here on earth)

sind wir selber Götter!
are we ourselves Gods!

Schubert   Winterreise
                  Winter Journey

                  23) Die Nebensonnen
                       The other suns

Drei Sonnen sah ich am Himmel stehn,
Three suns saw I in heaven stand,

hab lang' und fest sie angesehn,
have long and firmly them watched,

und sie auch standen da so stier,
and they also stood there so firm,

als wollten sie nicht weg von mir.
as wanted they not away from me.
(as if they did not want to leave me)

Ach, meine Sonnen seid ihr nicht!
Ah, my suns are you not!
(Ah, you are not my suns)

schaut andern doch ins Angesicht!
look others [but] in the face!

Ja, neulich hatt ich auch wohl drei;
Yes, lately had I also still three;

nun sind hinab die besten zwei.
now are gone down the best two.

Ging nur die dritt erst hinterdrein!
Would go but the third now afterwards!
                       (after them)

Im Dunkeln wird mir wohler sein.
In the darkness will me better be.
          (I will feel better)

Winterreise
         Winter Journey

              24) Der Leiermann
                   The organ-grinder

Drüben hinterm Dorfe steht ein Leiermann,
Yonder behind the village stands an organ-grinder,
    (outside)

und mit starren Fingern dreht er, was er kann.
and with stiff fingers grinds he, what he can.
                        (as best he can)

Barfuss auf dem Eise wankt er hin und her,
Barefoot on the ice staggers he to and fro,

und sein kleiner Teller bleibt ihm immer leer.
and his small plate remains [him] always empty.

Keiner mag ihn hören, keiner sieht ihn an,
Nobody likes him to hear, nobody looks him on,
         (to hear him)   (looks at him)

und die Hunde knurren um den alten Mann.
and the dogs growl around the old man.

Und er lässt es gehen alles, wie es will,
And he lets it go all, as it will,
(And he lets everything occur)

dreht, und seine Leier steht ihm nimmer still.
grinds, and his organ remains [him] never silent.

Wunderlicher Alter, soll ich mit dir gehn?
Strange old man, shall I with you go?

Willst zu meinen Liedern deine Leier drehn?
Will (you) for my songs your organ grind?

Schumann   Aufträge
                  Commissions
                  (Messages)

Nicht so schnelle,
Not so quick,

wart' ein wenig, kleine Welle!
wait a little, tiny wave!

Will dir einen Auftrag geben
(I) will you a message give

an die Liebste mein!
to the beloved mine!

Wirst du ihr vorüberschweben,
Will you her flow past,
(When you will flow past her)

grüsse sie mir fein!
greet her (from) me politely!

Sag' ich wäre mitgekommen,
Tell (her) I would have arrived with (you),

auf dir selbst herab geschwommen:
upon you myself down have swum:
(would have swum down with you)

für den Gruss
for the greeting

einen Kuss
a kiss

kühn mir zu erbitten;
daringly (for) me to request;

doch der Zeit
but [the] time's

Dringlichkeit
urgency

hätt' es nicht gelitten.
had it not permitted.

Schumann   Aufträge   (Continued)

Nicht so eilig! halt! erlaube,
Not so quick! stop! allow,

kleine, leichtbeschwingte Taube!
little, light-winged dove!

Habe dir was aufzutragen
Have you something to give

an die Liebste mein!
for the beloved mine!

Sollst ihr tausend Grüsse sagen,
Shall her thousand greetings tell,
(A thousand greetings you shall deliver to her)

hundert obendrein.
(a) hundred besides.
          (more)
Sag', ich wär' mit dir geflogen,
Tell (her) I would have with you flown,
                    (flown with you)

über Berg' und Strom gezogen:
over mountains and river moved:
(would have moved over mountains and river)

für den Gruss
for the greeting

einen Kuss
a kiss

kühn mir zu erbitten;
daringly (for) me to request;

doch der Zeit
but [the] time's

Dringlichkeit
urgency

hätt' es nicht gelitten.
had it not permitted.

Schumann   Aufräge   (Continued)

Warte nicht, dass ich dich treibe,
Wait not, that I you drive,
                    (push)

o, du träge Mondenscheibe!
oh, you indolent moon-disc!

weisst's ja, was ich dir befohlen
(you) know it indeed, what I you charged with

für die Liebste mein:
for the beloved mine:

durch das Fensterchen verstohlen
through the little window stealthily

grüsse sie mir fein!
greet her (from) me politely!

Sag', ich wär' auf dich gestiegen,
Tell (her), I would have you boarded,
                    (boarded you)

selber zu ihr hinzufliegen:
myself to her to fly:
(to fly to her)

für den Gruss
for the greeting

einen Kuss
a kiss

kühn mir zu erbitten,
daringly (for) me to request,

du seist Schuld,
(but) you are guilty,

Ungeduld
impatience

hätt' mich nicht gelitten.
had me not permitted.
(did not permit to do so)

Schumann   Dein Angesicht
                  Your face

Dein Angesicht, so lieb und schön,
Your face, so dear and beautiful,

das hab' ich jüngst im Traum geseh'n,
that have I recently in [the] dream seen,

es ist so mild und engelgleich,
it is so mild and angel-like,

und doch so bleich, so schmerzenreich.
and yet so pale, so sorrow-rich.
                  (full of sorrow)

Und nur die Lippen, die sind rot;
And only the lips, they are red;

bald aber küsst sie bleich der Tod.
soon but kisses them pale [the] death.
(soon death kisses them pale)

Erlöschen wird das Himmelslicht,
Fade away will the heaven's light,

das aus den frommen Augen bricht.
that from the gentle eyes breaks.
                  (shines)

Schumann   Der Nussbaum
                 The nut-tree

Es grünet ein Nussbaum vor dem Haus,
There grows a nut tree in front of the house,

duftig, luftig breitet er blätt'rig die Äste aus.
fragrantly, airy spreads it leafy the branches [out].

Viel liebliche Blüten stehen d'ran;
Many lovely buds stand thereon;

linde Winde kommen, sie herzlich zu umfah'n.
gentle breezes come, them cordially to embrace.

Es flüstern je zwei zu zwei gepaart,
There whisper each two at two paired,

neigend, beugend zierlich zum Kusse
inclining, bending gracefully for (a) kiss

die Häuptchen zart.
the little heads delicate.
(the little delicate heads)

Sie flüstern von einem Mägdlein,
They whisper of a young maiden,

das dächte die Nächte und Tage lang,
who thought [the] nights and days long,

wusste, ach! selber nicht, was.
knew, ah! herself not, what.
(knew not of what she was thinking)

Sie flüstern; wer mag versteh'n so gar leise Weis'?
They whisper; who can understand such very soft tune?

flüstern vom Bräut'gam und nächstem Jahr.
(they) whisper of bridegroom and next year.

Das Mägdlein horchet, es rauscht im Baum,
The young maiden listens, it rustles in the tree,

sehnend, wähnend sinkt es
longing, hoping sinks it
                   (she)

Schumann   Der Nussbaum   (Continued)

lächelnd in Schlaf und Traum.
smiling into sleep and dream.

Schumann   Dichterliebe
                Poet's love

        1)   Im wunderschönen Monat Mai
             In the wonderful month (of) May

Im wunderschönen Monat Mai,
In the wonderful month (of) May,

als alle Knospen sprangen,
when all buds burst,

da ist in meinem Herzen
there is in my heart
     (has)

die Liebe aufgegangen.
[the] love unfolded.

Im wunderschönen Monat Mai,
In the wonderful month (of) May,

als alle Vögel sangen,
when all birds sang,

da hab' ich ihr gestanden
there have I (to) her confessed

mein Sehnen und Verlangen.
my longing and desire.

Schumann   Dichterliebe
               Poet's love

               2)   Aus meinen Tränen spriessen
                    From my tears sprout

Aus meinen Tränen spriessen
From my tears sprout

viel blühende Blumen hervor,
many blooming flowers [out],

und meine Seufzer werden
and my sighs become

ein Nachtigallenchor.
a choir of nightingales.

Und wenn du mich lieb hast, Kindchen,
And when you me love, [-] little child,

schenk' ich dir die Blumen all',
present I to you the flowers all,

und vor deinem Fenster soll klingen
and before your window shall sound

das Lied der Nachtigall.
the song of the nightingale.

Schumann   Dichterliebe
                    Poet's love

          3) Die Rose, die Lilie
              The rose, the lily

Die Rose, die Lilie, die Taube, die Sonne,
The rose, the lily, the dove, the sun,

die liebt ich einst alle in Liebeswonne.
they loved I once all in love's bliss.

Ich lieb' sie nicht mehr, ich liebe alleine
I love them no more, I love alone

die Kleine, die Feine, die Reine, die Eine;
the little one, the fine one, the pure one, the one;

sie selber, aller Liebe Wonne,
she herself, all love's bliss,

ist Rose und Lilie und Taube und Sonne;
is rose and lily and dove and sun;

ich liebe alleine die Kleine,
I love alone the little one,

die Feine, die Reine, die Eine!
the fine one, the pure one, the one!

Schumann   Dichterliebe
                    Poet's love

                    4) Wenn ich in deine Augen seh'
                        When I into your eyes look

Wenn ich in deine Augen seh',
When I into your eyes look,

so schwindet all' mein Leid und Weh;
so disappears all my sorrow and pain;

doch wenn ich küsse deinen Mund,
but when I kiss your mouth,
                  (lips)

so werd ich ganz und gar gesund.
so get I wholly and completely well.

Wenn ich mich lehn' an deine Brust,
When I [myself] lean on your breast,

kommt's über mich wie Himmelslust;
comes it over me like heaven's delight;
(bliss overcomes me like heaven's delight)

doch wenn du sprichst: ich liebe dich!
but when you speak: I love you!

so muss ich weinen bitterlich.
then must I cry bitterly.

Schumann   Dichterliebe
                  Poet's love

          5) Ich will meine Seele tauchen
              I will my soul submerge

Ich will meine Seele tauchen
I will my soul submerge

in den Kelch der Lilie hinein;
into the cup of the lily [-];

die Lilie soll klingend hauchen
the lily shall ringingly breathe

ein Lied von der Liebsten mein.
a song from the beloved mine.

Das Lied soll schauern und beben,
The song shall thrill and shake,

wie der Kuss von ihrem Mund,
as the kiss from her mouth,
                        (lips)

den sie mir einst gegeben
which she me once has given

in wunderbar süsser Stund'!
in (a) wonderful sweet hour!

Schumann   Dichterliebe
                  Poet's love

                  6) Im Rhein
                  In the Rhine

Im Rhein, im heiligen Strome,
In the Rhine, in the holy river,

da spiegelt sich in den Well'n,
there reflects [itself] in the waves,

mit seinem grossen Dome,
with its great cathedral,

das grosse, heilige Cöln.
the great, holy Cologne.

Im Dom, da steht ein Bildnis,
In the cathedral, there stands a portrait,

auf goldenem Leder gemalt;
on golden leather painted;

in meines Lebens Wildnis
into my life's wilderness

hat's freundlich hinein gestrahlt.
has it friendly beamed.

Es schweben Blumen und Eng'lein
There hover flowers and little angels

um unsre liebe Frau;
around our beloved lady;

die Augen, die Lippen,
the eyes, the lips,

die Lippen, die Wänglein,
the lips, the little cheeks,

die gleichen der Liebsten genau.
they resemble (those) of the beloved exactly.
(they resemble exactly those of the beloved)

Schumann   Dichterliebe
Poet's love

7)   Ich grolle nicht
I chide (you) not

Ich grolle nicht, und wenn das Herz auch bricht,
I chide (you) not, and if the heart also breaks,

ewig verlor'nes Lieb, ich grolle nicht.
eternally lost love, I chide (you) not.

Wie du auch strahlst in Diamantenpracht,
As you [also] shine in diamond's splendor,

es fällt kein Strahl in deines Herzens Nacht,
[it] falls no ray into your heart's night,

das weiss ich längst.
that know I (a) long (time).

Ich grolle nicht und wenn das Herz auch bricht.
I chide (you) not and if the heart also breaks.

Ich sah dich ja im Traume,
I saw you [yes] in the dream,

und sah die Nacht in deines Herzens Raume,
and saw the night in your heart's room,

und sah die Schlang', die dir am Herzen frisst,
and saw the snake, which you at the heart gnaws,

ich sah, mein Lieb, wie sehr du elend bist.
I saw, my love, how very you miserable are.
                    (how very miserable you are)

Ich grolle nicht.
I chide (you) not.

455

Schumann   Dichterliebe
                  Poet's love

8)   Und wüssten's die Blumen
     And would know it the flowers
     (And would the flowers know it)

Und wüssten's die Blumen, die kleinen,
And would know [it] the flowers, the little ones,
(And would the flowers know it)

wie tief verwundet mein Herz,
how deeply wounded my heart,

sie würden mit mir weinen,
they would with me weep,

zu heilen meinen Schmerz.
to heal my pain.

Und wüssten's die Nachtigallen,
And would know [it] the nightingales,

wie ich so traurig und krank,
how I (am) so sad and ill,

sie liessen fröhlich erschallen
they would let cheerfully resound

erquickenden Gesang.
refreshing singing.

Und wüssten sie mein Wehe,
And would know they my grief,

die goldenen Sternelein,
the golden little stars,

sie kämen aus ihrer Höhe,
they would come from their height

und sprächen Trost mir ein.
and would speak comfort to me [-].

Sie alle können's nicht wissen,
They all can [it] not know,

nur Eine kennt meinen Schmerz;
only one knows my grief;

sie hat ja selbst zerrissen,
she has indeed [herself] torn,

zerrissen mir das Herz.
torn me the heart.
(torn my heart)

Schumann   Dichterliebe
Poet's love

9)   Das ist ein Flöten und Geigen
That is a flute-playing and fiddling

Das ist ein Flöten und Geigen,
That is a flute-playing and fiddling,

Trompeten schmettern darein;
trumpets blare into (it);

da tanzt wohl den Hochzeitreigen
there dances indeed the wedding-dance
(there my most beloved one dances)

die Herzallerliebste mein.
the most beloved one (of) mine.
(indeed the wedding-dance)

Das ist ein Klingen und Dröhnen,
That is a sounding and resounding,

ein Pauken und ein Schalmei'n;
a drumming and a shawm-playing;*

dazwischen schluchzen und stöhnen
among it sob and groan

die lieblichen Engelein.
the lovely little angels.

* shawm - an obsolete wind instrument of the oboe class

458

Schumann   Dichterliebe
                Poet's love

        10) Hör' ich das Liedchen klingen
             Hear I the little song sound

Hör' ich das Liedchen klingen,
Hear I the little song sound,

das einst die Liebste sang,
which once the beloved one sang,

so will mir die Brust zerspringen
then will me the breast burst

von wildem Schmerzensdrang.
from wild pain's force.

Es treibt mich ein dunkles Sehnen
[It] drives me a dark yearning

hinauf zur Waldeshöh',
up to the forest-hill,

dort löst sich auf in Tränen
there dissolves [itself -] into tears

mein übergrosses Weh'.
my oversized grief.

Schumann   Dichterliebe
                  Poet's love

                  11)   Ein Jüngling liebt ein Mädchen
                        A youth loved a maiden

Ein Jüngling liebt ein Mädchen,
A youth loved a maiden,

die hat einen Andern erwählt;
who has another (man) chosen;

der And're liebt eine Andre
the other (man) loves another (maiden)

und hat sich mit dieser vermählt.
and has [himself with] this one married.

Das Mädchen nimmt aus Ärger
The maiden takes out of anger

den ersten besten Mann,
the first best man,

der ihr in den Weg gelaufen;
who her in the path ran;
(who has crossed her path)

der Jüngling ist übel d'ran.
the youth is badly thereat.
          (is in a bad situation)

Es ist eine alte Geschichte,
It is an old story,

doch bleibt sie immer neu;
yet remains it always new;

und wem sie just passieret,
and to whom it just happens,

dem bricht das Herz entzwei.
him breaks the heart to pieces.
(his heart breaks to pieces)

Schumann   Dichterliebe
                   Poet's love

            12)   Am leuchtenden Sommermorgen
                On a shining summer morning

Am leuchtenden Sommermorgen
On a shining summer morning

geh ich im Garten herum.
walk I in the garden [about].

Es flüstern und sprechen die Blumen,
[It] whisper and speak the flowers,

ich aber wandle stumm.
I but walk silently.

Es flüstern und sprechen die Blumen,
[It] whisper and speak the flowers,

und schau'n mitleidig mich an:
and look pityfully me at:
                    (at me)

Sei unsrer Schwester nicht böse,
Be (with) our sister not angry,

du trauriger, blasser Mann.
you sad, pale man.

Schumann   Dichterliebe
                    Poet's love

                    13) Ich hab' im Traum geweinet
                         I have in the dream wept

Ich hab' im Traum geweinet,
I have in the dream wept,

mir träumte, du lägest im Grab.
me dreamt, you did lie in the tomb.

Ich wachte auf, und die Träne
I woke up, and the tear

floss noch von der Wange herab.
flowed still from the cheek [down].

Ich hab' im Traum geweinet,
I have in the dream wept,

mir träumt', du verliessest mich.
me dreamt, you deserted me.

Ich wachte auf, und ich weinte
I woke up, and I wept

noch lange bitterlich.
still long bitterly.

Ich hab' im Traum geweinet,
I have in the dream wept,

mir träumte, du wärst mir noch gut.
me dreamt, you were me still good.
                    (you still loved me)

Ich wachte auf, und noch immer
I woke up, and [yet] always

strömt meine Tränenflut.
flows my tears' torrent.

Schumann   Dichterliebe
                   Poet's love

                14)   Allnächtlich im Traume
                     Nightly in [the] dream

Allnächtlich im Traume seh' ich dich,
Nightly in [the] dream see I you,

und sehe dich freundlich grüssen,
and see you friendly greet,

und laut aufweinend stürz' ich mich
and loudly weeping rush I [myself]

zu deinen süssen Füssen.
to your sweet feet.

Du siehest mich an wehmütiglich
You look (at) me [-] sadly

und schüttelst das blonde Köpfchen;
and shake the blond little head;

aus deinen Augen schleichen sich
from your eyes steal away [themselves]

die Perlentränentröpfchen.
the pearl-like teardrops.

Du sagst mir heimlich ein leises Wort,
You say to me secretly a soft word,

und gibst mir den Strauss von Cypressen.
and gives me the bouquet of cypresses.

Ich wache auf, und der Strauss ist fort,
I wake up, and the bouquet is gone,

und's Wort hab' ich vergessen.
and the word have I forgotten.

Dichterliebe
Poet's love

15) Aus alten Märchen winkt es
From ancient fairy-tales beckons it

Aus alten Märchen winkt es
From ancient fairy-tales beckons it

hervor mit weisser Hand,
forth with white hand,

da singt es und da klingt es
there sings it and there sounds it

von einem Zauberland;
of a magic land;

wo bunte Blumen blühen
where colored flowers bloom

im gold'nen Abendlicht,
in the golden evening-light,

und lieblich duftend glühen,
and lovely scenting glow,

mit bräutlichem Gesicht;
with bridal face;

und grüne Bäume singen
and green trees sing

uralte Melodei'n,
very old melodies,

die Lüfte heimlich klingen,
the breezes secretly ring,

und Vögel schmettern drein;
and birds rejoice into it;

und Nebelbilder steigen
and images of mist rise

wohl aus der Erd' hervor,
right from the soil [out],

und tanzen luft'gen Reigen
and dance airy round-dance

im wunderlichen Chor;
in a strange choir;

und blaue Funken brennen
and blue sparks burn

an jedem Blatt und Reis,
on each leaf and sprig,

und rote Lichter rennen
and red lights run

im irren, wirren Kreis;
in erring, tangled circle;

und laute Quellen brechen
and noisy springs gush

aus wildem Marmorstein,
out (from) wild marblestone,

und seltsam in den Bächen
and peculiarly in the brooks
(and in the brooks peculiarly)

strahlt fort der Widerschein.
flashes on the reflection.
(continues flashing the reflection)

Ach! könnt' ich dorthin kommen
Ah! could I thereto come

und dort mein Herz erfreu'n,
and there my heart please,
(and there please my heart)

und aller Qual entnommen,
and (of) all agony relieved,

und frei und selig sein!
and free and blessed be!

Ach, jenes Land der Wonne,
Ah, that land of bliss,

das seh' ich oft im Traum,
that see I often in [the] dream,

doch kommt die Morgensonne,
but comes the morning-sun,

zerfliesst's wie eitel Schaum.
dissolves it as vain froth.

Schumann   Dichterliebe
                  Poet's love

                  16) Die alten, bösen Lieder
                       The ancient, bad songs

Die alten, bösen Lieder,
The ancient, bad songs,

die Träume bös' und arg,
the dreams bad and evil,

die lasst uns jetzt begraben,
those let us now bury,

holt einen grossen Sarg.
fetch a big coffin.

Hinein leg' ich gar Manches,
In it place I [quite] something,

doch sag' ich noch nicht was;
but say I yet not what;

der Sarg muss sein noch grösser
the coffin must be still bigger

wie's Heidelberger Fass.
than the Heidelberg barrel.

Und holt eine Totenbahre
And get a bier

von Brettern fest und dick;
of boards firm and thick;

auch muss sie sein noch länger,
also must it be still longer,

als wie zu Mainz die Brück'.
than [-] at Mainz the bridge.

Und holt mir auch zwölf Riesen,
And get me also twelve giants,

die müssen noch stärker sein,
they must still stronger be,

467

als wie der starke Christoph
than [-] the strong Christopher

im Dom zu Cöln am Rhein.
in the cathedral at Cologne on the Rhine.

Die sollen den Sarg forttragen,
They shall the coffin carry away,

und senken in's Meer hinab;
and sink into the sea down;
(and sink it down into the sea)

denn solchem grossen Sarge
for such (a) big coffin

gebührt ein grosses Grab.
is due a big tomb.

Wisst ihr, warum der Sarg wohl
Know you, why the coffin indeed
(Do you know, why the coffin)

so gross und schwer mag sein?
so big and heavy must be?
(must be indeed so big and heavy)

Ich senkt' auch meine Liebe
I sank also my love

und meinen Schmerz hinein.
and my grief into it.

Schumann   Die beiden Grenadiere
                 The both grenadiers
                 (The two grenadiers)

Nach Frankreich zogen zwei Grenadier',
To France marched two grenadiers,

die waren in Russland gefangen.
who were in Russia captured.
     (had been)

Und als sie kamen in's deutsche Quartier,
And when they came into the German camp,

sie liessen die Köpfe hangen.
they let the heads hang.

Da hörten sie beide die traurige Mär',
There heard they both the sad news,

dass Frankreich verloren gegangen,
that France lost went,

besiegt und geschlagen das tapfere Heer,
defeated and beaten the brave army,

und der Kaiser gefangen.
and the emperor captured.

Da weinten zusammen die Grenadier'
There wept together the grenadiers

wohl ob der kläglichen Kunde.
about the lamentable news.

Der Eine sprach: "Wie weh' wird mir,
The one spoke: "How sick gets me,
               (How sick I get)

wie brennt meine alte Wunde!"
how burns my old wound!"

Der Andre sprach: "Das Lied ist aus,
The other spoke: "The song is out,
               (has ended)

auch ich möcht' mit dir sterben,
also I like with you (to) die,

doch hab' ich Weib und Kind zu Haus,
but have I wife and child at the house,
                    (at home)

die ohne mich verderben. "
who without me perish. "
(who perish without me)

"Was schert mich Weib, was schert mich Kind,
"What bothers me wife, what bothers me child,

ich trage weit besser Verlangen;
I bear far better desire;
    (have)

lass sie betteln gehn, wenn sie hungrig sind -
let them beg go, when they hungry are -
            (go begging)

mein Kaiser, mein Kaiser gefangen!
my emperor, my emperor captured!

Gewähr' mir, Bruder, eine Bitt':
Grant me, brother, one request:

Wenn ich jetzt sterben werde,
When I now die [will],

so nimm meine Leiche nach Frankreich mit,
then take my corpse to France with (you),

begrab' mich in Frankreich's Erde.
bury me in France's soil.

Das Ehrenkreuz am roten Band
The cross of honor on the red ribbon

sollst du auf's Herz mir legen;
shall you on the heart me lay;

die Flinte gib mir in die Hand,
the musket give me in the hand,

und gürt' mir um den Degen.
and gird me around the sword.
(and around me gird the sword)

So will ich liegen und horchen still,
So will I lie and listen quietly,

wie eine Schildwach' im Grabe,
as a sentry in the grave,

bis einst ich höre Kanonengebrüll
till one day I hear (the) roar of cannons

und wiehernder Rosse Getrabe.
and neighing horses trot.

Dann reitet mein Kaiser wohl über mein Grab,
Then rides my emperor surely over my grave,

viel Schwerter klirren und blitzen,
many swords clash and flash,

dann steig' ich gewaffnet hervor aus dem Grab -
then rise I in arms forth from the grave -

den Kaiser, den Kaiser zu schützen!"
the emperor, the emperor to protect!"

Schumann   Die Lotosblume
                The lotus-flower

Die Lotosblume ängstigt sich
The lotus-flower fears [herself]

vor der Sonne Pracht,
[before] the sun's splendor,

und mit gesenktem Haupte
and with drooping head

erwartet sie träumend die Nacht.
awaits she dreamily the night.

Der Mond, der ist ihr Buhle,
The moon, he is her lover,

er weckt sie mit seinem Licht,
he wakes her with his light,

und ihm entschleiert sie freundlich
and to him unveils she friendly

ihr frommes Blumengesicht.
her gentle flower-face.

Sie blüht und glüht und leuchtet,
She blooms and glows and shines,

und starret stumm in die Höh';
and stares mute in the height;

sie duftet und weinet und zittert
she exhales and weeps and trembles

vor Liebe und Liebesweh.
of love and love's pain.

472

Schumann   Du bist wie eine Blume
                     You are like a flower

Du bist wie eine Blume,
You are like a flower,

so hold und schön und rein;
so lovely and fair and pure;

ich schau' dich an, und Wehmut
I look you on, and melancholy
        (at you)

schleicht mir in's Herz hinein.
creeps me into the heart [-].

Mir ist, als ob ich die Hände
To me (it) is, as if I the hands

auf's Haupt dir legen sollt',
upon the head (of) you lay should,
(upon your head should lay)

betend, dass Gott dich erhalte
praying, that God you preserve

so rein und schön und hold.
so pure and fair and lovely.

Schumann   Frauenliebe und -leben
                 Women's love and -life

         1)   Seit ich ihn gesehen
               Since I him have seen
               (Since I have seen him)

Seit ich ihn gesehen,
Since I him have seen,
(Since I have seen him)

glaub' ich blind zu sein;
believe I blind to be;

wo ich hin nur blicke,
where I to solely look,
(wherever I may look)

seh' ich ihn allein;
see I him only;

wie im wachen Traume
as in the awakened dream
            (day-dream)

schwebt sein Bild mir vor,
hovers his image me before,

taucht aus tiefstem Dunkel
surfaces from deepest darkness

heller, heller nur empor.
brighter, brighter yet [-].

Sonst ist licht- und farblos
Otherwise is light- and colorless

alles um mich her,
everything around me [-],

nach der Schwestern Spiele
for the sister's pleasures

nicht begehr' ich mehr,
not desire I more,

möchte lieber weinen,
prefer rather to weep,

still im Kämmerlein;
quietly in the little room;

seit ich ihn gesehen,
since I him have seen,

glaub' ich blind zu sein.
believe I blind to be.

Schumann   Frauenliebe und -leben
             Women's love and -life

        2)   Er, der Herrlichste von allen
              He, the noblest of all

Er, der Herrlichste von allen,
He, the noblest of all,

wie so milde, wie so gut!
how so gentle, how so good!

Holde Lippen, klares Auge,
Lovely lips, clear eye,
                    (eyes)

heller Sinn und fester Mut.
bright mind and firm courage.

So wie dort in blauer Tiefe,
So as there in blue depth,

hell und herrlich, jener Stern,
bright and glorious, that star,

also er an meinem Himmel,
thus (is) he in my heaven,

hell und herrlich, hehr und fern.
bright and glorious, sublime and distant.

Wandle, wandle deine Bahnen,
Go, go your paths,

nur betrachten deinen Schein,
(let me) only look (at) your brightness,

nur in Demut ihn betrachten,
only in devotion him look at,
                    (look at him)

selig nur, und traurig sein!
very happy then, and sad to be!

Höre nicht mein stilles Beten,
Hear not my silent praying,

deinem Glücke nur geweiht;
to your happiness only dedicated;
(dedicated only to your happiness)

darfst mich, nied're Magd, nicht kennen,
(you) should me, lowly maiden, not know,

hoher Stern der Herrlichkeit.
high star of splendor.

Nur die Würdigste von allen
Only the most dignified of all

darf beglücken deine Wahl,
may make happy your choice,
        (respond to)

und ich will die Hohe segnen
and I will the esteemed one bless

viele tausendmal.
many thousand times.

Will mich freuen dann und weinen,
Will [myself] delight then and weep,

selig, selig bin ich dann,
happy, (very) happy am I then,

sollte mir das Herz auch brechen,
should me the heart also break,

brich, o Herz, was liegt daran?
break, oh heart, what (do I) lay stress on it?
        (what does it matter)

Schumann   Frauenliebe und -leben
                              Women's love and -life

                     3)   Ich kann's nicht fassen
                           I can it not comprehend

Ich kann's nicht fassen, nicht glauben,
I can it not comprehend, not believe,

es hat ein Traum mich berückt;
it has a dream me charmed;
(a dream has charmed me)

wie hätt' er doch unter allen
how could have he [yet] among all (maidens)

mich Arme erhöht und beglückt?
me poor one lifted up and made happy?

Mir war's, er habe gesprochen:
To me was it, he had spoken:

"Ich bin auf ewig dein, "
"I am for ever yours, "

mir war's ich träume noch immer,
to me was it (as if) I dream still [on],

es kann ja nimmer so sein.
it can [but] never so be.

O lass im Traume mich sterben,
Oh let in [the] dream me die,

gewieget an seiner Brust,
cradled at his breast,

den seligen Tod mich schlürfen
[the] blissful death (let) me sip

in Tränen unendlicher Lust.
in tears (of) unending joy.

Schumann   Frauenliebe und -leben
                       Women's love and -life

                 4)   Du Ring an meinem Finger
                    You ring on my finger

Du Ring an meinem Finger,
You ring on my finger,

mein goldenes Ringelein,
my golden little ring,

ich drücke dich fromm an die Lippen,
I press you gently to the lips,

an das Herze mein.
to the heart (of) mine.

Ich hatt' ihn ausgeträumet,
I had [it] outdreamt,
       (ended)

der Kindheit friedlich schönen Traum,
[the] childhood's peacefully beautiful dream,

ich fand allein mich,
I found alone myself,

verloren im öden, unendlichen Raum.
lost in the empty, unending space.

Du Ring an meinem Finger,
You ring on my finger,

da hast du mich erst belehrt,
there have you me first taught,

hast meinem Blick erschlossen
have to my view opened up

des Lebens unendlichen, tiefen Wert.
[the] life's unending, deep value.

Ich will ihm dienen, ihm leben,
I will him serve, (for) him live,

ihm angehören ganz,
(to) him belong entirely,

hin selber mich geben
[-] (to him) myself [me] give

und finden verklärt mich in seinem Glanz.
and find transfigured myself in his glory.

Schumann   Frauenliebe und -leben
            Women's love and -life

        5) Helft mir, ihr Schwestern
            Help me, you sisters

Helft mir, ihr Schwestern, freundlich mich schmücken,
Help me, you sisters, kindly me (to) adorn,

dient der Glücklichen heute, mir!
serve the happy one today, me!

Windet geschäftig mir um die Stirne
Wind [busily] me around the forehead
            (around my forehead)

noch der blühenden Myrthe Zier.
[yet] the blooming myrtle's beauty.

Als ich befriedigt, freudigen Herzens,
When I satisfied, (with) joyful heart,
(When I lay satisfied with joyful heart)

sonst dem Geliebten im Arme lag,
[then] the beloved in the arm lay,
(in the beloved's arm)

immer noch rief er, Sehnsucht im Herzen,
always [yet] called he, longing in the heart,

ungeduldig den heutigen Tag.
impatiently for today's day.

Helft mir, ihr Schwestern,
Help me, you sisters,

helft mir verscheuchen eine törichte Bangigkeit;
help me banish [a] foolish anxiety;

dass ich mit klarem Aug' ihn empfange,
that I with clear eye him receive,

ihn, die Quelle der Freudigkeit.
him, the fountain of joy.

Bist, mein Geliebter, du mir erschienen,
Are, my beloved, you to me appeared,
(Have)

481

gibst du mir, Sonne, deinen Schein?
give you to me, sun, your shine?

Lass mich in Andacht, lass mich in Demut,
Let me in devotion, let me in humility,

lass mich verneigen dem Herren mein.
let me bow to the master (of) mine.

Streuet ihm, Schwestern, streuet ihm Blumen,
Scatter (for) him, sisters, scatter (for) him flowers,

bringet ihm knospende Rosen dar.
present to him budding roses [-].

Aber euch, Schwestern, grüss' ich mit Wehmut,
But you, sisters, greet I with sadness,

freudig scheidend aus eurer Schaar.
joyfully withdrawing from your group.

Schumann   Frauenliebe und -leben
                  Women's love and -life

                  6)   Süsser Freund
                         Sweet friend

Süsser Freund, du blickest mich verwundert an,
Sweet friend, you look (at)me in wonder [-],

kannst es nicht begreifen, wie ich weinen kann;
(you)can [it] not understand, how I weep [can];

lass der feuchten Perlen ungewohnte Zier
let the moist pearls unusual beauty

freudig hell erzittern in dem Auge mir.
joyfully bright shimmer in the eye (of)me.
                                   (in my eyes)

Wie so bang mein Busen, wie so wonnevoll!
How so fearful my bosom, how so full of bliss!

wüsst' ich nur mit Worten, wie ich's sagen soll;
knew I only with words, how I it say should;
(if I only knew, how to say it in words)

komm und birg dein Antlitz hier an meiner Brust,
come and hide your face here on my breast,

will in's Ohr dir flüstern alle meine Lust.
will in the ear to you whisper all my joy.

Weisst du nun die Tränen, die ich weinen kann,
Know you now the tears, which I cry can,
(Do you know now why I cry)

sollst du nicht sie sehen, du geliebter Mann!
should you not them see, you beloved man!
(you should)

Bleib an meinem Herzen, fühle dessen Schlag,
Remain on my heart, feel its beat,

dass ich fest und fester nur dich drücken mag,
that I firm and firmer only you press may,
(that I may press you firm and firmer)

fest und fester!
firm and firmer!

Hier an meinem Bette hat die Wiege Raum,
Here at my bed has the cradle space,
                    (is space for the cradle)

wo sie still verberge meinen holden Traum;
where it quietly hides my lovely dream;

kommen wird der Morgen, wo der Traum erwacht,
come will the morning, where the dream awakes,

und daraus dein Bildnis mir entgegen lacht.
and out of it your image me towards smiles.
                    (smiles towards me)

Schumann   Frauenliebe und -leben
                    Women's love and -life

               7)   An meinem Herzen
                   On my heart

An meinem Herzen, an meiner Brust,
On my heart, on my breast,

du meine Wonne, du meine Lust!
you my joy, you my delight!

Das Glück ist die Liebe, die Lieb' ist das Glück,
[The] happiness is [the] love, [the] love is [the] happiness,

ich hab's gesagt und nehm's nicht zurück.
I have it said and take it not back.

hab' überschwenglich mich geschätzt,
Have exuberantly myself valued,
(I have believed myself to be exuberant)

bin überglücklich aber jetzt.
am more than happy [but] now.

Nur die da säugt, nur die da liebt
Only who [there] feeds, only who [there] loves

das Kind, dem sie die Nahrung gibt,
the child, to whom she [the] nourishment gives,

nur eine Mutter weiss allein,
only a mother knows alone,

was lieben heisst und glücklich sein.
what (to) love means and happy (to) be.
(what it means, to love and to be happy)

O wie bedaur' ich doch den Mann,
Oh how pity I [yet] the man,

der Mutterglück nicht fühlen kann!
who mother's joy not feel can!
(who can not imagine a mother's joy)

Du lieber, lieber Engel du,
You dear, dear angel you,

Schumann   An meinem Herzen   (Continued)

du schauest mich an und lächelst dazu!
you look at me and smile at the same time!

An meinem Herzen, an meiner Brust,
On my heart, on my breast,

du meine Wonne, du meine Lust!
you my joy, you my delight!

Schumann   Frauenliebe und -leben
                 Women's love and -life

         8)   Nun hast du mir den ersten Schmerz
              getan
           Now have you to me the first sorrow
              done
           (given)

Nun hast du mir den ersten Schmerz getan,
Now have you to me the first sorrow done,
                        (given)

der aber traf.
that one really hurt.

Du schläfst, du harter, unbarmherz'ger Mann,
You sleep, you hard, merciless man,

den Todesschlaf.
the sleep of death.

Es blicket die Verlass'ne vor sich hin,
[It] looks the deserted one before herself [-],

die Welt ist leer, ist leer.
the world is empty, is empty.

Geliebet hab' ich und gelebt,
Loved have I and lived,

ich bin nicht lebend mehr.
I am not living more.

Ich zieh' mich in mein Inn'res still zurück,
I withdraw [myself] into my inner self quietly [-],
(I withdraw quietly into my inner self)

der Schleier fällt,
the curtain falls,

da hab' ich dich und mein verlornes Glück,
there have I you and my lost happiness,

du meine Welt!
you my world!

Schumann   Marienwürmchen
                      Ladybird
                      (Ladybug)

Marienwürmchen, setze dich auf meine Hand,
Ladybird, sit yourself on my hand,
(Ladybug)

ich tu' dir nichts zu Leide.
I do you nothing to harm.

Es soll dir nichts zu Leid gescheh'n,
It shall you nothing to harm (be) done,
(Nothing shall be done to harm you)

will nur deine bunten Flügel seh'n,
want only your colorful wings to see,

bunte Flügel meine Freude.
colorful wings (are)my joy.

Marienwürmchen, fliege weg,
Ladybird, fly away,

dein Häuschen brennt,
your little house burns,

die Kinder schrei'n so sehre, wie so sehre.
the children scream so much, how so much.

Die böse Spinne spinnt sie ein,
The wicked spider spins them in,
                    (envelops your children by spinning)

Marienwürmchen, flieg' hinein,
ladybird, fly into (it),

die Kinder schreien sehre.
the children scream (so)much.

Marienwürmchen, fliege hin zu Nachbars Kind,
ladybird, fly there to neighbor's children,

sie tun dir nichts zu Leide.
they do you nothing to harm.

Es soll dir da kein Leid gescheh'n,
[It] shall to you [there] no harm (be) done,

sie wollen deine bunten Flügel seh'n,
they want your colorful wings to see,

und grüss' sie alle beide.
and greet them [all] both.

Schumann　　　　　Mondnacht
　　　　　　　　　　Moon-night

Es war, als hätt' der Himmel
It was, as had [the] heaven

die Erde still geküsst,
the earth quietly kissed,

dass sie im Blütenschimmer
that it in the flowers' splendor
(the earth)

von ihm nur träumen müsst'.
of him only dream must.
(the heaven)

Die Luft ging durch die Felder,
The breeze went through the fields,

die Ähren wogten sacht,
the wheat heads waved gently,

es rauschten leis' die Wälder,
[it] rustled softly the forests,

so sternklar war die Nacht.
so starlight was the night.

Und meine Seele spannte
And my soul spread

weit ihre Flügel aus,
wide its wings [out],

flog durch die stillen Lande,
flew through the silent lands,

als flöge sie nach Haus.
as (if) flying [herself to] home.

490

Schumann   Stille Tränen
                   Silent tears

Du bist vom Schlaf erstanden
You are from sleep awakened

und wandelst durch die Au,
and walk through the meadow,

da liegt ob allen Landen
there lies over all lands

der Himmel wunderblau.
the heaven wondrously blue.

So lang du ohne Sorgen
As long(as) you without sorrow

geschlummert schmerzenlos,
slumbered free of pains,

der Himmel bis zum Morgen
the heaven till the morning

viel Tränen niedergoss.
many tears poured down.

In stillen Nächten weinet
In silent nights cries
(In silent nights many a one)

oft mancher aus den Schmerz,
often many a one out the pain,
(often cries away the pain)

und morgens dann ihr meinet,
and in the morning then you think,

stets fröhlich sei sein Herz.
always happy has been his heart.

Schumann   Volksliedchen
                Folk song

Wenn ich früh in den Garten geh'
When I early to the garden go

in meinem grünen Hut,
in my green hat,

ist mein erster Gedanke,
is my first thought,

was nun mein Liebster tut?
what now my beloved does?

Am Himmel steht kein Stern,
In heaven stands no star,

den ich dem Freund nicht gönnte.
which I to the friend not would allow.
(which I would not give to my friend)

Mein Herz gäb' ich ihm gern,
My heart gave I to him willingly,
(My heart I would give to him willingly)

wenn ich's heraustun könnte.
if I it take out could.
(if I could take it out)

Schumann   Wanderlied
                    Wander-song

Wohlauf! noch getrunken den funkelnden Wein!
Your health! still (let us) drink the sparkling wine!

Ade nun, ihr Lieben! geschieden muss sein.
Good-bye now, you dear ones! departed (we) must be.

Ade nun, ihr Berge, du väterlich Haus!
Good-bye now, you mountains, you paternal house!

Es treibt in die Ferne mich mächtig hinaus.
It drives into the distance me powerfully out.
(The wanderlust drives me powerfully into the distance)

Die Sonne, sie bleibet am Himmel nicht steh'n,
The sun, [she] remains in heaven not motionless,

es treibt sie, durch Länder und Meere zu geh'n.
it drives her, across lands and oceans to pass.
(the wanderlust) (sun)

Die Woge nicht haftet am einsamen Strand,
The wave not clings to the lonely beach,

die Stürme, sie brausen mit Macht durch das Land.
the storms, they roar with power through the land.

Mit eilenden Wolken der Vogel dort zieht
With speeding clouds the bird there moves
                            (flies)

und singt in der Ferne ein heimatlich Lied.
and sings in the distance a home-like song.

So treibt es den Burschen durch Wälder und Feld,
So drives it the youth through forest and field,

zu gleichen der Mutter, der wandernden Welt.
to resemble the mother, the wandering world.

Da grüssen ihn Vögel bekannt über'm Meer,
There greet him birds well-known over the sea,
                    (well-known birds)

sie flogen von Fluren der Heimath hieher;
they flew from fields of the homeland hither;

da duften die Blumen vertraulich um ihn,
there smell sweet the flowers familiarly around him,
(there the familiar flowers smell sweet around him)

sie trieben vom Lande die Lüfte dahin.
they drove from land the breezes across.

Die Vögel, die kennen sein väterlich Haus,
The birds, they know his paternal house,

die Blumen, die pflanzt er der Liebe zum Strauss,
the flowers, them plants he for love to a bouquet,
            (he plants them for a bouquet for love)

und Liebe, die folgt ihm, sie geht ihm zur Hand:
and love, it follows him, it goes him at hand:

so wird ihm zur Heimat das ferneste Land.
thus becomes (for)him as home the most distant land.

Wohlauf! noch getrunken den funkelnden Wein!
Your health! still (let us) drink the sparkling wine!

Ade nun, ihr Lieben! geschieden muss sein.
Good-bye now, you dear ones! departed (we) must be.

Ade nun, ihr Berge, du väterlich Haus!
Good-bye now, you mountains, you paternal house!

Es treibt in die Ferne mich mächtig hinaus!
It drives into the distance me powerfully out!
(The wanderlust drives me powerfully into the distance)

Schumann   Widmung
                Dedication

Du meine Seele, du mein Herz,
You my soul, you my heart,

du meine Wonn', o du mein Schmerz,
you my joy, oh you my pain,

du meine Welt, in der ich lebe,
you my world, in which I live,

mein Himmel du, darein ich schwebe,
my heaven you, therein I hover,

o du mein Grab, in das hinab
oh you my grave, into which [down]

ich ewig meinen Kummer gab!
I eternally my grief gave!

Du bist die Ruh', du bist der Frieden,
You are [the] rest, you are [the] peace,

du bist vom Himmel mir beschieden.
you are from heaven me given.

Dass du mich liebst, macht mich mir wert,
That you me love, makes myself to me worthy,

dein Blick hat mich vor mir verklärt,
your glance has myself to me transfigured,
(your glance has transfigured myself to me)

du hebst mich liebend über mich,
you lift me lovingly above myself,

mein guter Geist, mein bess'res Ich!
my good spirit, my better self!

Strauss   Allerseelen
                All-soul's day

Stell' auf den Tisch die duftenden Reseden,
Put on the table the fragrant mignonettes,

die letzten roten Astern trag' herbei,
the last red asters bring in,

und lass uns wieder von der Liebe reden,
and let us again of [the] love speak,

wie einst im Mai.
as once in May.

Gieb mir die Hand, dass ich sie heimlich drücke,
Give me the hand, that I it secretly press,

und wenn man's sieht, mir ist es einerlei,
and if one it sees, to me is it the same,
                        (I do not care)

gieb mir nur einen deiner süssen Blicke,
give me only one of your sweet glances,

wie einst im Mai.
as once in May.

Es blüht und duftet heut' auf jedem Grabe,
[It] blooms and smells sweet today upon each grave,

ein Tag im Jahr ist ja den Toten frei,
one day in the year is [indeed] to the dead free,
                        (reserved for the dead)

komm an mein Herz, dass ich dich wieder habe
come to my heart, that I you again have

wie einst im Mai.
as once in May.

Strauss   Befreit
               Freed

Du wirst nicht weinen.   Leise,
You will not weep.   Gently,

leise wirst du lächeln und wie zur Reise
gently will you smile and as to (a) voyage
                        (as leaving on a voyage)

geb ich dir Blick und Kuss zurück.
return (I to) your glance and kiss [-].

Unsere lieben vier Wände, du hast sie bereitet,
Our dear four walls, you have them readied,

ich habe sie dir zur Welt geweitet;
I have them (for)you to a world expanded;

o Glück!
oh happiness!

Dann wirst du heiss meine Hände fassen
Then will you hotly my hands grasp
                        (warmly)

und wirst mir deine Seele lassen,
and will to me your soul leave,

lässt unsern Kindern mich zurück.
leave to our children me behind.

Du schenktest mir dein ganzes Leben,
You donated me your whole life,

ich will es ihnen wiedergeben;
I will it (to) them give back;
(I will give it back to them)

o Glück!
oh happiness!

Es wird sehr bald sein, wir wissen's Beide,
It will very soon be, we know it both,

wir haben einander befreit vom Leide,
we have each other freed from suffering,

so geb' ich dich der Welt zurück!
thus give I you to the world back!

Dann wirst du mir nur noch im Traum erscheinen
Then will you to me solely [yet] in the dream appear
(Then will you appear to me solely in dreams)

und mich segnen und mit mir weinen;
and (will) me bless and with me weep;

o Glück!
oh happiness!

Strauss   Breit über mein Haupt dein schwarzes Haar
                            Spread over my head your black hair

Breit über mein Haupt dein schwarzes Haar,
Spread over my head your black hair,

neig' zu mir dein Angesicht,
bend to me your face,

da strömt in die Seele so hell und klar
there flows into the soul so bright and clear

mir deiner Augen Licht.
[me] your eyes' light.

Ich will nicht droben der Sonne Pracht,
I desire not above the sun's splendour,
                            (the sun's splendour above)

noch der Sterne leuchtenden Kranz,
nor the stars shining garland,

ich will nur deiner Locken Nacht
I desire only your curl's night

und deiner Blicke Glanz.
and your glances' luster.
            (eyes)

Strauss   Cäcilie
                Cecily

Wenn du es wüsstest, was träumen heisst
If you [it] would know, what (to) dream means

von brennenden Küssen. von Wandern
of burning kisses, of wandering

und Ruhen mit der Geliebten,
and resting with the beloved,

Aug' in Auge und kosend und plaudernd,
eye in eye and caressing and talking,

wenn du es wüsstest, du neigtest dein Herz!
if you [it] knew, you would incline your heart!
                      (give)

Wenn du es wüsstest, was bangen heisst
If you [it] would know, what (to) fear means

in einsamen Nächten, umschauert vom Sturm,
in lonely nights, shaken by the storm,

da niemand tröstet milden Mundes die kampfmüde Seele,
since nobody comforts (with)gentle mouth the fight-worn soul,
                      (lips)

wenn du es wüsstest, du kämest zu mir.
if you [it] knew, you would come to me.

Wenn du es wüsstest, was leben heisst,
If you [it] would know, what (to) live means,

umhaucht von der Gottheit weltschaffendem Atem,
breathed on by the deity's world-creating breath,

zu schweben empor, lichtgetragen, zu seligen Höh'n,
to surge upwards, carried by the light, to blessed heights,

wenn du es wüsstest, du lebtest mit mir.
if you [it] knew, you would live with me.

Strauss Die Nacht
The night

Aus dem Walde tritt die Nacht,
From the forest treads the night,

aus den Bäumen schleicht sie leise,
from the trees creeps she quietly,

schaut sich um in weitem Kreise,
looks [herself] around in(a) wide circle,

nun gib acht.
now pay attention.

Alle Lichter dieser Welt,
All lights of this world,

alle Blumen, alle Farben
all flowers, all colors

löscht sie aus und stiehlt die Garben
extinguishes she [-] and steals the sheaves

weg vom Feld.
away from the field.

Alles nimmt sie, was nur hold,
Everything takes she, which [only] lovely,
(is)

nimmt das Silber weg des Stroms,
takes the silver away from the river,

nimmt vom Kupferdach des Doms
takes from the copper-roof of the cathedral

weg das Gold.
away the gold.

Ausgeplündert steht der Strauch,
Plundered stands the shrub,

rücke näher, Seel' an Seele;
move nearer, soul to soul;

o die Nacht, mir bangt, sie stehle
oh the night, me fear, she steals
                    (I)

dich mir auch.
you (from) me also.

Strauss   Freundliche Vision
                  Friendly vision

Nicht im Schlafe hab ich das geträumt,
Not in sleep have I this dreamt,

hell am Tage sah ich's schön vor mir:
brightly in the day saw I it beautiful before me:

Eine Wiese voller Margeriten;
A meadow full of marguerites;

tief ein weisses Haus in grünen Büschen;
deep a white house in green bushes;
(a white house deep in the green thicket)

Götterbilder leuchten aus dem Laube.
Images of the Gods shine from the foliage.

Und ich geh' mit Einer, die mich lieb hat,
And I go with one, who (for)me love has,
                        (loves me)

ruhigen Gemütes in die Kühle dieses weissen Hauses,
(with)calm heart into the coolness of this white house,

in den Frieden, der voll Schönheit wartet,
into the peace, which full of beauty waits,

dass wir kommen.
that we come.
(for us to come)

Und ich geh' mit Einer, die mich lieb hat,
And I go with one, who me loves [-],

in den Frieden voll Schönheit!
into the peace full of beauty!

Strauss   Heimkehr
Homeward

Leiser schwanken die Äste,
More quietly sway the branches,

der Kahn fliegt uferwärts,
the boat rushes shoreward,

heim kehrt die Taube zum Neste,
home comes the dove to the nest,

zu dir kehrt heim mein Herz.
to you comes home my heart.

Genug am schimmernden Tage,
Enough of the glittering day,

wenn rings das Leben lärmt,
when around [the] life roars,
(when life becomes noisy around us)

mit irrem Flügelschlage
with erring wingbeat

ist es in's Weite geschwärmt.
is it to the distance flown.

Doch nun die Sonne geschieden
But now (as) the sun (has) departed

und Stille sich senkt auf den Hain,
and silence [itself] sinks upon the grove,

fühlt es: bei dir ist der Frieden,
feels it: near you is [the] peace,
   (the heart)

die Ruh' bei dir allein.
[the] rest near you alone.

Strauss   Heimliche Aufforderung
               Secret invitation

Auf, hebe die funkelnde Schale
Arise, lift the sparkling goblet

empor zum Mund,
up to the mouth,
        (lips)

und trinke beim Freudenmahle
and drink at the feast of joy
(and at the feast of joy drink)

dein Herz gesund.
your heart sound.
(that your heart may recover)

Und wenn du sie hebst, so winke
And when you it lift, then beckon
        (lift it)

mir heimlich zu,
to me secretly [-],

dann lächle ich und dann trinke
then smile I and then drink

ich still wie du...
I silently like you...

und still gleich mir betrachte
and silently like myself watch

das Heer
the host

der trunknen Schwätzer - verachte
of drunken gossips - despise

sie nicht zu sehr.
them not too much.

Nein, hebe die blinkende Schale,
No, lift the gleaming goblet,

505

gefüllt mit Wein,
filled with wine,

und lass beim lärmenden Mahle
and let at the noisy feast
(and at the noisy feast let)

sie glücklich sein.
them happy be.
(them be happy)

Doch hast du das Mahl genossen,
But have you the meal enjoyed,

den Durst gestillt,
the thirst quenched,

dann verlasse der lauten Genossen
then leave the loud companions

festfreudiges Bild
festive display

und wandle hinaus in den Garten
and walk out into the garden

zum Rosenstrauch,
to the rosebush,

dort will ich dich dann erwarten
there will I you [then] await

nach altem Brauch,
according (to an) old custom,

und will an die Brust dir sinken,
and will on the bosom [you] sink,

eh' du's gehofft,
before you it hoped,

und deine Küsse trinken,
and (will) your kisses drink,

wie ehmals oft
as formerly often

und flechten in deine Haare
and (will) weave into your hair

der Rose Pracht -
the rose's splendor -

o komm, du wunderbare,
oh come, you wonderful,

ersehnte Nacht!
longed for night!

Strauss   Kornblumen
                  Cornflowers

Kornblumen nenn' ich die Gestalten,
Cornflowers call I the creatures,

die milden mit den blauen Augen,
the gentle ones with the blue eyes,

die, anspruchslos, in stillem Walten
who, unassuming, in quiet deed

den Tau des Friedens, den sie saugen
the dew of peace, which they draw

aus ihren eignen, klaren Seelen,
from their own, clear souls,

mitteilen allem, dem sie nah'n,
communicate to all, which they approach,

bewusstlos der Gefühlsjuwelen,
unconscious of the jewels of sentiment,

die sie von Himmelshand empfah'n.
which they from heaven's hand received.

Dir wird so wohl in ihrer Nähe,
You get so well in their nearness,

als gingest du durch ein Saatgefilde,
as went you through a seeded field,

durch das der Hauch des Abends wehe,
through which the breath of evening blows,

voll frommen Friedens und voll Milde.
full (of) gentle peace and full (of) mildness.

Strauss   Mit deinen blauen Augen
                 With your blue eyes

Mit deinen blauen Augen
With your blue eyes

siehst du mich lieblich an,
look you (at) me charmingly [-],

da ward mir so träumend zu Sinne,
then was me so dreamily in the mind,
        (became I)   (my thoughts)

dass ich nicht sprechen kann.
that I not speak can.
        (can not speak)

An deine blauen Augen
Of your blue eyes

gedenk' ich allerwärts:
think I everywhere:

Ein Meer von blauen Gedanken
A sea of blue thoughts

ergiesst sich über mein Herz.
pours [itself] over my heart.

Strauss   Morgen
      Tomorrow

Und morgen wird die Sonne wieder scheinen
And tomorrow will the sun again shine

und auf dem Wege, den ich gehen werde,
and on the road, which I go shall
      (shall go)

wird uns, die Glücklichen, sie wieder einen
will us, the happy ones, it again unite
      (the sun)

inmitten dieser sonnenatmenden Erde...
in the midst of this sun-breathing earth...

und zu dem Strand, dem weiten, wogenblauen,
and to the beach, the wide, wave-blue one,

werden wir still und langsam niedersteigen,
shall we silently and slowly descend,

stumm werden wir uns in die Augen schauen,
mute shall we us in the eyes look,

und auf uns sinkt des Glückes stummes Schweigen.
and upon us sinks [the] happiness' mute silence.

Strauss   Nachtgang
           Nightwalk

Wir gingen durch die stille, milde Nacht,
We walked through the quiet, mild night,

dein Arm in meinem, dein Auge in meinem.
your arm in mine, your eye(s) in mine.

Der Mond goss silbernes Licht über dein Angesicht,
The moon poured silvery light over your face,

wie auf Goldgrund ruhte dein schönes Haupt.
as on golden background rested your beautiful head.

Und du erschienst mir wie eine Heilige,
And you appeared to me like a Saint,

mild, mild und gross und seelenübervoll,
gentle, gentle and great and soulful,

heilig und rein, wie die liebe Sonne.
holy and pure, like the dear sun.

Und in die Augen schwoll mir
And in the eyes swelled [me]

ein warmer Drang wie Tränenahnung.
a warm urge like foreboding of tears.

Fester fasst' ich dich und küsste,
Firmer grasped I you and kissed,

küsste dich ganz leise.
kissed you very softly.

Meine Seele weinte.
My soul wept.

Strauss   Ruhe, meine Seele
                  Rest, my soul

Nicht ein Lüftchen regt sich leise,
Not a little breeze moves [itself] softly,

sanft entschlummert ruht der Hain;
gently slumbering rests the grove;

durch der Blätter dunkle Hülle
through the foliage's dark cover

stiehlt sich lichter Sonnenschein.
steals [itself] bright sunshine.

Ruhe, ruhe, meine Seele,
Rest, rest, my soul,

deine Stürme gingen wild;
your storms went fiercely;

hast getobt und hast gezittert,
(you) have raged and have trembled,

wie die Brandung, wenn sie schwillt!
as the breakers, when they swell!

Diese Zeiten sind gewaltig,
These times are violent,

bringen Herz und Hirn in Not -
bring heart and mind into misery -

Ruhe, ruhe, meine Seele,
Rest, rest, my soul,

und vergiss, was dich bedroht!
and forget, what you threatens!
                  (threatens you)

Strauss   Ständchen
              Serenade

Mach' auf, mach' auf, doch leise, mein Kind,
Open up (the door), open up, but quietly, my child,

um keinen vom Schlummer zu wecken;
for no one from slumber to wake;

kaum murmelt der Bach, kaum zittert im Wind
hardly murmurs the brook, hardly trembles in the wind

ein Blatt an den Büschen und Hecken.
a leaf on the bushes and hedges.

Drum leise, mein Mädchen, dass nichts sich regt,
Therefore quietly, my maiden, that nothing [itself] moves,

nur leise die Hand auf die Klinke gelegt.
just quietly the hand on the latch laid.
               (lay the hand on the latch)

Mit Tritten wie Tritte der Elfen so sacht,
With steps like steps of fairies so soft,

um über die Blumen zu hüpfen,
as over the flowers to hop,

flieg' leicht hinaus in die Mondscheinnacht
fly lightly out into the moonshine-night

zu mir in den Garten zu schlüpfen.
to me in the garden to slip.

Rings schlummern die Blüten am rieselnden Bach
Around slumber the blossoms at the murmuring brook

und duften im Schlaf, nur die Liebe ist wach!
and smell sweet in [the] sleep, only [the] love is awake!

Sitz' nieder, hier dämmert's geheimnisvoll
Sit down, here grows dark it mysteriously

unter den Lindenbäumen,
under the linden trees,

die Nachtigall uns zu Häupten soll
the nightingale us to the heads shall
            (above our heads)

von uns'ren Küssen träumen,
of our kisses dream,

und die Rose, wenn sie am Morgen erwacht,
and the rose, when it in the morning awakes,

hoch glühn von den Wonneschauern der Nacht.
(shall) high glow from the thrills of bliss of the night.
      (brightly)

Strauss   Traum durch die Dämmerung
                 Dream through [the] twilight

Weite Wiesen im Dämmergrau;
Wide meadows in the grey dusk;

die Sonne verglomm, die Sterne ziehn,
the sun sets, the stars move on,

nun geh' ich hin zu der schönsten Frau,
now go I there to the most beautiful woman,

weit über Wiesen im Dämmergrau,
far over meadows in the grey dusk,

tief in den Busch von Jasmin.
deep in the bush of jasmine.

Durch Dämmergrau in der Liebe Land;
Through grey dusk into [the] love's land;

ich gehe nicht schnell, ich eile nicht;
I go not fast, I hasten not;

mich zieht ein weiches sammtenes Band
me draws a soft velvety ribbon
(a soft velvety ribbon draws me)

durch Dämmergrau in der Liebe Land,
through grey dusk into [the] love's land,

in ein blaues, mildes Licht.
into a blue, mild light.

Strauss   Wie sollten wir geheim sie halten
             How should we secret it keep
             (How should we keep it secret)

Wie sollten wir geheim sie halten,
How should we secret it keep,
(How should we keep it secret)

die Seligkeit, die uns erfüllt?
the happiness, which us fills?

Nein, bis in seine tiefsten Falten
No, till into its deepest folds

sei allen unser Herz enthüllt!
be (to) all our heart unveiled!

Wenn zwei in Liebe sich gefunden,
When two in love themselves (have) found,

geht Jubel hin durch die Natur,
goes jubilation [there] through [the] nature,

in längern, wonnevollen Stunden
in longer, blissful hours

legt sich der Tag auf Wald und Flur.
lays [itself] the day upon forest and field.
(sinks)

Selbst aus der Eiche morschem Stamm,
Even from the oak's rotten trunk,

die ein Jahrtausend überlebt,
which a thousand years survived,

steigt neu des Wipfels grüne Flamme
rises anew the tree-top's green flame

und rauscht von Jugendlust durchbebt.
and rustles of joy of youth trembling.
             (trembling of joy of youth)

Zu höhern Glanz und Dufte brechen
To higher luster and scent burst

die Knospen auf beim Glück der Zwei
the buds open at the happiness of the two (of us)

und süsser rauscht es in den Bächen
and sweeter murmur [it in] the brooks

und reicher blüht und reicher glänzt der Mai.
and richer blooms and richer shines [the] May.

Strauss   Zueignung
                Dedication

Ja, du weisst es, teure Seele,
Yes, you know it, dear soul,

dass ich fern von dir mich quäle,
that I far from you myself torment,

Liebe macht die Herzen krank,
love makes [the] hearts sick,

habe Dank.
have thanks.
(be thanked)

Einst hielt ich, der Freiheit Zecher,
Once held I, the freedom's drinker,
              (the drinker to freedom)

hoch den Amethisten Becher
high the amethyst goblet

und du segnetest den Trank,
and you blessed the drink,

habe Dank.
have thanks.
(be thanked)

Und beschworst darin die Bösen,
And (you) conjured therein [the] demons,

bis ich, was ich nie gewesen,
till I, what I never had been,

heilig, heilig an's Herz dir sank,
solemnly, solemnly at the heart you sank,
(sank solemnly on your heart)

habe Dank.
have thanks.
(be thanked)

Tchaikowsky   Adieu, forêts, from "Jeanne d'Arc"
                   Farewell, forests, from "Joan of Arc"

Oui, Dieu le veut! Je dois suivre ton ordre,
Yes, God it wants! I must follow your order,

obéir à ton appel, sainte Vierge!
obey your call, saint Virgin!

Pourquoi, mon coeur, pourquoi bats-tu si fort?
Why, my heart, why beat you so strong?
(Why, my heart, why do you beat so fast)

Pourquoi frémir? L'effroi remplit mon âme!
Why tremble? Fright fills my soul!

Adieu, forêts, adieu, prés fleuris, champs d'or,
Farewell, forests, farewell, meadows flowered, fields of gold,
(Farewell, forests, farewell, flowering meadows, golden
    fields)

Et vous, paisibles vallons, adieu!
And you, peaceful valleys, farewell!

Jeanne aujourd'hui vous dit à jamais adieu.
Joan today to you says forever farewell.
(Today Joan says goodbye to you forever)

Oui, pour toujours, toujours, adieu!
Yes, forever, forever, farewell!

Mes prés fleuris et mes forêts ombreuses,
My meadows flowered and my forests shady,
(My flowering meadows and my shady forests)

Vous fleurirez pour d'autres que pour moi.
You will bloom for others than for me.

Adieu, forêts, eau pure de la source: Je vais partir
Farewell, forests, water pure of the spring: I am going to
    leave

Et ne vous verrai plus, Jeanne vous fuit, et pour jamais.
and you will see no longer, Joan you flees, and forever.
(and will see you no longer, Joan flees from you forever)

519

Tchaikowsky   Adieu... (Continued)

O doux vallon où j'ai connu la joie!
Oh sweet valley where I have known joy!

Aujourd'hui je te quitte, doux vallon!
Today I you leave, sweet valley!

Et mes agneaux, dans les vertes prairies
And my lambs, in the green pastures

demanderont en vain leur guide!
will ask in vain (for) their guide!
(in vain will call out for their guide)

Au champ d'honneur je dois guider les braves,
To the field of honor I am to guide the brave (ones),
(I am going to the battlefield to lead brave men)

cueillir les palmes sanglantes de la victoire!
to gather (the) palms bloody of victory!

Je vais où les voix m'appellent, Voix saintes,
I go where the voices me call, Voices saint,
(I am going where my voices call me, holy Voices)

Seigneur, vous voyez au fond de mon âme!
Lord, you see to the depth of my soul!

Mon coeur se brise, Mon âme souffre, mon coeur saigne!
My heart is breaking, My soul suffers, my heart bleeds!

O monts aimés, adieu, forêts ombreuses,
Oh mountains loved, farewell, forests shady,
(Oh beloved mountains, farewell, shady forests)

Et vous, paisibles vallons, adieu!
And you, peaceful valleys, farewell!

Jeanne aujourd'hui vous dit à jamais adieu!
Joan today says goodbye to you forever!

Oui, pour toujours, adieu.
Yes, forever, farewell.

Prés fleuris, arbres verts, Si chers à mon enfance,
Meadows flowering, trees green, So dear to my childhood,

520

Tchaikowsky   Adieu... (Continued)

Vous fleurissez pour d'autres que pour moi.
You bloom for others than for me.

Adieu, mes champs, adieu, vallon, source pure,
Farewell, my fields, farewell, valley, spring pure,

Il faut partir et pour toujours!
It is necessary to leave and forever!
(I must leave and forever)

Ah! recevez mon éternel adieu!
Ah! receive my eternal farewell!

Thomas   Connais-tu le pays, from "Mignon"
                     Know you the land, from "Darling"

Connais-tu le pays où fleurit l'oranger,
Know you the land where blossoms the orange tree,

Le pays des fruits d'or et des roses vermeilles,
The land of fruits of gold and of roses vermilion,

Où la brise est plus douce, et l'oiseau plus léger,
Where the breeze is more sweet, and the bird more light,

Où dans toute saison butinent les abeilles,
Where in all season gather the bees,
(Where the bees gather honey in every season)

Où rayonne et sourit, comme un bienfait de Dieu,
Where radiates and smiles, like a favor from God,

Un éternel printemps sous un ciel toujours bleu?
An eternal spring beneath a sky always blue?

Hélas! que ne puis-je te suivre
Alas! why not may I you follow
(Alas! why may I not follow you)

Vers ce rivage heureux, d'où le sort m'exila!
Toward this bank happy, from where fate me exiled!
(To this happy shore, from which fate has exiled me)

C'est là, que je voudrais vivre,
It is there, that I would like to live,

Aimer, aimer et mourir! C'est là! oui, c'est là!
To love, to love and to die! It is there! yes, it is there!

Connais-tu la maison où l'on m'attend là-bas,
Know you the house where one me awaits over there,
(Do you know the house down there where people wait for
    me)

La salle aux lambris d'or, où des hommes de marbre
The hall with panels of gold, where some men of marble

M'appellent dans la nuit en me tendant les bras?
Me call in the night in me holding out the arms?
(Hold out their arms to me and call me in the night)

Thomas   Connais-tu...(Continued)

Et la cour où l'on danse à l'ombre d'un grand arbre?
And the courtyard where one dances in the shade of a large
   tree?

Et le lac transparent, où glissent sur les eaux
And the lake transparent, where glides over the waters
(And the transparent lake where a thousand weightless boats)

Mille bateaux légers, pareils à des oiseaux!
A thousand boats light, similar to birds!
(Glide over the water like birds)

Vers ce pays lointain d'où le sort m'exila!
Toward this land faraway from where the fate me exiled!
(To this faraway land from which fate has exiled me)

Thomas Elle ne croyait pas, from "Mignon"
She did not believe, from "Darling"

Elle ne croyait pas, dans sa candeur naïve,
She believed not, in her artlessness naïve,
(She did not believe, in her naïveté)

Que l'amour innocent qui dormait dans son coeur,
That the love innocent that slept in her heart,

Dût se changer un jour en une ardeur plus vive
Should be changed one day in an ardor more alive
(Would change one day to a more fervent desire)

Et troubler à jamais son rêve de bonheur.
And trouble forever her dream of happiness.

Pour rendre à la fleur épuisée
To give to the flower exhausted
(Give the withered flower)

Sa fraîcheur, son éclat vermeil,
Its freshness, its sparkle vermilion,

O printemps, donne-lui ta goutte de rosée!
Oh springtime, give it your drop of dew!
(Oh springtime, by giving it a drop of dew)

O mon coeur, donne-lui ton rayon de soleil!
Oh my heart, give it your ray of sun!

C'est en vain que j'attends un aveu de sa bouche,
It is in vain that I await a confession from her mouth,

Je veux connaître en vain ses secrètes douleurs,
I want to know in vain her secret sorrows,

Mon regard l'intimide et ma voix l'effarouche,
My gaze her intimidates and my voice her frightens,

Un mot trouble son âme et fait couler ses pleurs!
A word troubles her soul and makes flow her tears!

Thomas   Je suis Titania, from "Mignon"
                I am Titania, from "Darling"

Oui! pour ce soir, je suis reine des fées!
Yes, for tonight, I am queen of the fairies!

Voici mon sceptre d'or et voici mes trophées!
Here is my scepter of gold and here are my trophies!

Je suis Titania la blonde
I am Titania the blond (one)

Je suis Titania fille de l'air
I am Titania daughter of the air

En riant je parcours le monde,
In laughing I skirt the world,

Plus vive que l'oiseau,
More lively than the bird,

plus prompte que l'éclair!
more prompt than lightening!

La troupe folle des lutins suit mon char qui vole et
The troop crazy of sprites follows my chariot that flies and

dans la nuit Fuit! autour de moi toute ma cour,
in the night Flees! about me all my court,

court, chantant le plaisir et l'amour,
runs, singing of pleasure and of love,

du rayon de Phoebé qui luit!
from the ray of Phoebus that shines!

Parmi les fleurs que l'aurore Fait éclore,
Among the flowers that the dawn Causes to open,

Par les bois et par les prés Diaprés
Through the woods and through the meadows dappled

Sur les flots couverts d'écume, dans la brume,
On the water covered with foam, in the fog,

Thomas   Je suis... (Continued)

On me voit d'un pied léger voltiger!
One me sees with a foot light flying!
(I can be seen in my lightfooted flight)

D'un pied léger par les bois, par les prés
With a foot light through the woods, through the meadows
(Lightly through the woods and over the meadows)

Et dans la brume on me voit voltiger, ah!
And in the fog one me sees flying about, ah!
(I can be seen flying about in the fog, ah)

Voilà Titania!   En riant je parcours le monde,
There is Titania!   In laughing I skirt the world,

Plus vive que l'oiseau, plus prompte que l'éclair.
Livelier than the bird, faster than lightening.

Je suis Titania, fille de l'air.
I am Titania, daughter of the air.

Thomas   O vin, dissipe la tristesse, from "Hamlet"
                        Oh wine, dissipate the sadness

O vin, dissipe la tristesse
Oh wine, dissipate the sadness

Qui pèse sur mon coeur! A moi les rêves de l'ivresse
That weighs upon my heart! For me the dreams of
    drunkeness

Et le rire moqueur!
And the laugh mocker!
(And the mocking laughter)

O liqueur enchanteresse,
Oh drink of enchantment,

Verse l'ivresse Et l'oubli dans mon coeur!
Pour drunkeness And forgetfulness in my heart!

Douce liqueur! O liqueur enchanteresse!
Sweet drink! Oh drink of enchantment!

Verse l'ivresse dans mon coeur!
Pour drunkeness in my heart!

O liqueur enchanteress! Verse l'ivresse
Oh drink of enchantment! Pour drunkeness

Et l'oubli dans mon coeur!
And forgetfulness in my heart!

La vie est sombre, Les ans sont courts;
Life is dark, The years are short;

De nos beaux jours Dieu sait le nombre.
Of our beautiful days God knows the number.
(God has numbered our happy days)

Chacun, hélas! Porte ici-bas Sa lourde chaîne,
Each one, alas! Carries down here (on earth) His heavy
    chain,

Cruels devoirs, Longs désespoirs De l'âme humaine!
Cruel duties, Long despairs Of the heart human!

Loin de nous, Noirs présages!
Far from us, Black forebodings!

Les plus sages Sont les fous! ah!
The most wise Are (the) madmen! ah!

Le vin dissipe la tristesse Qui pèse sur mon coeur!
Wine dissipates the sadness That weighs upon my heart!

A moi les rêves de l'ivresse Et le rire moqueur!
For me the dreams of drunkeness And the laughter mocking!

O liqueur enchanteresse, Verse l'ivresse
Oh drink of enchantment, Pour drunkeness

Et l'oubli dans mon coeur! Douce liqueur,
And forgetfulness in my heart! Sweet drink,

O liqueur enchanteresse, Verse l'ivresse dans mon coeur!
Oh drink of enchantment, Pour drunkeness in my heart!

O liqueur enchanteresse!
Oh drink of enchantment!

Verse l'ivresse Et l'oubli dans mon coeur,
Pour drunkeness And forgetfulness in my heart,

versenous l'ivresse!
pour us drunkeness!

Wagner   Allmächt'ge Jungfrau, from "Tannhäuser"
                   Almighty Virgin

Allmächt'ge Jungfrau, hör' mein Flehen!
Almighty Virgin, hear my supplication!

Zu dir, Gepries'ne, rufe ich!
To Thee, Praised one, call I!

Lass mich im Staub vor dir vergehen,
Let me in the dust before Thee perish,

o! nimm von dieser Erde mich!
oh! take from this earth me!

Mach' dass ich rein und engelgleich
Make that I pure and angel-like

eingehe in dein selig Reich!
enter into Thy blessed kingdom!

Wenn je, in tör'gem Wahn befangen,
If ever, in foolish illusion captured,

mein Herz sich abgewandt von dir,
my heart [itself] turned away from Thee,

wenn je ein sündiges Verlangen,
if ever a sinful desire,

ein weltlich Sehnen keimt' in mir:
a worldly longing sprang up in me:

so rang ich unter tausend Schmerzen,
so struggled I in thousand pains,

dass ich es töd' in meinem Herzen.
that I it kill in my heart.
    (kill it)

Doch konnt' ich jeden Fehl nicht büssen,
But, could I each wrong not atone,

so nimm dich gnädig meiner an!
so accept Thou mercifully me [-]!

Dass ich mit demutvollem Grüssen
That I with humble salutations

als würd'ge Magd dir nahen kann:
as worthy maiden to Thee approach can:
(can approach Thee as (a) worthy maiden)

um deine gnadenreichste Huld
for Thy most merciful favor

nur anzuflehn für seine Schuld!
solely to implore for his offense!
                    (Tannhäuser's)

Wagner   Dich, teure Halle, from "Tannhäuser"
                You, dear hall

Dich, teure Halle, grüss' ich wieder,
You, dear hall, greet I again,

froh grüss' ich dich, geliebter Raum!
gladly greet I you, beloved room!

In dir erwachen seine Lieder
In you awake his songs
    (I still hear)

und wecken mich aus düst'rem Traum.
and waken me from gloomy dream.
(which)

Da er aus dir geschieden,
As he from you departed,

wie öd' erschienst du mir!
how desolate appeared you to me!

Aus mir entfloh der Frieden,
From me fled [the] peace,

die Freude zog aus dir!
[the] joy moved from you!

Wie jetzt mein Busen hoch sich hebet,
As now my bosom high [itself] lifts,

so scheinst du jetzt mir stolz und hehr;
so seem you now to me proud and lofty;
(to me you seem now proud and lofty)

der mich und dich so neu belebet,
who me and you so newly enlivened,
(he who has enlivened you and me)

nicht weilt er ferne mehr!
not tarries he far [more]!
(tarries no longer in the distance)

Sei mir gegrüsst, sei mir gegrüsst!
Be (by) me greeted, be (by) me greeted!

Wagner   Dich, teure Halle... (Continued)

Du, teure Halle, sei mir gegrüsst!
You, dear hall, be (by) me greeted!

Wagner   Du bist der Lenz, from "Die Walküre"
          You are [the] spring

Du bist der Lenz, nach dem ich verlangte
You are [the] spring, for which I longed

in frostigen Winters Frist.
in frosty winter's time.

Dich grüsste mein Herz mit heiligem Grau'n,
You greeted my heart with holy horror,
(My heart greeted you with holy horror)

als dein Blick zuerst mir erblühte.
when your glance first me bloomed.
                    (fell on me)

Fremdes nur sah ich von je,
Strange (things) only saw I at all times,

freundlos war mir das Nahe;
friendless was to me [the] nearness;
(nearness was hostile to me)

als hätt' ich nie es gekannt,
as had I never [it] known,
(whatever happened to me was as if)

war, was immer mir kam.
was, what ever to me came.
(I had never known it)

Doch dich kannt' ich deutlich und klar;
But you knew I plainly and clearly;
          (I knew)

als mein Auge dich sah, warst du mein Eigen;
when my eye you saw, were you my own;
(when my eye recognized you, you were my own)

was im Busen ich barg, was ich bin,
what in the bosom I hid, what I am,
(that which I hid in my bosom and what I am)

hell wie der Tag taucht' es mir auf,
bright as the day turns it [to me] up,
(became as bright as the day to me)

533

wie tönender Schall schlug's an mein Ohr,
as (a) resonant sound rings it in my ear,

als in frostig öder Fremde
as in frosty deserted foreign land

zuerst ich den Freund ersah.
first I the friend saw.

Wagner   Einsam in trüben Tagen, from "Lohengrin"
        Lonely in sad days

Einsam in trüben Tagen
Lonely in sad days

hab' ich zu Gott gefleht,
have I [to] God implored,

des Herzens tiefstes Klagen
the heart's deepest lament

ergoss ich im Gebet,
poured I into prayer,

da drang aus meinem Stöhnen
there came up from my groaning

ein Laut so klagevoll,
a sound so grief-filled,

der zu gewalt'gen Tönen
which to powerful ringing

weit in die Lüfte schwoll:
far into the air swelled:

ich hört' ihn fern hin hallen,
I heard it (from) far resound,

bis kaum mein Ohr er traf;
till hardly my ear it reached;

mein Aug' ist zugefallen,
my eye [is] closed,

ich sank in süssen Schlaf.
I sank into sweet slumber.

In lichter Waffen Scheine
In bright arm's shine
   (armor's)

ein Ritter nahte da,
a knight approached then,

so tugendlicher Reine
(of) such virtuous pureness

ich keinen noch ersah.
I no one yet saw.
(as I had never seen)

Ein golden Horn zur Hüften,
A golden bugle at the hip,

gelehnet auf sein Schwert,
leaned on his sword,
(leaning)

so trat er aus den Lüften
thus stepped he from the air
                              (sky)

zu mir, der Recke wert;
to me, the warrior worthy;
          (the worthy warrior)

mit züchtigem Gebahren
with modest manners

gab Tröstung er mir ein:
gave comfort he to me [-]:

des Ritters will ich wahren,
for the knight will I care,

er soll mein Streiter sein!
he shall my warrior be!

Hört, was dem Gottgesandten
Hear, what to the envoy of God

ich biete für Gewähr:
I offer as surety:
          (prize)

in meines Vaters Landen
in my father's lands

die Krone trage er,
the crown bear he,
(he shall wear the crown)

mich glücklich soll ich preisen,
myself happy shall I esteem,

nimmt er mein Gut dahin,
accepts he my possession [-],

will er Gemahl mich heissen,
wants he spouse me to call,
(if he wants me to be his spouse)

geb' ich ihm, was ich bin!
give I him, what I am!

Wagner   Morgenlich...

Morgenlich leuchtend, from "Die Meistersinger"
At daybreak shining

Morgenlich leuchtend im rosigen Schein,
At daybreak shining in [the] rosy light,

von Blüt' und Duft
of blossom and fragrance

geschwellt die Luft,
swollen the air,
(filled)

voll aller Wonnen
full of all joys
(full of never)

nie ersonnen,
never imagined,
(imagined joys)

ein Garten lud mich ein,
a garden invited me [-],

dort unter einem Wunderbaum,
there under a magic tree,

von Früchten reich behangen,
with fruits richly hung,
(richly hung with fruits)

zu schau'n im sel'gen Liebestraum,
to see in blissful dream of love,

was höchstem Lustverlangen
what (to) highest desire of joy

Erfüllung kühn verhiess,
fulfilment daringly promised,

das schönste Weib, Eva, im Paradies!
the most beautiful woman, Eva, in paradise!

Abendlich dämmernd umschloss mich die Nacht;
At nightfall duskily encircled me [the] night;

auf steilem Pfad
on steep path

war ich genaht
was I gone close
(did I approach)

zu einer Quelle
to a spring's

reiner Welle,
pure wave,
    (ripple)

die lockend mir gelacht:
which alluringly at me smiled:

dort unter einem Lorbeerbaum,
there under a laurel tree,

von Sternen hell durchschienen,
by stars brightly shone through,
                    (illuminated)

ich schaut' im wachen Dichtertraum,
I viewed in the waking dream of a poet,
(I saw in a poet's daydream)

von heilig holden Mienen,
with holy gentle features,
(a muse with holy gentle features)

mich netzend mit dem edlen Nass,
me refreshing with the precious liquid,
(who refreshed me)

das hehrste Weib: die Muse des Parnass!
the most sublime woman: the muse of Parnassus!

Huldreichster Tag,
Most graceful day,

dem ich aus Dichter's Traum erwacht!
on (which) I from poet's dream awakened!

Dass ich erträumt, das Paradies,
That I dreamed of, the paradise,

in himmlisch neu verklärter Pracht
in heavenly new transfigured splendor

hell vor mir lag,
brightly before me lay,

dahin lachend nun der Quell den Pfad mir wies;
to where smilingly now the spring the path to me pointed;

die, dort geboren,
she, there born,

mein Herz erkoren,
(who has) my heart chosen,

der Erde lieblichstes Bild,
the earth's loveliest image,

als Muse mir geweiht,
as muse me given,

so heilig ernst als mild,
so sacredly earnest as (she is) gentle,

ward kühn von mir gefreit;
was daringly by me courted;

am lichten Tag der Sonnen,
on the bright day of the suns,

durch Sanges Sieg gewonnen:
through singing's victory won:

Parnass und Paradies!
Parnassus and paradise!

Wagner   O du mein holder...

O du mein holder Abendstern, from "Tannhäuser"
Oh you my lovely evening star

Wie Todesahnung Dämm'rung deckt die Lande;
Like foreboding of death twilight covers the lands;

umhüllt das Tal mit schwärzlichem Gewande,
wraps up the valley with blackish gown,

der Seele, die nach jenen Höh'n verlangt,
the soul, which for those heights longs,

vor ihrem Flug durch Nacht und Grausen bangt.
before its flight through night and horror (is) afraid.
(is frightened before its flight through night and horror)

Da scheinest du, o! lieblichster der Sterne,
There shine you, oh! loveliest of the stars,
(There you shine)

dein sanftes Licht entsendest du der Ferne,
your soft light send you to the distance,

die nächt'ge Dämm'rung teilt dein lieber Strahl,
the nightly twilight divides your dear beam,
                    (is divided by your dear beam)

und freundlich zeigst du den Weg aus dem Tal.
and friendly show you the path from the valley.

O du mein holder Abendstern,
Oh you my lovely evening star,

wohl grüsst' ich immer dich so gern;
[indeed] greet I always you so willingly;

vom Herzen, das sie nie verriet,
from the heart, which her never betrayed,
                    (Elisabeth)

grüsse sie, wenn sie vorbei dir zieht,
greet her, when she passes you by,

wenn sie entschwebt dem Tal der Erden,
when she flies from the valley of the earth,

541

Wagner   O du mein... (Continued)

ein sel'ger Engel dort zu werden.
a blessed angel there to become.

Wagner   Träume
                Dreams

Sag, welch wunderbare Träume
Say, what wonderful dreams

halten meinen Sinn umfangen,
hold my mind encompassed,

dass sie nicht wie leere Schäume
that they not like empty froth

sind in ödes Nichts vergangen?
are into deserted nothingness vanished?
(have)

Träume, die in jeder Stunde,
Dreams, which in each hour,

jedem Tage schöner blüh'n,
each day bloom more beautifully

und mit ihrer Himmelskunde
and with their heaven's message

selig durch's Gemüte ziehn!
blissful through the soul move!

Träume, die wie hehre Strahlen
Dreams, which like sublime beams

in die Seele sich versenken,
into the soul [themselves] sink,

dort ein ewig Bild zu malen:
there an eternal image to paint:

Allvergessen, Eingedenken!
Forgetting all, remembering (all)!

Träume, wie wenn Frühlingssonne
Dreams, as if spring-sun

aus dem Schnee die Blüten küsst,
from the snow the blossoms kisses,
(is kissing the blossoms out of the snow)

dass zu nie geahnter Wonne
that to never imagined joy

sie der neue Tag begrüsst,
they the new day greets,

dass sie wachsen, dass sie blühen,
that they (may) grow, that they (may) bloom,

träumend spenden ihren Duft,
dreamily spend their scent,

sanft an deiner Brust verglühen,
gently at your bosom cease to glow

und dann sinken in die Gruft.
and then sink into the tomb.

Winterstürme wichen dem Wonnemond, from "Die Walküre"
Winterstorms gave way to the month of May

Winterstürme wichen dem Wonnemond,
Winterstorms gave way to the month of May,

in mildem Lichte leuchtet der Lenz;
in mild light shines the spring;

auf linden Lüften, leicht und lieblich,
on gentle breezes, light and lovely,

Wunder webend er sich wiegt;
miracles weaving it [itself] cradles;
(spring floats and weaves miracles)

durch Wald und Auen weht sein Atem,
through forest and meadows blows its breath,

weit geöffnet lacht sein Aug';
wide opened smiles its eye;

aus sel'ger Vöglein Sange süss es tönt,
from joyful little birds singing sweet it sounds,

holde Düfte haucht er aus;
gentle fragrances exhales it [-];

seinem warmen Blut entblühen wonnige Blumen,
from its warm blood blossom delightful flowers,

Keim und Spross entspringt seiner Kraft.
germ and sprout arise from its power.

Mit zarter Waffen Zier bezwingt er die Welt,
With delicate arm's radiance conquers it the world,

Winter und Sturm wichen der starken Wehr:
winter and storm gave way to the strong might:

wohl musste den tapfern Streichen
surely must to the valiant blows

die strenge Türe auch weichen,
the strong door [even] give way,

die trotzig und starr uns trennte von ihm.
which defiantly and rigidly us separated from it.
                              (spring)

Zu seiner Schwester schwang er sich her;
To its sister sweeps he [itself] hither;

die Liebe lockte den Lenz:
[the] love lured [the] spring:

in uns'rem Busen barg sie sich tief;
in our bosom hid it [itself] profoundly;
                (love)

nun lacht sie selig dem Licht.
now smiles it joyful to the light.

Die bräutliche Schwester befreite der Bruder;
The bridely sister freed the brother;

zertrümmert liegt, was je sie getrennt;
in pieces lies, what ever them separated;

jauchzend grüsst sich das junge Paar:
exultingly greets [itself] the young pair:

vereint sind Liebe und Lenz!
united are love and spring!

Weber   Durch die Wälder...

Durch die Wälder, durch die Auen, from "Der Freischütz"
Through the forests, through the meadows - "The Free-
    shooter"

Nein! länger trag' ich nicht die Qualen,
No! longer bear I not the agonies,

die Angst, die jede Hoffnung raubt.
the fear, which each hope takes away.
        (which takes away all hope)

Für welche Schuld muss ich bezahlen?
For what guilt must I pay?

Was weiht dem falschen Glück mein Haupt?
What dooms to false luck my head?

Durch die Wälder, durch die Auen
Through the forests, through the meadows

zog ich leichten Sinns dahin!
moved I (with) light mind on!
        (heart)

Alles, was ich konnt erschauen,
Everything, which I could see,

war des sichern Rohr's Gewinn.
was the trust-worthy gun's prize.

Abends bracht' ich reiche Beute,
In the evening brought I rich prey

und wie über eig'nes Glück,
and as about (her) own happiness,

drohend wohl dem Mörder, freute
threatening surely the murderer, gladdened
(Agathe's glance of love gladdened)

sich Agathe's Liebesblick.
[itself] Agathe's glance of love.
(even threatening me the "murderer")

Hat denn der Himmel mich verlassen?
Has then [the] heaven me deserted?

Die Vorsicht ganz ihr Aug' gewandt?
[The] prudence totally its eye(s) turned?
(Has caution totally turned its eyes)

Soll das Verderben mich erfassen?
Shall [the] ruin me seize?

Verfiel ich in des Zufalls Hand?
Fell I into [the] chance's hand?

Jetzt ist wohl ihr Fenster offen,
Now is perhaps her window open,

und sie horcht auf meinen Tritt,
and she listens for my step,

lässt nicht ab vom treuen Hoffen:
lets not go of true hope:

Max bringt gute Zeichen mit.
Max brings good signs (with) him.
                    (omens)

Wenn sich rauschend Blätter regen,
When [itself] rustling leaves move,

wähnt sie wohl, es sei mein Fuss,
imagines she perhaps, it (to) be my foot,

hüpft vor Freuden, winkt entgegen
jumps for joy, waves towards

nur dem Laub den Liebesgruss.
[only] the foliage the greeting of love.

Doch mich umgarnen finstre Mächte,
But me ensnare sinister powers,
(But I am ensnared by sinister powers)

mich fasst Verzweiflung, foltert Spott!
me takes despair, (me) torments mockery!
(despair overtakes me, mockery torments me)

548

O dringt kein Strahl durch diese Nächte?
Oh penetrates no ray through these nights?

herrscht blind das Schicksal?   lebt kein Gott?
reigns blindly [the] fate?   lives no God?

mich fasst Verzweiflung, foltert Spott!
me takes despair, (me) torments mockery!
(despair overtakes me, mockery torments me)

Weber   Leise, leise...

Leise, leise, fromme Weise, from "Der Freischütz"
Softly, softly, gentle melody - "The Free-shooter"

Wie nahte mir der Schlummer
How approaches me [the] slumber
(How can slumber approach me)

bevor ich ihn gesehn?
before I him seen?
(before I have seen him)

Ja, Liebe pflegt mit Kummer
Yes, love uses with grief
(Yes, love usually goes hand)

stets Hand in Hand zu gehn.
always hand in hand to go.
(in hand with grief)

Ob Mond auf seinem Pfad wohl lacht?
If (the) moon on his path may smile?

Wie schön die Nacht!
How beautiful the night!

Leise, fromme Weise,
Softly, gentle melody,

schwing' dich auf zum Sternenkreise!
swing yourself up to the circle of stars!

Lied erschalle, feiernd walle
Song resound, solemnly ascends

mein Gebet zur Himmelshalle!
my prayer to heaven's hall!

O wie hell die gold'nen Sterne,
Oh how bright the golden stars,

mit wie reinem Glanz sie glühn!
with what pure shine they glow!

Nur dort in der Berge Ferne
Only there in the mountain's distance

550

scheint ein Wetter aufzuziehn,
seems a storm to draw up,
              (build up)

dort am Wald auch schwebt ein Heer
there at the woods also hovers a host

dunkler Wolken dumpf und schwer.
(of) dark clouds damp and heavy.
(of damp and heavy clouds)

Zu dir wende ich die Hände,
To you turn I the hands,

Herr, ohn' Anfang und ohn' Ende.
Lord, without beginning and without end.

Vor Gefahren uns zu wahren,
From dangers us to protect,

sende deine Engelschaaren!
send your legions of angels!

Alles pflegt schon längst der Ruh!
All attend already long to rest!
(Everyone has already slept for a long time)

Trauter Freund, wo weilest du?
Trusted friend, where linger you?

Ob mein Ohr auch eifrig lauscht,
Whether my ear even eagerly listens,

nur der Tannen Wipfel rauscht,
only the pines' tree-tops rustle,

nur das Birkenlaub im Hain
only the foliage of birches in the grove

flüstert durch die hehre Stille,
whispers through the sublime silence,

nur die Nachtigall und Grille
only the nightingale and cricket

551

scheint der Nachtluft sich zu freu'n.
seem the night breeze [themselves] to enjoy.

Doch wie! täuscht mich nicht mein Ohr?
But how! deceives me not my ear?
(But how come)

Dort klingt's wie Schritte!
There sounds it like steps!

Dort aus der Tannen Mitte
There from the pines' midst

kommt was hervor!
comes something out!

Er ist's! die Flagge der Liebe mag weh'n!
He is it! the flag of love may wave!
(It is he)

Dein Mädchen wacht
Your maiden wakes

noch in der Nacht!
yet in the night!

Er scheint mich noch nicht zu sehn.
He seems me still not to see.

Gott! täuscht das Licht
God! deceives the light

des Mond's mich nicht,
of the moon me not,

so schmückt ein Blumenstrauss den Hut!
so adorns a flower-bouquet the hat!

Gewiss, er hat den besten Schuss getan;
Certainly, he has the best shot done;

das kündet Glück für morgen an!
that announces happiness for tomorrow [-]!

O süsse Hoffnung!   Neu belebter Mut!
Oh sweet hope!   Newly revived courage!

All' meine Pulse schlagen,
All my pulses beat

und das Herz wallt ungestüm
and the heart agitates impetuously

süss entzückt entgegen ihm!
sweetly charmed towards him!

Konnt' ich das zu hoffen wagen?
Could I this to hope dare?
(Could I dare to hope for this)

Ja! es wandte sich das Glück
Yes!   it turned [itself the] happiness
(Yes, happiness returned)

zu dem teuren Freund zurück,
to the dear friend back,
(to the dear friend)

will sich morgen treu bewähren!
will itself tomorrow faithfully prove!
(will tomorrow faithfully prove itself)

Ist's nicht Täuschung, ist's nicht Wahn?
Is it not delusion, is it not illusion?

Himmel, nimm des Dankes Zähren
Heaven, accept [the] thanks' tears

für dies Pfand der Hoffnung an!
for this pledge of hope [-]!

Weber   Und ob die...

Und ob die Wolke sie verhülle, from "Der Freischütz"
And if the cloud it veils - "The Free-shooter"

Und ob die Wolke sie verhülle,
And if the cloud it veils,

die Sonne bleibt am Himmelszelt,
the sun remains in [the] heaven's canopy,

es waltet dort ein heil'ger Wille,
it reigns there a holy will,

nicht blindem Zufall dient die Welt.
not (to) blind chance serves the world.

Das Auge, ewig rein und klar,
The eye, eternally pure and clear,

nimmt aller Wesen liebend wahr.
perceives all beings lovingly [-].

Für mich wird auch der Vater sorgen,
For me will also the Father care,

dem kindlich Herz und Sinn vertraut,
to whom childly heart and mind (are) entrusted,

und wär' dies auch mein letzter Morgen,
and would this even (be) my last morning,

rief mich sein Vaterwort als Braut.
should call me His Father's word as bride.
(should He call me to heaven as His bride)

Wolf   Alle gingen, Herz, zur Ruh
              All have gone, heart, to [the] rest

Alle gingen, Herz, zur Ruh,
All have gone, heart, to [the] rest,

alle schlafen, nur nicht du.
all sleep, but not you.

Denn der hoffnungslose Kummer
For the hopeless grief

scheucht von deinem Bett den Schlummer,
frightens from your bed the slumber,

und dein Sinnen schweift in stummer
and your thoughts wander in mute

Sorge seiner Liebe zu.
anxiety towards its love [-].

Wolf Anakreons Grab
Anacreon's grave

Wo die Rose hier blüht,
Where the rose here blooms,

wo Reben und Lorbeer sich schlingen,
where vines and laurel [themselves] entwine,

wo das Turtelchen lockt,
where the turtle-dove calls,

wo sich das Grillchen ergötzt,
where itself the cricket enjoys,
(where the cricket enjoys itself)

welch ein Grab ist hier,
what a grave is here,
(whose)

das alle Götter mit Leben
that all Gods with life

schön bepflanzt und geziert?
beautifully planted and adorned?

Es ist Anakreons Ruh.
It is Anacreon's rest.

Frühling, Sommer und Herbst
Spring, summer and autumn

genoss der glückliche Dichter;
enjoyed the happy poet;

vor dem Winter hat ihn endlich
from the winter has him finally

der Hügel geschützt.
the mound protected.

Wolf   Auch kleine Dinge
               Even little things

Auch kleine Dinge können uns entzücken,
Even little things can us delight,

auch kleine Dinge können teuer sein.
even little things can dear be.

Bedenkt, wie gern wir uns mit Perlen schmücken,
Think, how willingly we ourselves with pearls adorn,

sie werden schwer bezahlt und sind nur klein.
they are heavily paid (for) and are only small.

Bedenkt, wie klein ist die Olivenfrucht,
Think, how small is the olive's fruit,

und wird um ihre Güte doch gesucht.
and is for its goodness nevertheless sought.

Denkt an die Rose nur, wie klein sie ist,
Think of the rose only, how small it is,

und duftet doch so lieblich, wie ihr wisst.
and smells [but] so lovely, as you know.

Wolf   Auf dem grünen Balkon
                     On the green balcony

Auf dem grünen Balkon mein Mädchen
On the green balcony my maiden

schaut nach mir durchs Gitterlein.
looks for me through the little trellis.

Mit den Augen blinzelt sie freundlich,
With the eyes winks she friendly,

mit dem Finger sagt sie mir: Nein!
with the finger says she to me: No!

Glück, das nimmer ohne Wanken
Happiness, that never without wavering

junger Liebe folgt hienieden,
young love follows here below,
(follows young love here below)

hat mir eine Lust beschieden,
has me a joy given,

und auch da noch muss ich schwanken.
and even then still must I waver.

Schmeicheln hör ich oder Zanken,
Flattering hear I or quarrelling

komm ich an ihr Fensterlädchen.
come I to her window-shutter.

Immer nach dem Brauch der Mädchen
Always according to the custom of [the] maidens

träuft ins Glück ein bischen Pein.
seeps into happiness a little torment.

Mit den Augen blinzelt sie freundlich,
With the eyes winks she friendly,

mit dem Finger sagt sie mir: Nein!
with the finger says she to me: No!

Wie sich nur in ihr vertragen
How themselves [then in her] behave

ihre Kälte, meine Glut?
her coldness, my fire?

Weil in ihr mein Himmel ruht,
Since in her my heaven rests,

seh ich Trüb und Hell sich jagen.
see I dimness and light themselves hunt.
                    (hunt themselves)

In den Wind gehn meine Klagen,
Into the wind go my complaints,

dass noch nie die süsse Kleine
that still never the sweet little one

ihre Arme schlang um meine;
her arms entwined around mine;
                    (with)

doch sie hält mich hin so fein,
but she keeps me waiting so nicely,

mit den Augen blinzelt sie freundlich,
with the eyes winks she friendly,

mit dem Finger sagt sie mir: Nein!
with the finger says she to me: No!

Wolf Auf ein altes Bild
About an old painting

In grüner Landschaft Sommerflor,
In green landscape's summer-blooming,

bei kühlem Wasser, Schilf und Rohr,
by cool water, reed and cane,

schau, wie das Knäblein sündelos
look, how the little boy sinless

frei spielet auf der Jungfrau Schoss!
freely plays upon the Virgin's lap!

Und dort im Walde wonnesam,
And there in the wood blissfully,

ach, grünet schon des Kreuzes Stamm!
ah, greens already the cross' beam!
    (grows)

Wolf   Bedeckt mich mit Blumen
                    Cover me with flowers

Bedeckt mich mit Blumen,
Cover me with flowers,

ich sterbe vor Liebe.
I die of love.

Dass die Luft mit leisem Wehen
That the breeze with soft blowing

nicht den süssen Duft mir entführe,
not the sweet fragrance (from) me carry away,

bedeckt mich!
cover me!

Ist ja alles doch dasselbe,
Is surely everything but the same,

Liebesodem oder Düfte von Blumen.
love's breath or scent of flowers.

Von Jasmin und weissen Lilien
Of jasmine and white lilies

sollt ihr hier mein Grab bereiten,
should you here my grave prepare,

ich sterbe.
I die.

Und befragt ihr mich:
And ask you me:

Woran? sag ich:
Of what? say I:

Unter süssen Qualen vor Liebe,
Among sweet torments of love,

vor Liebe.
of love.

Wolf   Das verlassene Mägdlein
              The deserted maiden

Früh, wann die Hähne krähn,
Early in the morning, when the cocks crow,

eh die Sternlein schwinden,
before the little stars disappear,

muss ich am Herde stehn,
must I at the cookstove stand,
(must I stand at the cookstove)

muss Feuer zünden.
must fire kindle.
(must kindle the fire)

Schön ist der Flammen Schein,
Beautiful is the flames' shine,
                    (brightness)

es springen die Funken;
[it] jump the sparks;

ich schaue so darein,
I look thus into it,

in Leid versunken.
in grief sunken.

Plötzlich, da kommt es mir,
Suddenly, there comes it to me,
                    (the thought comes to me)

treuloser Knabe,
faithless boy,

dass ich die Nacht von dir
that I (during) the night of you

geträumet habe.
dreamt have.
(have dreamt)

Träne auf Träne dann
Tear upon tear then

stürzet hernieder;
rushes down;

so kommt der Tag heran -
thus comes the day [up] -

o, ging er wieder!
oh, would go it again!
(oh, would it pass again)

Wolf   Denk es, o Seele
                  Think (of) it, oh soul

Ein Tännlein grünet wo, wer weiss, im Walde,
A little fir tree grows somewhere, who knows, in the
   forest,

ein Rosenstrauch, wer sagt, in welchem Garten?
a rosebush, who tells, in which garden?

Sie sind erlesen schon, denk es, o Seele,
They are selected already, think (of) it, oh soul,

auf deinem Grab zu wurzeln und zu wachsen.
on your grave to take root and to grow.

Zwei schwarze Rösslein weiden auf der Wiese,
Two black little horses gaze on the meadow,

sie kehren heim zur Stadt in muntern Sprüngen.
they return home to the city (with) gay prancing.

Sie werden schrittweis gehn mit deiner Leiche;
They will step by step go with your corpse;

vielleicht noch eh an ihren Hufen
perhaps (this will occur) still before on their hoofs

das Eisen los wird, das ich blitzen sehe!
the iron loosens, which I flashing see!
(the horse-shoes loosen, which I see flashing)

Wolf   Der Gärtner
                The gardener

Auf ihrem Leibrösslein,
Upon her very own steed,

so weiss wie der Schnee,
so white as [the] snow,

die schönste Prinzessin
the most beautiful princess

reit't durch die Allee.
rides through the alley.

Der Weg, den das Rösslein
The road, which the little horse

hintanzet so hold,
dances along so gracefully,

der Sand, den ich streute,
the sand, which I strewed,

er blinket wie Gold!
it glitters like gold!

Du rosenfarb's Hütlein
You rose-colored little hat

wohl auf und wohl ab,
now up and now down,

o wirf eine Feder
oh throw a feather

verstohlen herab!
secretly down!

Und willst du dagegen
And want you for it

eine Blüte von mir,
a blossom from me,

nimm tausend für eine,
take thousand for one,

Wolf   Der Gärtner   (Continued)

nimm alle dafür!
take all (of them) for it!

Wolf   Der Mond...

Der Mond hat eine schwere Klag erhoben
The moon has a grave complaint uttered

Der Mond hat eine schwere Klag erhoben
The moon has a grave complaint uttered

und vor dem Herrn die Sache kund gemacht:
and before the Lord the case proclaimed:

Er wolle nicht mehr stehn am Himmel droben,
She would no longer stand in heaven above,

du habest ihn um seinen Glanz gebracht.
you had her of her lustre deprived.

Als er zuletzt das Sternenheer gezählt,
When he last the host of stars counted,

da hab es an der vollen Zahl gefehlt;
there had it on the full number lacked;
(the full number was not complete)

zwei von den schönsten habest du entwendet:
two of the most beautiful have you stolen:

die beiden Augen dort,
[the] both eyes there,
     (two)

die mich verblendet.
which me dazzled.

Wolf   Der Musikant
              The minstrel

Wandern lieb ich für mein Leben,
(To) wander love I for my life,
(I am exceedingly fond of wandering)

lebe eben, wie ich kann,
live just, as I can,

wollt ich mir auch Mühe geben,
would I [me] even pains take,
(would I even take pains)

passt es mir doch garnicht an.
suits it me but not at all.
(it would not suit me at all)

Schöne alte Lieder weiss ich,
Beautiful old songs know I,

in der Kälte ohne Schuh,
in the cold without shoe(s),

draussen in die Saiten reiss ich,
outdoors [in] the strings pluck I,

weiss nicht, wo ich abends ruh!
know not, where I in the evening rest!

Manche Schöne macht wohl Augen,
Many a belle makes surely (big) eyes,

meinet, ich gefiel ihr sehr,
thinks, I pleased her much,

wenn ich nur was wollte taugen,
if I only a bit would be good for,
(if I only would be useful for something)

so ein armer Lump nicht wär!
such a poor vagabond not would be!

Mag dir Gott ein'n Mann bescheren,
May to you God a man present,
(May God give you a man)

wohl mit Haus und Hof versehn!
well with house and home provided!

Wenn wir zwei zusammen wären,
If we two together were,

möcht mein Singen mir vergehn.
might my singing [me] pass away.

Wolf   Der Tambour
                The drummer

Wenn meine Mutter hexen könnt',
If my mother bewitch could,
        (could practice sorcery)

da müsst sie mit dem Regiment,
then must she (go) with the regiment,

nach Frankreich überall mit hin,
to France everywhere with (us) there,

und wär' die Marketenderin.
and (she) would be the canteen-woman.

Im Lager, wohl um Mitternacht,
In the camp, around midnight,

wenn niemand auf ist als die Wacht,
when nobody up is but the watch,

und alles schnarchet, Ross und Mann,
and all snore, horse and man,

vor meiner Trommel säss' ich dann:
at my drum would sit I then:

die Trommel müsst' eine Schüssel sein,
the drum must a bowl be,

ein warmes Sauerkraut darein,
a warm sauerkraut in it,

die Schlegel Messer und Gabel,
the drumsticks (must be) knife and fork,

eine lange Wurst mein Sabel,
a big sausage my sabre,

mein Tschako wär' ein Humpen gut,
my sako would be a tankard fine,

den füll' ich mit Burgunderblut.
which fill I with burgundy blood.
(which I fill with burgundy wine)

Und weil es mir an Lichte fehlt,
And as it me of light lacks,
(And as I have no light)

da scheint der Mond in mein Gezelt;
there shines the moon into my tent;

scheint er auch auf Franzö'sch herein,
shines he even in French into it,
   (the moon)   (the tent)

mir fällt doch meine Liebste ein:
me think yet (of) my sweetheart [-]:
(I remember yet my sweetheart)

ach weh! jetzt hat der Spass ein End'!
ah woe! now has the fun an end!

Wenn nur meine Mutter hexen könnt'!
If only my mother bewitch could!
           (could practice sorcery)

Wolf   Elfenlied
                       Elf's song

Bei Nacht im Dorfe der Wächter rief: Elfe! *
At night in the village the watchman cried: Eleven!

Ein ganz kleines Elfchen im Walde schlief
A very small little elf in the forest slept

wohl um die Elfe!
around [the] eleven[th hour]!

Und meint, es rief ihm aus dem Tal
And thinks, [it] calls him from the valley

bei seinem Namen die Nachtigall,
by his name the nightingale,

oder Silpelit hätt ihm gerufen.
or Silpelit had him called.

Reibt sich der Elf die Augen aus,
Rubs [itself] the elf the eyes clear,

begibt sich vor sein Schneckenhaus
goes [itself] before his snail's house

und ist als wie ein trunken Mann,
and is like a drunken man,

sein Schläflein war nicht voll getan,
his little nap was not fully completed,

und humpelt also, tippe, tapp,
and (he) hobbles then, tippy, tap,

durchs Haselholz ins Tal hinab,
through the hazel-wood into the valley down,

schlupft an der Mauer hin so dicht,
slips by the wall there so closely,
(creeps)

da sitzt der Glühwurm Licht an Licht.
there sits the glow-worm light by light.

"Was sind das helle Fensterlein?
"What are those (for) bright little windows?

Da drin wird eine Hochzeit sein:
There inside will a wedding be:
                    (a wedding goes on)

die Kleinen sitzen beim Mahle,
the little ones sit at the meal,

und treibens in dem Saale:
and carry on in the hall:

Da guck ich wohl ein wenig 'nein!"
There peep I just a little in!"
(There peep I in just a little)

Pfui, stösst den Kopf an harten Stein!
Pfui, knocks the head on (the) hard stone!
                    (his)

Elfe, gelt, du hast genug?
Elf, how about, you have enough?
                    (did you have enough of it)

Gukuk!
Cuckoo!

*In the German language the same word "Elf" is used for
an "elf' as well as for the number "eleven."

Wolf
Er ist's
He is it
(It is he)

Frühling lässt sein blaues Band
Spring lets its blue ribbon

wieder flattern durch die Lüfte;
again flutter through the breezes;

süsse, wohlbekannte Düfte
sweet, well-known fragrances

streifen ahnungsvoll das Land.
graze full of foreboding the land.

Veilchen träumen schon,
Violets dream already,

wollen balde kommen.
want soon to come up.

Horch, von fern ein leiser Harfenton!
Listen, from afar a soft tone of the harp!

Frühling, ja du bist's!
Spring, yes you are it!
(it is you)

Dich hab ich vernommen,
You have I perceived,

ja du bist's!
yes you are it!

Wolf   Führ' mich, Kind, nach Bethlehem!
                   Lead me, Child, to Bethlehem!

Führ' mich, Kind, nach Bethlehem!
Lead me, Child, to Bethlehem!

dich, mein Gott, dich will ich sehn.
Thee, my God, Thee will I see.

Wem geläng' es, wem,
Whom (is) given it, whom,
(Who can go to Thee, God)

ohne dich zu dir zu gehn!
without Thee to Thee to go!
(without Thy guidance)

Rüttle mich, dass ich erwache,
Shake me, that I awake,

rufe mich, so will ich schreiten;
call me, so will I walk;

gib die Hand mir, mich zu leiten,
give the hand to me, me to guide,

dass ich auf den Weg mich mache.
that I on the way [myself] start.

Dass ich schaue Bethlehem,
That I (may) look (at) Bethlehem,

dorten meinen Gott zu sehn.
there my God to see.

Wem geläng' es, wem,
Whom (is) given it, whom,
(Who can go to Thee, God)

ohne dich zu dir zu gehn!
without Thee to you to go!
(without Thy guidance)

Von der Sünde schwerem Kranken
From [the] sin's grave sickness

bin ich träg und dumpf beklommen.
am I indolently and wearily anxious.

Willst du nicht zu Hülfe kommen,
Would Thou not to help come,

muss ich straucheln, muss ich schwanken.
(then) must I stumble, must I stagger.

Leite mich nach Bethlehem,
Lead me to Bethlehem,

dich, mein Gott, dich will ich sehn.
Thee, my God, Thee must I see.

Wem geläng' es, wem,
Whom (is) given it, whom,

ohne dich zu dir zu gehn!
without Thee to Thee to go!

Wolf   Fussreise
                Walking tour

Am frisch geschnittnen Wanderstab,
With the fresh-cut traveller's staff,

wenn ich in der Frühe
when I in the morning

so durch Wälder ziehe,
[thus] through woods go,

Hügel auf und ab:
hills up and down:

dann, wie's Vöglein im Laube
then, as the little bird in the foliage

singet und sich rührt,
sings and [itself] moves,

oder wie die goldne Traube
or as the golden grape

Wonnegeister spürt
spirits of joy feels

in der ersten Morgensonne:
in the first morning-sun:
        (early)

so fühlt auch mein alter, lieber
thus feels also my old, dear

Adam Herbst- und Frühlingsfieber,
Adam Fall- and Spring-fever,

gottbeherzte,
God-given,

nie verscherzte
never forfeited

Erstlings- Paradieseswonne.
first joy of paradise.

Also bist du nicht so schlimm, o alter
Thus are you not so bad, oh old

Adam, wie die strengen Lehrer sagen;
Adam, as the austere teachers say;

liebst und lobst du immer doch,
love and praise you always yet,
(yet always you continue to love and praise)

singst und preisest immer noch,
(you) sing and extol always yet,
(to sing and to extol)

wie an ewig neuen Schöpfungstagen,
as on eternal new days of creation,

deinen lieben Schöpfer und Erhalter.
your dear Creator and Supporter.

Möcht es dieser geben,
May [it] this one give,
(God willing)

und mein ganzes Leben
and my whole life

wär im leichten Wanderschweisse
would be in light wander-sweat

eine solche Morgenreise!
a such morning walk!
(such a)

Wolf   Gebet
                  Prayer

Herr! schicke was du willt,
Lord! send what you will,

ein Liebes oder Leides;
[an] affection or grief;

ich bin vergnügt, dass beides
I am delighted, that both

aus deinen Händen quillt.
from your hands flow.

Wollest mit Freuden
Do with joy

und wollest mit Leiden
and do with sorrow

mich nicht überschütten!
me not overwhelm!

Doch in der Mitten
But in the middle

liegt holdes Bescheiden.
lies gentle contentment.

Wolf   Gesang Weylas
                        Song of Weila

Du bist Orplid, mein Land!
You are Orplid, my land!

das ferne leuchtət;
that distantly shines;

vom Meere dampfet dein besonnter Strand
from the sea steams your sunny shore
(from your shore the mist rises)

den Nebel, so der Götter Wange feuchtet.
the mist, which the Gods' cheek moistens.
(to moisten the Gods' cheek)

Uralte Wasser steigen
Age-old waters rise

verjüngt um deine Hüften, Kind!
rejuvenated around your hips, child!

Vor deiner Gottheit beugen
Before your deity bow

sich Könige, die deine Wärter sind.
[themselves] kings, who your attendants are.
(kings, who are your servants)

Wolf   Gesegnet sei
                  Blessed be (the Lord)

Gesegnet sei, durch den die Welt entstund;
Blessed be, through whom the world originated;

wie trefflich schuf er sie nach allen Seiten!
how excellently created He it at all sides!

Er schuf das Meer mit endlos tiefem Grund,
He created the sea with endless deep ground,

er schuf die Schiffe, die hinübergleiten,
He created the vessels, which glide over (it),

er schuf das Paradies, mit ew'gem Licht,
He created the paradise, with eternal light,

er schuf die Schönheit und dein Angesicht.
He created [the] beauty and your face.

Wolf   Herr, was trägt der Boden hier
                        Lord, what bears the soil here

Herr, was trägt der Boden hier,
Lord, what bears the soil here,
(Lord, what will the soil bring forth)

den du tränkst so bitterlich?
which you moisten so bitterly?
                        (tearfully)

"Dornen, liebes Herz, für mich,
"Thorns, dear heart, for me,

und für dich der Blumen Zier."
and for you the flowers' beauty."

Ach, wo solche Bäche rinnen,
Ah, where such brooks (of tears) flow,

wird ein Garten da gedeihn?
will a garden there thrive?

"Ja, und wisse! Kränzelein,
"Yes, and know! Little wreaths,

gar verschiedene, flicht man drinnen."
many different ones, twines one within."

O mein Herr, zu wessen Zier
Oh my Lord, for whose adornment

windet man die Kränze? sprich!
twines one the wreaths? say!

"Die von Dornen sind für mich,
"Those of thorns are for me,

die von Blumen reich ich dir."
those of flowers pass I to you."
                        (offer)

Wolf   Ich hab in Penna einen Liebsten wohnen
                      I have in Penna one lover residing

Ich hab in Penna einen Liebsten wohnen,
I have in Penna one lover residing,
(I have one lover who lives in Penna)

in der Maremmenebne einen andern,
in the Maremma-plain another,

einen im schönen Hafen von Ancona,
one in the beautiful port of Ancona,

zum vierten muss ich nach Viterbo wandern;
to the fourth one must I to Viterbo wander;

ein andrer wohnt in Casentino dort,
another dwells in Casentino [there],

der nächste lebt mit mir am selben Ort,
the next lives with me at the same place,

und wieder einen hab ich in Magione,
and again one have I in Magione,

vier in La Fratta, zehn in Castiglione.
four in La Fratta, ten in Castiglione.

Wolf   In dem Schatten meiner Locken
                In the shadow of my curls

In dem Schatten meiner Locken
In the shadow of my curls

schlief mir mein Geliebter ein.
fell asleep [me] my beloved [-].

Weck ich ihn nun auf? Ach nein!
Wake I him now up? Ah no!

Sorglich strählt ich meine krausen
Carefully combed I my curly

Locken täglich in der Frühe,
locks daily in the early morning,

doch umsonst ist meine Mühe,
but in vain is my effort,

weil die Winde sie zerzausen.
as the winds them rumple.

Lockenschatten, Windessausen
Curls' shadow, wind's rustling

schläferten den Liebsten ein.
lulled the beloved in.
              (to sleep)

Weck ich ihn nun auf? Ach nein!
Wake I him now up? Ah no!

Hören muss ich, wie ihn gräme,
Hear must I, how him grieves,
(I must hear how sorry he is)

dass er schmachtet schon so lange,
that he languishes [already] so long,
          (pines)

dass ihm Leben geb und nehme
that him life gives and takes
(that my brown cheeks)

diese meine braune Wange.
this my brown cheek.
(are life-giving or life-taking)

Und er nennt mich seine Schlange,
And he calls me "his snake,"

und doch schlief er bei mir ein.
and yet fell asleep he by me [-].
                        (in my presence)

Weck ich ihn nun auf?   Ach nein!
Wake I him now up?   Ah no!

Wolf   In der Frühe
                        In the early morning

Kein Schlaf noch kühlt das Auge mir,
No sleep yet cools the eye me,
                        (my eyes)

dort gehet schon der Tag herfür
there comes already [the] day [up]

an meinem Kammerfenster.
at my bedroom window.

Es wühlet mein verstörter Sinn
It moves my troubled mind
(Amidst doubts my troubled)

noch zwischen Zweifeln her und hin
[yet] amidst doubts to and fro
(mind moves to and fro)

und schaffet Nachtgespenster.
and creates night-ghosts.

Ängst'ge, quäle
Alarm, torment

dich nicht länger, meine Seele!
yourself not longer, my soul!
            (no more)

Freu dich!   Schon sind da und dorten
Rejoice [yourself]!   Already are there and yonder

Morgenglocken wach geworden.
morning-bells awakened.

586

Wolf   Lebe wohl
              Farewell

Lebe wohl! Du fühlest nicht,
Farewell!   You feel not,

was es heisst, dies Wort der Schmerzen;
what it means, this word of pains;

mit getrostem Angesicht
with confident face

sagtest du's und leichtem Herzen.
said you it and (with) light heart.

Lebe wohl!
Farewell!

Ach tausendmal
Ah (a) thousand times

hab ich mir es vorgesprochen,
have I to me it told,

und in nimmersatter Qual
and in never ending torment

mir das Herz damit gebrochen!
me the heart with it broken!

Wolf   Mausfallen - Sprüchlein
                        Mousetrap - Verses

Kleine Gäste, kleines Haus,
Tiny guests, tiny house,

liebe Mäusin oder Maus,
dear Miss Mouse or Mr. Mouse,

stelle dich nur kecklich ein
arrive you but boldly [-]
(boldly come in)

heute Nacht bei Mondenschein!
this night by moon shine!

Mach aber die Tür fein hinter dir zu,
Close [but] the door fine behind you [-],
                        (securely)

hörst du?
hear you?

Dabei hüte dein Schwänzchen!
Thereby watch your little tail!

hörst du?   Dein Schwänzchen!
hear you?   Your little tail!

Nach Tische singen wir,
After table sing we,
        (supper we sing)

nach Tische springen wir
after table leap we
        (supper we leap around)

und machen ein Tänzchen!
and do a little dance!

Witt, witt!
Witt, witt!

Meine alte Katze tanzt wahrscheinlich mit,
My old cat dances probably with(us),

hörst du?
hear you?

588

Wolf   Michelangelo Lieder
                   Michelangelo songs

               1)   Wohl denk' ich oft
                  Surely think I often

Wohl denk' ich oft an mein vergang'nes Leben,
Surely think I often of my past life,

wie es vor meiner Liebe für dich war;
how it before my love for you was;
(how it was before I loved you)

kein Mensch hat damals Acht auf mich gegeben,
no human being had then care for me given,

ein jeder Tag verloren für mich war;
each and every day lost for me was;
(each day was lost for me)

Ich dachte wohl, ganz dem Gesang zu leben,
I thought indeed, entirely for singing to live,

auch mich zu flüchten aus der Menschen Schar...
even [myself] to flee from [the] men's throng...
                                 (company)

genannt in Lob und Tadel bin ich heute,
mentioned in praise and blame am I today,

und, dass ich da bin, wissen alle Leute!
and, that I here am, know all people!
        (exist)

Wolf   Michelangelo Lieder
                                Michelangelo songs

                          2)   Alles endet, was entstehet
                              Everything ends, which begins

Alles endet, was entstehet.
Everything ends, which begins.

Alles, alles rings vergehet,
Everything, everything around perishes,

denn die Zeit flieht, und die Sonne sieht,
for [the] time flees, and the sun perceives,

dass alles rings vergehet,
that everything around perishes,

Denken, Reden, Schmerz und Wonne;
 thinking, speaking, pain and joy;

und die wir zu Enkeln hatten
and those we as grandchildren had
(and those grandchildren we had)

schwanden wie bei Tag die Schatten,
disappeared as at daytime the shadows,

wie ein Dunst im Windeshauch.
as a haze in the wind's breath.

Menschen waren wir ja auch,
Men were we surely too,

froh und traurig, so wie ihr,
gay and sad, just as you,

und nun sind wir leblos hier,
and now are we lifeless here,

sind nur Erde, wie ihr sehet.
are only earth, as you see.
           (dust)

Alles endet, was entstehet.
Everything ends, which begins.

Wolf   Alles endet... (Continued)

Alles, alles rings vergehet.
Everything, everything around perishes.

Wolf   Michelangelo Lieder
                Michelangelo songs

                3) Fühlt meine Seele
                    Feels my soul

Fühlt meine Seele das ersehnte Licht
Feels my soul the longed-for light

von Gott, der sie erschuf?
of God, who it created?
                (the soul)

ist es der Strahl
is it the beam

von and'rer Schönheit aus dem Jammertal,
of other beauty from the valley of misery,

der in mein Herz Erinnerung weckend bricht?
which [in] my heart memories arousing penetrates?
(which penetrates my heart - arousing memories)

ist es ein Klang, ein Traumgesicht,
is it a sound, a dream-face,

das Aug' und Herz mir füllt mit einem Mal
which eye(s) and heart me fills at once

in unbegreiflich glüh'nder Qual,
in inconceivable burning torment,

die mich zu Tränen bringt?
which me to tears brings?
(which cause my tears to flow)

Ich weiss es nicht.
I know it not.

Was ich ersehne, fühle, was mich lenkt,
What I long for, feel, what me guides,

ist nicht in mir:
is not in me:

sag' mir, wie ich's erwerbe?
tell me, how I it acquire?

592

Mir zeigt es wohl nur eines And'ren Huld;
To me shows it [indeed] only another's favor;

darein bin ich, seit ich dich sah, versenkt.
in which am I, since I you saw, submerged.
                         (saw you)

Mich treibt ein Ja und Nein,
Me drives a "Yes" and "No,"
(It drives me a "Yes" and "No")

ein Süss und Herbe -
a sweetness and (a) bitterness -

daran sind, Herrin, deine Augen Schuld.
that are, mistress, your eyes' fault.

Wolf   Mignon

see: Beethoven: Mignon

Wolf   Nimmersatte Liebe
                 Never satisfied love

So ist die Lieb!
Such is [the] love!

Mit Küssen nicht zu stillen:
With kisses not to appease:

wer ist der Tor und will ein Sieb
who is the fool and wants a sieve
                       (to fill)

mit eitel Wasser füllen?
with just water fill?
(a sieve with water only)

Und schöpfst du an die tausend Jahr,
And draw you up to thousand years,
(And would you draw water for a thousand years)

und küssest ewig, ewig gar,
and would kiss eternally, eternally even,

du tust ihr nie zu Willen.
you do her never to will.
(you never satisfy her wishes)

Die Lieb, die Lieb hat alle Stund
[The] love, [the] love has at all hours

neu wunderlich Gelüsten;
new strange desires;

wir bissen uns die Lippen wund,
we bit [us] the lips sore,

da wir uns heute küssten.
as we [us] today kissed.

Das Mädchen hielt in guter Ruh,
The maiden held still in good composure,

wie's Lämmlein unterm Messer;
as the little lamb under the knife;

ihr Auge bat: nur immer zu,
her eye(s) begged: go on,

je weher, desto besser!
the more painful, the better!
(the more it hurts, the better)

So ist die Lieb, und war auch so,
Such is [the] love, and was always thus,

wie lang es Liebe gibt,
as long as love exists,

und anders war Herr Salomo,
and otherwise was Mr. Solomon,
(and in no other way was)

der Weise, nicht verliebt.
the sage, not in love.
(Mr. Solomon in love)

Wolf   Nun wandre, Maria
                       Now wander, Mary

Nun wandre, Maria, nun wandre nur fort.
Now wander, Mary, now wander [just] on.

Schon krähen die Hähne, und nah ist der Ort.
Already crow the cocks and near is the place.

Nun wandre, Geliebte, du Kleinod mein,
Now wander, beloved, you jewel of mine,

und balde wir werden in Bethlehem sein.
and soon we will in Bethlehem be.

Dann ruhest du fein und schlummerst dort.
Then rest you fine and slumber there.
                       (comfortably)

Schon krähen die Hähne, und nah ist der Ort.
Already crow the cocks and near is the place.

Wohl seh ich, Herrin, die Kraft dir schwinden;
Well see I, mistress, the strength of you disappear;
                       (your strength disappear)

kann deine Schmerzen, ach, kaum verwinden.
can your pains, ah, hardly endure.

Getrost! wohl finden wir Herberg dort;
Be confident! surely find we shelter there;

schon krähn die Hähne und nah ist der Ort.
already crow the cocks and near is the place.

Wär erst bestanden dein Stündlein, Marie,
Were only passed your hour, Mary,

die gute Botschaft gut lohnt ich sie.
the good news well will reward I it.

Das Eselein hie gäb ich drum fort!
The little donkey here gave I for it away!
(For the good news I would give away the little donkey)

Schon krähen die Hähne, komm, nah ist der Ort.
Already crow the cocks, come, near is the place.

597

Wolf
Schlafendes Jesuskind
Sleeping Christ-child*

Sohn der Jungfrau, Himmelskind!
Son of the Virgin, heaven's child!

am Boden auf dem Holz der Schmerzen eingeschlafen,
on the floor on the wood of pains fallen asleep,
(as of the cross)

das der fromme Meister, sinnvoll spielend
that the pious master, meaningfully playing
(painter)   (painting)

deinen leichten Träumen unterlegte.
your light dreams underlaid.
(has laid under your light dreams)

Blume du, noch in der Knospe
Flower you, still in the bud
(Baby you are)

dämmernd eingehüllt
sleepily enfolded

die Herrlichkeit des Vaters!
the excellence of the Father!

O wer sehen könnte,
Oh who see could,
(could see)

welche Bilder hinter dieser Stirne,
what pictures behind this forehead,
(what kind of pictures behind this forehead)

diesen schwarzen Wimpern,
(behind) these black eyelashes,

sich in sanften Wechsel malen!
[themselves] in gentle succession paint!
(are painted in gentle succession)

Sohn der Jungfrau, Himmelskind!
Son of the Virgin, heaven's child!

*This is the description of a painting depicting the sleeping
Christ-child.

598

Wolf   Über Nacht
                        Over night

Über Nacht, über Nacht
During (the) night, during (the) night

kommt still das Leid,
comes quietly [the] grief,

und bist du erwacht,
and are you awakened,
(and when you awaken)

o traurige Zeit,
oh sad time,

du grüssest den dämmernden Morgen
you greet the dawning morning

mit Weinen und mit Sorgen.
with weeping and with sorrows.

Über Nacht, über Nacht
During (the) night, during (the) night

kommt still das Glück,
comes quietly [the] happiness,

und bist du erwacht,
and are you awakened,

o selig Geschick,
oh blissful fate,

der düstre Traum ist zerronnen,
the somber dream is dissolved,
                        (has vanished)

und Freude ist gewonnen.
and joy is won.

Über Nacht, über Nacht
over night, over night

kommt Freud und Leid,
comes joy and grief,

und eh du's gedacht,
and before you it thought,
(and before you think of it)

verlassen dich beid
leave you both
(both leave you)

und gehen dem Herrn zu sagen,
and (they) go to the Lord to tell,
                              (report)

wie du sie getragen.
how you them endured.

Wolf   Und willst du deinen Liebsten sterben sehen
                And want you your beloved to die see
                (Do you want to see your beloved dying)

Und willst du deinen Liebsten sterben sehen,
And want you your beloved to die see,
(Do you want to see your beloved dying)

so trage nicht dein Haar gelockt, du Holde.
so carry not your hair in locks, you gentle one.

Lass von den Schultern frei sie niederwehen;
Let from the shoulders freely them flow down;

wie Fäden sehn sie aus von purem Golde.
like threads look they [-] of pure gold.
(They look like threads of pure gold)

Wie goldne Fäden, die der Wind bewegt,
Like golden threads, which the wind moves,

schön sind die Haare, schön ist, die sie trägt!
beautiful is the hair, beautiful is, who it wears!

Goldfäden, Seidenfäden, ungezählt,
Golden threads, silken threads, uncountable,

schön sind die Haare, schön ist, die sie strählt!
beautiful is the hair, beautiful is (the one), who it combs!

Wolf   Verborgenheit
       Concealment

Lass, o Welt, o lass mich sein!
Let, oh world, oh let me be!

locket nicht mit Liebesgaben,
tempt (me) not with love's gifts,

lasst dies Herz alleine haben
let this heart alone have

seine Wonne, seine Pein!
its joy, its torment!

Was ich traure, weiss ich nicht,
What I mourn, know I not,

es ist unbekanntes Wehe;
it is unknown grief;

immerdar durch Tränen sehe
continuously through tears see

ich der Sonne liebes Licht.
I the sun's dear light.

Oft bin ich mir kaum bewusst
Often am I [me] hardly conscious

und die helle Freude zücket
and [the] bright joy pulsates

durch die Schwere, so mich drücket,
through the heaviness, that me burdens,
     (sorrow)

Wonniglich in meiner Brust.
blissfully into my bosom.

Wolf   Zitronenfalter im April
                        Lemon (colored) butterfly in April

Grausame Frühlingssonne,
Cruel spring-sun,

du weckst mich vor der Zeit,
you awaken me before the time,
(you awoke me too early)

dem nur in Maienwonne
for whom only in May's bliss

die zarte Kost gedeiht!
the tender food thrives!

Ist nicht ein liebes Mädchen hier,
Is not a dear maiden here,

das auf der Rosenlippe mir
who on the rosy lip me

ein Tröpfchen Honig beut,
a little drop (of) honey offers,

so muss ich jämmerlich vergehn,
then must I wretchedly pass away,

und wird der Mai mich nimmer sehn
and will [the] May me never see

in meinem gelben Kleid.
in my yellow gown.

Wolf   Zur Ruh, zur Ruh!
                    (Go) To rest, (go) to rest!

Zur Ruh, zur Ruh ihr müden Glieder!
(Go) to rest, (go) to rest you tired limbs!

schliesst fest euch zu, ihr Augenlider!
close firmly [yourselves -], you eyelids!

ich bin allein, fort ist die Erde;
I am alone, gone is the earth;
                    (the earth has vanished)

Nacht muss es sein, dass Licht mir werde,
Night must it be, that light me will be,
                    (I shall see)

o führt mich ganz, ihr innern Mächte!
oh guide me completely, you inner powers!

hin zu dem Glanz der tiefsten Nächte.
[there] to the luster of the deepest nights.

Fort aus dem Raum der Erdenschmerzen,
Away from the place of earthly pains,

durch Nacht und Traum zum Mutterherzen!
through night and dream to the mother's heart!

B

C

D

E

F

G

H

I

J

M

N

O

T

CPSIA information can be obtained at www.ICGtesting.com
Printed in the USA
BVOW08*0034030816

457341BV00004B/1/P